PAUL D. SANSONE, O.F.M.

Uncovering Ancient Stones

H. Neil Richardson

Uncovering Ancient Stones

Essays in Memory
of
H. Neil Richardson

edited by
Lewis M. Hopfe

Eisenbrauns
Winona Lake, Indiana
1994

Library of Congress Cataloging-in-Publication Data

Uncovering ancient stones : essays in memory of H. Neil Richardson / edited by Lewis
   M. Hopfe.
      p.   cm.
   Includes bibliographical references and indexes.
   ISBN 0-931464-73-0 (alk. paper)
   1. Bible. O.T.—Criticism, interpretation, etc.   2. Bible. O.T.—Antiquities.
3. Bible. O.T.—Use.   I. Richardson, H. Neil (Henry Neil), 1916–1988.
II. Hopfe, Lewis M.
BS1171.2.U49   1994
221.6—dc20   94-6464
                                                                   CIP

The paper used in this publication meets the minimum requirements of the American
National Standard for Information Sciences—Permanence of Paper for Printed Library
Materials, ANSI Z39.48-1984.♾™

Contents

Contents

Preface

❧ ⦿ ❧

THIS VOLUME IS A COLLECTION OF essays written by the students and friends of H. Neil Richardson. They are our attempt to remember his many contributions to our lives and to the fields of Old Testament studies and archaeology. The authors of these essays knew Neil at various stages in his long career as a professor at Syracuse University and at Boston University. Some of us knew him as a colleague at excavation sites in Jordan, Israel, or Cyprus. Many of the contributors have expressed in print or in private conversation Neil's concern for them and something of the impression he made upon their lives.

I first met Neil Richardson in 1961 when I was a doctoral candidate in Old Testament at Boston University. One of the things that impressed me most about him was his demand for excellence. I entered on a course with him that was charitably known as "Directed Study." In this course Neil worked out a reading list for me. Once a week I would meet with him for an hour in his office and the class would begin with: "What have you read?" No student ever felt more naked than I in those encounters. There was no place to hide! Neil had read the book in question and many of the books in the bibliography. It was likely that he knew the author and the author's friends. He had probably debated certain points with the author at a professional meeting or on a plane to the Middle East. After one or two such sessions I learned that the only possible preparation was complete preparation. Even that was not enough.

Throughout my five years at Boston University Neil Richardson kept up the pressure in the classroom. Yet outside the class I found him to be a warm friend and a loving father to his family. Neil and his family invited the Hopfes to dinner at their home and accepted invitations to days at the Rockport beaches. It was Neil and Faith Richardson who loaned me their Hebrew alphabet typewriter for the notes in my dissertation. It was Neil who inspired me to do archaeology and gave me the information on a touring archaeological classroom that in 1963 gave me my first digging experience.

Twenty years after my graduation I dug with Neil at Dor. Then he was within a few years of his death and fighting a debilitating disease that left him at half strength. At that point in my career I had worked for six seasons at other sites in Israel. I had been an area supervisor, written field notes and reports, read several tons of pottery, authored a college textbook, and published in an archaeological journal. Yet at Dor Neil gave me my best lesson in the basic art of balk trimming. In small matters and great Neil was as always my teacher.

We lovingly and respectfully dedicate these essays to the memory of H. Neil Richardson.

Lewis Moore Hopfe†
Wichita, Kansas
Pentecost 1991

Publisher's Note

We regret to report that the editor of this volume, Lewis Hopfe, passed away on September 2, 1992, while this volume was in production. The completion of the production was carried out by the Eisenbrauns editorial staff.

Some time has passed since most of the essays in this volume were completed; the articles are published here without major modification, though some authors have made some minor revisions and included more recent bibliographical information.

Abbreviations

❧ ❧

AASOR	Annual of the American Schools of Oriental Research
AB	Anchor Bible
AnBib	Analecta Biblica
ANET	J. B. Pritchard (ed.), *Ancient Near Eastern Texts Relating to the Old Testament* (3d ed.)
AnOr	Analecta orientalia
AOAT	Alter Orient und Altes Testament
ARM	Archives royales de Mari
AV	Authorized Version
BA	*Biblical Archaeologist*
BAR	*Biblical Archaeologist Reader*
BAR Int. Series	British Archaeological Reports, International Series
BASOR	*Bulletin of the American Schools of Oriental Research*
BDB	F. Brown, S. R. Driver, and C. A. Briggs, *Hebrew and English Lexicon of the Old Testament*
BHS	Biblia Hebraica Stuttgartensia
Bib	*Biblica*
BibOr	Biblica et Orientalia
BWANT	Beiträge zur Wissenschaft vom Alten und Neuen Testament
BZAW	Beihefte zur ZAW
BZNW	Beihefte zur ZNW
CAD	*The Assyrian Dictionary of the Oriental Institute of the University of Chicago*
CBQ	*Catholic Biblical Quarterly*
CBQMS	Catholic Biblical Quarterly Monograph Series
CT	Cuneiform Texts from the British Museum
DJD	Discoveries in the Judaean Desert
EAEHL	Encyclopaedia of Archaeological Excavations in the Holy Land
ErIsr	Eretz-Israel

HALAT	L. Koeher and W. Baumgartner et al., *Hebräisches und aramäisches Lexikon zum Alten Testament*
HSM	Harvard Semitic Monographs
IB	*Interpreter's Bible*
ICC	International Critical Commentary
IDB	G. A. Buttrick (ed.), *Interpreter's Dictionary of the Bible*
IDBSup	Supplementary volume to *IDB*
IEJ	*Israel Exploration Journal*
Int	*Interpretation*
IOS	*Israel Oriental Studies*
JANES(CU)	*Journal of the Ancient Near Eastern Society (of Columbia University)*
JAOS	*Journal of the American Oriental Society*
JB	A. Jones (ed.), *Jerusalem Bible*
JBL	*Journal of Biblical Literature*
JJS	*Journal of Jewish Studies*
JNES	*Journal of Near Eastern Studies*
JPSV	Jewish Publication Society Version
JQR	*Jewish Quarterly Review*
JR	*Journal of Religion*
JSOT	*Journal for the Study of the Old Testament*
JSOTSup	Journal for the Study of the Old Testament Supplement Series
JTS	*Journal of Theological Studies*
KAI	H. Donner and W. Röllig, *Kanaanäische und aramäische Inschriften*
KAT	Kommentar zum Alten Testament
KJV	King James Version
LCL	Loeb Classical Library
LSJ	Liddell-Scott-Jones, *Greek-English Lexicon*
LXX	Septuagint
MT	Masoretic Text
NAB	New American Bible
NCB	New Century Bible
NEB	New English Bible
NIV	New International Version
NJB	H. Wansbrough (ed.), *New Jerusalem Bible*
NKJV	New King James Version
NovT	*Novum Testamentum*
NRSV	New Revised Standard Version
OBO	Orbis biblicus et orientalis
OBT	Overtures to Biblical Theology
OIP	Oriental Institute Publications
OrAnt	*Oriens antiquus*
OTL	Old Testament Library
PAAJR	*Proceedings of the American Academy of Jewish Research*

Abbreviations

PEQ	*Palestine Exploration Quarterly*
PJ	*Palästina-Jahrbuch*
QDAP	*Quarterly of the Department of Antiquities in Palestine*
RB	*Revue biblique*
REJ	*Revue des études juives*
RQ	*Römische Quartalschrift für christliche Altertumskunde und Kirchengeschichte*
RSV	Revised Standard Version
SBLDS	SBL Dissertation Series
SBLSBS	SBL Sources for Biblical Study
TDNT	G. Kittel and G. Friedrich (eds.), *Theological Dictionary of the New Testament*
TDOT	G. J. Botterweck and H. Ringgren (eds.), *Theological Dictionary of the Old Testament*
Tg.	Targum
TSSI	J. C. L. Gibson, *Textbook of Syrian Semitic Inscriptions* (3 vols.)
TToday	*Theology Today*
UT	C. H. Gordon, *Ugaritic Textbook*
Vg.	Vulgate
VT	*Vetus Testamentum*
VTSup	Vetus Testamentum Supplements
WBC	Word Biblical Commentary
ZA	*Zeitschrift für Assyriologie*
ZAW	*Zeitschrift für die Alttestamentliche Wissenschaft*
ZNW	*Zeitschrift für die Neutestamentliche Wissenschaft*

Biographical Sketch:
H(enry) Neil Richardson

෨ᦾ

H. NEIL RICHARDSON WAS BORN IN Pendleton, Oregon, on May 21, 1916, elder son of Edwin Ira and Iter Georgina Neil Richardson. Soon after, the family moved to Tacoma, Washington, and there Neil was educated in the public schools and then at the University of Puget Sound, receiving an A.B. with dual majors in Religious Education and Drama.

Following college graduation in 1940, Neil matriculated at Boston University School of Theology and, upon receiving the S.T.B. in 1943, was awarded the Lucinda Bidwell Beebe Fellowship and enrolled as a doctoral candidate in Old Testament Studies at Boston University Graduate School. In 1951 a Ph.D. was awarded to him after completion of a dissertation entitled *Ugaritic Parallels to the Old Testament.*

In 1945 Neil received an appointment at Syracuse University, where he was Associate Professor of Bible and Religion until 1957. In the fall of 1958 he began a 24-year teaching career as Professor of Old Testament at Boston University School of Theology and Graduate School.

The archaeology "bug" bit Neil in 1953–54 when he spent fourteen months as a Fellow of the American Schools of Oriental Research and participated in a dig at Dhiban and at Tell es-Sultan (Jericho) under Kathleen Kenyon. Infatuation with biblical archaeology never left him!

Neil was appointed Annual Professor for 1956–57 and Director for 1957–58 at the W. F. Albright Institute of Archaeological Research in Jerusalem. Although the family of five was forced to leave the area at the outbreak of hostilities during the Suez Crisis, Neil returned to fulfill his responsibilities and participated in excavations at Jericho, Tell el-Jib (Gibeon), Beth-zur, Khirbet Fahil (Pella), and Tell Balatah (Shechem).

He took his sabbatical year of 1966–67 in Israel and further familiarized himself with the Holy Land from Dan to Beersheba and beyond, as well as working on a special week-long project designed to find the Solomonic Gate at Tell Gezer.

In 1971 he joined with G. Ernest Wright and others to excavate at Dhali (Idalion), Cyprus, and continued with this project through 1974. From 1980 to 1987 he worked with Ephraim Stern on the Senior Staff at Tel Dor, Israel.

Dr. Richardson's many scholarly articles and lectures reflect not only his avid interest in biblical archaeology but his love of Semitic and other ancient languages. This knowledge undergirded his insight into the canonical writings, which he gladly shared with students, academic colleagues, and groups of clergy and laity.

H. Neil Richardson, archaeologist, Semitic-language scholar, teacher, and ordained United Methodist minister, was married to C. Faith Simpson, his partner and research assistant, for almost fifty years. Neil Richardson died in Boston, Massachusetts, on December 19, 1988. A memorial service was held in Marsh Chapel at Boston University on Sunday afternoon, January 15, 1989.

Curriculum Vitae:
H. Neil Richardson

Born

May 21, 1916, Pendleton, Oregon, son of Edwin Ira and Iter Georgina Neil Richardson.

Died

December 19, 1988, Beth Israel Hospital, Boston, Massachusetts.

Family

Married C. Faith Simpson in Tacoma, Washington, April 9, 1939.

Three daughters: Joan Christine Harrington Wrenn of Hayward, California; Marsha Ruth Richardson and Marla Faith Richardson of Newton, Massachusetts.

Two grandchildren: Drew Marshall Harrington and Erryn Faith Harrington.

Two great-grandsons: Jacob Daniel Harrington and Jaret Edward Harrington.

Education

Tacoma (Washington) Public Schools.

A.B., University of Puget Sound, 1940.

Classes at Harvard University and Episcopal Divinity School.

S.T.B. (cum laude), Boston University, 1943.

Ph.D., Boston University, 1951.

Fellowships/Honors

Lucinda Bidwell Beebe Fellow, Boston University, 1943–44.

Graduate Assistant in Old Testament, Boston University School of Theology, 1943–45.

Fellow, W. F. Albright Institute of Archaeological Research, Jerusalem, 1952–53.

Post-doctoral Fellow, Nelson Glueck Institute, Jerusalem, 1966–67.

Honorary Associate, W. F. Albright Institute of Archaeological Research, Jerusalem, 1966–67.

Visiting Scholar, Near Eastern Languages and Culture, Harvard University, 1981–82.

Honorary Trustee, W. F. Albright Institute of Archaeological Research, 1985–88.

Academic Positions

Instructor—Associate Professor of Bible and Religion, Syracuse University, 1945–57; Acting Chairman of Department of Bible and Religion, 1950–51.

Director, Institute of Religious Education, Syracuse University, summer 1955; co-director, summer 1956.

Annual Professor, W. F. Albright Institute of Archaeological Research, Jerusalem, 1956–57 (on leave from Syracuse University).

Curriculum Vitae: H. Neil Richardson

Director, W. F. Albright Institute of Archaeological Research, Jerusalem, 1957–58 (on leave from Boston University).

Associate Professor—Professor of Old Testament, Boston University (School of Theology and Graduate School), 1957–81; Professor Emeritus, 1981–88.

Church Affiliation

Ordained Deacon, The Methodist Church, 1942, by Bishop G. Bromley Oxnam.

Ordained Elder, The Methodist Church, 1947, by Bishop W. Earl Ledden.

Member, Pacific Northwest Annual Conference, The Methodist Church, 1940–68.

Member, New Hampshire Annual Conference, The United Methodist Church, 1968–88.

Pastoral Experience

Student pastor, Gig Harbor (Washington) M. E. Church, 1938–39; LeSourd Methodist Church, Tacoma, Washington, 1939–40.

Pastor, Evangelical Congregational Church, Dunstable, Massachusetts, 1941–44; Trinity Methodist Church, Cambridge, Massachusetts, 1944–45.

Interim Pastor, Geddes Congregational Church, Syracuse, New York, 1945–46, 1947–48; Plymouth Congregational Church, Syracuse, New York, 1950–51; Constantia (New York) Congregational Church, Nov. 1956–May 1957.

Positions Held

Chair, Leadership Training, Religious Education and Radio Committees, Council of Churches of Syracuse and Onondaga County (New York), 1945–52.

Corresponding Secretary, National Association of Hebrew Professors, 1950–51.

President, Theta Chi Beta (Bible Honorary), 1950–52.

Chair, Membership Committee, American Academy of Religion, 1952–54.

Chair, Liberal Arts Curriculum Committee, Syracuse University, 1954–56.

Book Editor, *Journal of Bible and Religion*, 1954–62.

Chair, Visual Aids Committee, American Schools of Oriental Research, 1954–59.

President, Alumni and Friends, American Schools of Oriental Research, 1955, 1960.

Co-director, World Council of Churches Workcamp in Gizeh, Egypt, August 1956.

Vice-President, American Academy of Religion, 1957.

President, Board of Trustees, Palestine Archaeological Museum, Jerusalem, 1958.

President, American Academy of Religion, 1958.

Lecturer, School for Accepted Supply Pastors of The Methodist Church, 1958, 1965.

Representative of Boston University at International Congress of Old Testament Scholars at Oxford, England, Summer 1959.

Chair, University Lectures Committee, Boston University, 1960–61.

Associate Trustee, American Schools of Oriental Research, 1961–62.

Archaeological Research Editor, *Journal of Bible and Religion*, 1964–67.

President, New England Section, Society of Biblical Literature, 1969.

Representative of Boston University at Consortium of Hebrew Union College Biblical and Archaeological School in Jerusalem, Israel, March 1969.

Chair, Continuing Education Committee, Board of Ordained Ministry, New Hampshire Annual Conference, 1969–80.

Chair, Zion Research Foundation/ASOR Summer Fellowship Committee, 1971.

Co-chair, Section on Philology: Hebrew and Cognate Languages, Society of Biblical Literature, 1971–72.

Associate-in-Council, Society of Biblical Literature, 1971–72.

Chair, Visiting Committee to Weston College for Massachusetts Board of Higher Education, 1971–72.

Chair, Committee to Evaluate Internship Program at Boston University School of Theology, 1973–74.

Chair, Section on Archaeology, Society of Biblical Literature, 1973–79.
Representative of Boston University Faculty on Committee on Hunger Project of the Massachusetts Foundation for Humanities and Public Policy, 1974–76.
Chair, Mutual Ministry and Community Committee, Boston University School of Theology, 1975–77.
Chair, Comprehensive Examination Committee, Biblical Studies, Boston University Graduate School, 1976–77.
Trustee, W. F. Albright Institute of Archaeological Research, 1976–77.
Secretary, Corporation of the American Schools of Oriental Research, 1976–80.
Consultant, Christian Science Publishing House, 1977–80.
Consultant, National Endowment for the Humanities, 1980–88.

Archaeological Activity

Area Supervisor: Dhiban, Jordan, 1952, 1953; Tell es-Sultan (Jericho), 1953, 1958; Tell el-Jib (Gibeon), 1956, 1959; Tell Gezer (Gezer), Israel, 1967.
Archaeological Advisor, Beth-zur, 1957.
Co-director, Khirbet Fahil (Pella), Jordan, 1958.
Assistant Field Director and Area Supervisor, 1971; Administrative Director, Director of Field School, 1972, 1974, Dhali (Idalion), Cyprus.
Senior Staff, Tell Balatah (Shechem), 1957, 1960; Tel Dor, Israel, 1980–87.

Memberships in Learned Societies at Time of Death

American Schools of Oriental Research
Catholic Biblical Association of America
Israel Exploration Society
National Geographic Society
Society of Biblical Literature

Publications

"A Ugaritic Letter of a King to His Mother," *Journal of Biblical Literature* 66, 1947.
"Some Literary Parallels between Ugaritic and the Old Testament," *Journal of Bible and Religion* 20, 1952.
"God's Search for Man in Biblical Thought," *Journal of Bible and Religion* 23, 1955.
"Some Notes on ליץ and Its Derivatives" and "Two Addenda to 'Some Notes on ליץ and Its Derivatives,' " *Vetus Testamentum* 5, 1955.
"With Pick and Trowel," *Adult Student*, 1955.
"Some Notes on 1QSa," *Journal of Biblical Literature* 76, 1957.
"The Historical Reliability of Chronicles," *Journal of Bible and Religion* 26, 1958.
"The 1958 Sounding at Pella," *Biblical Archaeologist*, 1958, with Robert W. Funk.
"Report of the Director of the School at Jerusalem," *Bulletin of the American Schools of Oriental Research* 152, 1958.
"A Decade of Archaeology in Palestine," *Journal of Bible and Religion* 27, 1959. (Presidential Address, American Academy of Religion, 1958.)
"Kh. Fahil (Pella)" in Chronique Archaeologique, *Revue Biblique* 67, 1960.
"A New Seventh Century Hebrew Ostracon," *Journal of Bible and Religion* 29, 1961.
Reader's Guide for Haggai—Zechariah 1–8—Malachi. Nashville: Board of Education of The Methodist Church, 1962.
"Agriculture" and numerous short articles, *Interpreter's Dictionary of the Bible*, 1962.
"Biblical Law Basis for Modern Law, *The Boston Globe*, Summer 1963.
"Studies in Genesis," International Lesson Series, *Adult Student* 22/7–8, 1963.
"Koinonia in Deed," *The Christian Century*, February 12, 1964.
"The Way of Israel," *Adult Bible Course*, 1964–65.

Handbook for the Study of Biblical Aramaic, 1965, rev. 1971.
Mould, E. W. K., *Essentials of Bible History,* rev. by Richardson and Berkey, 1966.
"A Critical Note on Amos 7:14," *Journal of Biblical Literature,* 1966.
"A Stamped Handle from Khirbet Yarmuk," *Bulletin of the American Schools of Oriental Research* 192, 1968.
"Apart from Justice and Righteousness There Is No Life: An Exegetical Study of Amos 5," *Wesleyan Studies in Religion,* 1969–70.
"The Last Words of David: Some Notes on II Samuel 23:1–7," *Journal of Biblical Literature* 90, 1971.
Articles on Esther, Judith, Tobit, and Additions to the Book of Esther in *The Interpreter's One-Volume Commentary on the Bible,* 1971.
Annotated Bibliography on the Old Testament, *Nexus* 46, 1972–73.
"SKT (Amos 9:11): 'Booth' or 'Succoth'," *Journal of Biblical Literature* 92/3, 1973.
"Cyprus" in *Interpreter's Dictionary of the Bible,* Supplementary Volume, 1976.
"Archaeology: Theory and Practice with Particular Reference to Idalion, Cyprus," *Nexus,* 1977.
"Origins of God's Chosen People," *Adult Bible Series,* 1982.
"Building a Model of Solomon's Temple," *Nexus* 54, 1977.
"Amos 2:13–16: Its Structure and Function in the Book," *Seminar Papers, Society of Biblical Literature,* 1978.
Handbook of Readings for the Study of Dor, 1984, rev. 1985.
"The Old Testament Background of Jesus as Begotten of God," *Bible Review,* Fall 1986.
"Psalm 106: "Yahweh's Succoring Love Saves from the Death of a Broken Covenant," *Love and Death in the Ancient Near East,* Essays in Honor of Marvin H. Pope, 1987.
"Hope and Judgment: Four Visions in the Book of Amos," in *Bible Review.*

Reviews

Johnson, *Prayer in the Apocrypha and Pseudepigrapha* in *Journal of Bible and Religion* 17, 1949.
Young, *An Introduction to the Old Testament* in *Journal of Bible and Religion* 18, 1950.
Thiessen, *Introductory Lectures in Systematic Theology* in *Journal of Bible and Religion* 19, 1951.
Two Hebrew grammars in *Vetus Testamentum* 3, 1953.
The Apocrypha in *Journal of Bible and Religion* 23, 1955.
Mendelsohn, ed., *Religions of the Ancient Near East* in *Journal of Bible and Religion* 23, 1955.
Rowley, *The Relevance of Apocalyptic* in *Journal of Bible and Religion* 23, 1955.
Canadian Journal of Theology in *Journal of Bible and Religion* 23, 1955.
Pritchard, *Ancient Near Eastern Texts* in *Journal of Bible and Religion* 24, 1956.
Braden, *These Also Believe* in *Journal of Bible and Religion* 25, 1957.
Murphy, *The Dead Sea Scrolls and the Bible* in *Journal of Bible and Religion* 25, 1957.
Wright, *Biblical Archaeology* in *Journal of Bible and Religion* 25, 1957.
Confraternity of Christian Doctrine, *The Holy Bible,* III in *Journal of Bible and Religion* 25, 1957.
Graystone, *The Dead Sea Scrolls and the Originality of Christ* in *Journal of Bible and Religion* 25, 1957.
Mowinckel, *He That Cometh* in *Journal of Bible and Religion* 26, 1958.
Moscati, *Ancient Semitic Civilizations* in *Journal of Bible and Religion* 27, 1959.
Davis, *Understanding Judaism* in *Journal of Bible and Religion* 27, 1959.
Deere, *The Twelve Speak* in *Journal of Bible and Religion* 27, 1959.
Kuhner, *Encyclopedia of the Papacy* in *Journal of Bible and Religion* 27, 1959.
Zimmermann, *The Book of Tobit* in *Journal of Bible and Religion* 27, 1959.

Baillie, *Our Knowledge of God* in *Journal of Bible and Religion* 27, 1959.
Coffin, *The Meaning of the Cross* in *Journal of Bible and Religion* 27, 1959.
Hume, *The World's Living Religions* in *Journal of Bible and Religion* 27, 1959.
Walker, *A History of the Christian Church* in *Journal of Bible and Religion* 27, 1959.
Williams, *What Present-Day Theologians Are Thinking* in *Journal of Bible and Religion* 27, 1959.
Beare, *First Epistle of Peter* in *Journal of Bible and Religion* 27, 1959.
Cadbury, *The Making of Luke–Acts* in *Journal of Bible and Religion* 28, 1960.
Johnson, *Psychology of Religion* in *Journal of Bible and Religion* 28, 1960.
J. E. and C. F. Holley, *Pictorial Profile of the Holy Land* in *Journal of Bible and Religion* 28, 1960.
Pritchard, *Gibeon: Where the Sun Stood Still* in *Religion in Life*, Spring 1963.
Franken and Franken-Battershill, *A Primer of Old Testament Archaeology* in *Journal of Bible and Religion* 32, 1964.
Gray, *I & II Kings: A Commentary* in *Journal of Bible and Religion* 33, 1965.
Finegan, *Handbook of Biblical Chronology* in *Journal of Bible and Religion* 33, 1965.
Herrmann, *Yarih und Nikkal und der Preis der Kutarat-Gottinnen: Ein kultisch magischer Text aus Ras Schamra* in *Journal of Biblical Literature* 87, 1968.
Rosenthal and Sivan, *Ancient Lamps in the Schloessinger Collection* in *Journal of the American Oriental Society*, 1981.
Avigad, *Discovering Jerusalem* in *Journal of Biblical Literature* 104, 1985.
Murphy-O'Connor, *The Holy Land, An Archaeological Guide from Earliest Times to 1700* (second, revised edition) and Doyle, *The Pilgrim's New Guide to the Holy Land* in *Journal of Biblical Literature.*

Unpublished Works/Lectures

"Ugaritic Parallels to the Old Testament," doctoral dissertation, Boston University, 1951.
"The Importance of Archaeology for the Humanities," Syracuse University Humanities Lecture Series, 1953.
"The Dead Sea Scrolls," lecture given by invitation to the Theological Faculty and Students at St. Lawrence University, 1955.
"The Prophets," "Archaeology and the Bible," Cape Cod Council of Churches, Fall 1958.
"Contemporary Near East Problems," St. Paul Methodist Church, Concord, New Hampshire, Fall 1958.
"Future Tasks of Old Testament Scholarship," paper read by invitation at New England Section of the Society of Biblical Literature, 1960.
"Archaeological Aspects of Canaanite-Aegean Relations," illustrated lecture given by invitation at New England Section of the Society of Biblical Literature, 1968.
"An Alternative to the Proposition 'God Reveals Himself in His Mighty Acts,'" lecture given by invitation at West Virginia Wesleyan College, 1968.
"The Ten Commandments," Newton Centre Ecumenical Lenten Gathering, 1969.
"Revelation and History: Language-Event as the Channel of God's Self-Revelation," Lowell Lecture, Boston University, 1970.
"International Trade in the Late Bronze Age (1550–1200 B.C.E.)," Feinsilver Lecture, Hebrew College, 1984.

Hobbies

Photography, collecting and listening to classical recordings, flower gardening.

Travel

Israel, Jordan, Egypt, Cyprus, Syria, Lebanon, Turkey, Iraq, Greece, Mexico, Canada, and most of the U.S.A. and western European countries.

THE HEBREW BIBLE IN ITS TIME

The Slaying of the Fleeing, Twisting Serpent: Isaiah 27:1 in Context

Bernhard W. Anderson

❧•❧

THIS STUDY FOCUSES ON A SINGLE VERSE found in the so-called Apocalypse of Isaiah, which the JPSV translates:

> In that day the Lord will punish
> With His great, cruel, mighty sword
> Leviathan the Elusive Serpent—
> Leviathan the Twisting Serpent;
> He will slay the Dragon of the Sea.
>
> Isa 27:1[1]

Footnotes to the translation indicate that the meaning of the Hebrew words
translated 'elusive' (*bāriaḥ*) and 'twisted' (*ᶜăqallātôn*) is uncertain.

The approach to this study is methodological, that is to say, Isa 27:1 may
be illuminated by various approaches: the study of the history of religions; a
form-critical analysis of the pericope; stylistic or rhetorical criticism of the
verse in its literary context; the placement of the passage within the structure
of Isaiah 24–27; and finally, determination of the function of the Isaiah
Apocalypse, which contains this crucial verse, within the canonical whole of

---

Author's Note: I gratefully dedicate this essay, originally presented in a graduate seminar at
Boston University School of Theology, to my esteemed colleague, Neil Richardson, who
would have enjoyed participating in the discussion.

1. *Tanakh: A New Translation of the Holy Scriptures According to the Traditional Hebrew
Text* (Philadelphia: Jewish Publication Society, 1985), also abbreviated JPSV.

---

the book of Isaiah. In this manner it is possible to move around the verse in concentric hermeneutical circles, as it were. Each of these steps, I hope to show, is important in the exegetical process.

The Myth of the *Chaoskampf*

In his seminal work *Shöpfung und Chaos in Urzeit und Endzeit*, published in 1895, Hermann Gunkel drew scholarly attention to the significance of the serpent motif in the history of religions.[2] A few years earlier, in 1873, a copy of the Babylonian creation story was found during the excavation of the library of Ashurbanapal at the site of ancient Nineveh. In this story the origin of the cosmos is traced to a fierce duel between the divine warrior Marduk and the monster of chaos Tiamat, in consequence of which the victorious god was crowned king in the heavenly council. Gunkel drew attention to echoes of the dragon myth and traditions regarding the primeval sea in the Old Testament. Israel's interpreters, he observed, used mythical language to portray a typological correspondence between, on the one hand, the divine triumph over the forces of chaos in the beginning and, on the other hand, the new creation at the consummation of time. Thus *Urzeit gleich Endzeit* ("primeval time corresponds to eschatological time").

Gunkel maintained that this myth of the conquest of the powers of chaos had its source in Babylonia. Since the discovery of the Ugaritic texts, however, it has become evident that the Israelites inherited this mythical view more directly from the Canaanites, in whose midst they dwelled. In these texts we read about a victory over a serpent *ltn*, usually vocalized *Lotan*[3] and identified with biblical *liwyātān*, Leviathan. In one case the victory is attributed to the goddess Anath on behalf of Baal. The passage is redolent of imagery used of the Divine Warrior Yahweh in various biblical texts: "rider of clouds," "sea" (*yam*), "river, flood" (*nahar*), the "seven-headed crooked serpent." H. L. Ginsberg translates:

2. Hermann Gunkel, *Shöpfung und Chaos in Urzeit und Endzeit* (1895); abbreviated translation by Charles A. Muenchow, "The Influence of Babylonian Mythology upon the Biblical Creation Story," in *Creation in the Old Testament* (ed. Bernhard W. Anderson; Philadelphia: Fortress, 1984) 25–52.

3. However, J. A. Emerton proposes *litanu*, going back via *liyatanu* to an original *liwyatanu* ("Leviathan and *LTN*: The Vocalization of the Ugaritic Word for the Dragon," *VT* 32 [1982] 327–31).

> What enemy's ris[en] 'gainst Baal,
> What foe 'gainst the Rider of Clouds [*rkb. ᶜrpt*]?
> Crushed I not El's Belov'd Yamm?
> Destroyed I not El's Flood [*nhr*] Rabbim?
> Did I not, pray, muzzle the Dragon [*tnn*]?
> I did crush the crooked serpent [*bṭn. ᶜqltn*],
> Shalyat the seven-headed.[4]

In another text that has even closer linguistic affinities with Isa 27:1, the triumph is attributed to Baal:

> If thou smite Lotan,
> the serpent slant [*ltn. bṭn. brḥ*]
> Destroy the Serpent tortuous [*bṭn. ᶜqltn*],
> Shalyat of the seven heads.
>
> *UT* 67:1–3

John Gray translates:

> 'Though thou didst smite *Ltn* the Primaeval Serpent,
> And didst annihilate the Crooked Serpent,
> The close-coiling-One of Seven Heads,
> The heavens will dry up, yea, languish;
> I shall pound thee, consume thee, and eat thee,
> Cleft, forspent, and exhausted.
> Thou shalt indeed go down into the throat of Mt
> the son of El.[5]

The dependence of Isa 27:1 on the Ugaritic texts is very close: *liwyātān nāḥāš bāriaḥ / liwyātān nāḥāš ᶜăqallātôn / hāttannîn ᵓăšer bayyām*. The passage, observes William R. Millar, "is almost a direct quote from Ugaritic text 5.1.1–5."[6] The close affinity, however, does not necessarily indicate that the poet had the Ugaritic texts at hand. It seems, rather, that the Ugaritic myth influenced the Israelite poetic tradition from early times, perhaps as early as the Song of the Sea (Exod 15:1–18), and in all likelihood by the time of the cultic recitations connected with the acclamation of Yahweh as King in Zion

---

4. H. L. Ginsberg, "Poems about Baal and Anath," *ANET* (ed. James B. Pritchard; Princeton: Princeton University Press, 1969) 137, D:30:9–10. For the Ugaritic text, see Cyrus Gordon, ᶜnt:III:34 (*Ugaritic Textbook* [AnOr 38: Rome: Pontifical Biblical Institute, 1967] 320–21) and John Gray, *The Legacy of Canaan* (2d ed.; VTSup 5; Leiden: Brill, 1965) 27–30.

5. Gray, *Legacy*, 30.

6. William R. Millar, *Isaiah 24–27 and the Origin of Apocalyptic* (HSM 11; Missoula: Scholars Press, 1976) 55.

(e.g., Psalm 93). In a community lament (Psalm 74), a hymnic interlude is found:

> Yet God my King is from of old,
>   working salvation in the earth.
> You divided the sea by your might;
>   you broke the heads of the dragons in the waters.
> You crushed the heads of Leviathan,
>   you gave him as food for the creatures of the
>   wilderness.
>
>   Psalm 74:12–14, NRSV; cf. Ps 89:9–13

Outside of cultic contexts the myth of the serpent appears, for instance, in an apostrophe to the victorious arm of the Divine Warrior in Isa 51:9 and in a meditation on the power of the Creator in Job 26:12–13:

> By his power he stilled the Sea,
>   by his understanding he struck down Rahab.
> By his wind the heavens were made fair;
>   his hand pierced the fleeing serpent [*nāḥāš bārîaḥ*].

In all these biblical texts, the issue is not whether Israel was influenced by the myth of the *Chaoskampf,* of which there were variations in the ancient world; rather, the question is how the myth was interpreted in the poetry of Israel's religion. I turn then from the context of history of religions to a consideration of Isa 27:1 in its own literary context.

Delimitation of the Literary Unit

In the exegesis of a biblical text, the first task is to determine the literary unit. Following the method of form criticism, it is usual first to determine the scope of the literary genre, then to seek to determine its *Sitz im Leben,* and finally, to compare it with other genres of the same sort, either biblical or extrabiblical literature.

Some commentators maintain that in this case the literary unit is Isa 27:1–5, but that is questionable on form-critical grounds. There is much to be said for regarding this verse as a literary unit that "stands by itself," as Ronald Clements remarks.[7] The verse has a decided beginning, the cliché "in that day," and is bounded by the beginning of v. 2, "in that day." Moreover, 27:1 has its own thematic integrity: the victory of the divine warrior over the

7. Ronald E. Clements, *Isaiah 1–39* (NCB; Grand Rapids: Eerdmans, 1981).

monster of chaos. The ensuing unit, 27:2–5[6], does not treat that theme at all but is a separate literary genre with another theme: a vineyard song announcing an eschatological reversal of the Song of the Vineyard found in Isa 5:1–7. It is tempting to analyze the literary parallels between this eschatological song and the earlier one: in both, the vineyard is regarded as potentially fertile (5:1, 27:2); in both, the vineyard is threatened by 'thorns' and 'briars' (*šāmîr* [*wā*] *šāyit*, the same word-pair in both cases: 5:6, 27:4); and in both, Yahweh is the Keeper of the Vineyard, though in 27:4 with this difference: "Of wrath I have none." But all of that is beyond the scope of this paper. Suffice it to say that the Song of the Vineyard is not intrinsically related to the announcement of the Victory of the Divine Warrior. As I shall seek to prove, the victory of the Divine Warrior (27:1) connects with the foregoing poem at the end of chapter 26.

Often Isa 27:1 is regarded as prose but, if it is prose, it is a prose that is close to poetry and is so regarded in the JPSV translation.[8] In the past, some commentators have interpreted the text prosaically to refer to three monsters, each of which symbolizes an oppressing nation such as Egypt, Babylon, and Greece—the three domains of Alexander the Great.[9] A similar historicizing view is found in the recent commentary by John Watts who, though translating as poetry, maintains that the monster refers to Tyre.[10] However, the linguistic parallels with ancient Ugaritic poetry are sufficient to invalidate a prosaic interpretation. The subject of Isa 27:1 is not three monsters but one, a monster who symbolizes the powers of evil at work in human history, manifest in any of the oppressive nations.

In Ugaritic texts the weapon of the Divine Warrior apparently is a club or mace that crushes the heads of the sea monster, whereas in the Isaiah text, Yahweh wields a mighty sword (see also the apocalyptic passage, Isa 34:5–6). This is true also in Isa 51:9, where the poet gives an appeal to the mighty "arm" of the Divine Warrior:

> Awake, awake, clothe yourself with splendor,
> O arm of the Lord!
> Awake as in days of old,
> As in former ages!
>
> Isa 51:9, JPSV

---

8. Millar notes that the verse should be read "either as prose or as long poetic lines, run on" (*Isaiah 24–27*, 54–55).

9. So Otto Procksch, *Jesaia I* (KAT 9; Leipzig: W. Scholl, 1930).

10. John D. W. Watts, *Isaiah 1–33* (WBC 24; Waco, Tex.: Word, 1985).

The poet goes on to speak of Yahweh's victory over [the] Sea, over the *Tĕhôm Rabbāh* 'Great Deep'. While the text of Isa 27:1 varies the myth slightly, the poetic parallelism is retained: Leviathan the fleeing serpent, Leviathan the twisting serpent. Although the *Kethiv* of the first modifier is unusual for an adjectival form (which ordinarily is spelled with a *yod*), the *Qere* may call for that form. The participial reading in the 1QIsa[a] manuscript (*bôrēaḥ*) and LXX *pheugonta* 'fleeing', also suggest that the archaic word describes some characteristic of the serpent. Albright's proposal of 'prehistoric' or 'primeval'[11] does not offer an appropriate parallel to the archaic term *ᶜăqallātôn* 'crooked, twisting, coiling'.

The Larger Literary Unit

Form criticism, however, has its limitations. For one thing, Isa 27:1 does not seem to reflect the requisite *Sitz im Leben*, unless it is indirectly related to the cultic situation of the enthronement of Yahweh celebrated in some of the psalms. Furthermore, form criticism tends in the direction of dividing material into smaller literary units rather than perceiving larger literary wholes. It is difficult to believe that this single verse of scripture really stands alone, as Clements maintains. It seems to me that this situation substantiates further the claim that the approach to the literature of scripture must be "form criticism and beyond," to cite the title of a presidential address to the Society of Biblical Literature by James Muilenburg.[12] Even Clements apparently senses this need to go beyond the immediate literary unit when he states that this verse was "almost certainly" added "in order to sum up the message of assurance given in 26:19" (promise of victory over the power of death), and that "it is, therefore, a further response to the lament of 26:7–18."[13]

What lies "beyond" form criticism, though not repudiating its gains, is rhetorical criticism. This mode of criticism is concerned with *Sitz im Text*, as one of my students, Edgar Conrad, puts it:[14] the function of the text in its literary context, the style and pattern of the literary unit, and the various

11. W. F. Albright, "Are the Ephod and the Teraphim Mentioned in Ugaritic Literature?" *BASOR* 83 (1941) 39–42.

12. James Muilenburg, "Form Criticism and Beyond," *JBL* 88 (1969) 1–18.

13. Clements, *Isaiah 1–39*, 218.

14. Edgar W. Conrad, "The Community as King in Second Isaiah," *Understanding the Word: Essays in Honor of Bernhard W. Anderson* (ed. James T. Butler, Edgar W. Conrad, and Ben C. Ollenburger; JSOTSup 37; Sheffield: JSOT, 1985) 99–111.

devices that bind the whole together (e.g., *inclusio*, chiasm, word-plays, alliteration, assonance, etc.).

Consider now the possibility suggested earlier that Isa 27:1 belongs with the poetic material at the end of chapter 26 rather than with the ensuing eschatological Song of the Vineyard. The presence of the words "in that day" does not necessarily militate against this proposal. An examination of the uses of that cliché reveals that it is not confined solely to introductory oracles; it may introduce a concluding eschatological promise, or it may be found in the middle of an oracle.

In his commentary published in 1941, Edward J. Kissane connected this verse with the foregoing verse (26:21).[15] The same connection was made by William Millar in his poetic analysis.[16] This association is suggested by the content, since the announcement (introduced by 'behold', *kî-hinnēh*) that Yahweh is prepared to go forth from his heavenly citadel or sanctuary (*māqôm*) connects nicely with the assertion that "in that day" the Divine Warrior will triumph over the power of evil. The poetic unit may even begin at 26:20, just after the announcement that death does not have the final verdict:

> Come, my people, enter your chambers,
>   and shut your doors behind you;
> hide yourselves for a little while
>   until the wrath is past.
> For the Lord comes out from his place
>   to punish the inhabitants of the earth for their iniquity;
> the earth will disclose the blood shed upon it,
>   and will no longer cover its slain.
> On that day the Lord with his
>   cruel and great and strong sword,
> will punish Leviathan the fleeing serpent,
>   Leviathan the twisting serpent,
> and he will kill the dragon that is in the sea.
>
> Isa 26:20–27:1, NRSV

Notice that the linkage of 27:1 to the foregoing poetic strophe is established by a rhetorical device, namely, the repeated use of the verb *pāqad* 'visit, punish' (see 27:3, 'harm'). The motif of divine visitation is found in the earlier passage introduced by "in that day" (24:21–23), where Yahweh will punish "the host of heaven" and "the kings on earth." According to 26:21 Yahweh will go forth from his celestial bulwark to punish the inhabitants of the earth for

---

15. Edward J. Kissane, *The Book of Isaiah* (2 vols.; Dublin: Browne and Nolan, 1960) 1.284.
16. Millar, *Isaiah 24–27,* 54–55.

their iniquity; and according to 27:1 the Divine Warrior will punish with his mighty sword the powers of evil at work in human history. What is the relation between 'the iniquity' (*ʿāwōn*) of the earth's inhabitants and the power of evil symbolized by Leviathan? When read in the larger context of the Isaiah Apocalypse, this iniquity is the violence that has oppressed the poor and help-less. Yahweh the Warrior comes to "punish" the power of evil. Notice too that the exhortation to the suffering people to hide "until the wrath is past" (26:20) anticipates the time of eschatological reversal when the day of judgment is past and Yahweh says, "I have no more wrath" (27:4), thereby suggesting that interconnecting motifs run through the larger literary whole.

The Literary Pattern of the Isaiah Apocalypse

I turn now to a rhetorical study of the cluster of chapters, Isaiah 24–27, which for many years scholars have regarded as a separate section in the book of Isaiah interpolated between the oracles against the nations (chaps. 13–23) and the conclusion of the original book of Isaiah (chaps. 28–32/33). Some doubt whether this section is apocalyptic in the same way that Daniel and similar literature is, but it is surely prophetic, well on the way to becoming apocalyptic. It is at this point that form criticism and rhetorical criticism may be supplemented with *Redaktionsgeschichte*, in attempting to trace the genesis of the Isaiah Apocalypse. Commenting on the key text, Isa 27:1 (which he regards as standing alone), Clements observes that this piece was "added to the Groundwork of chs. 24–27 at a late stage," as is evidenced by the redac-tional formula "in that day."[17]

Since the approach of this study is primarily methodological, it is unnec-essary to summarize all of the debates surrounding the study of Isaiah 24–27.[18] Suffice it to say that one of the noteworthy features of the Isaiah apoca-lypse is the interspersing of the oracles of impending divine judgment with lyrical poems or liturgical songs:

24:13–16a	Hymnic Praise of Yahweh's Majesty
25:1–5	Psalm of Thanksgiving
26:1–6	Eschatological Song
26:7–19	Community Lament
27:2–6	Eschatological Song of the Vineyard

17. Clements, *Isaiah 1–39*, 218.
18. See G. W. Anderson, "Isaiah XXIV–XXVII Reconsidered," *Congress Volume: Bonn 1962* (VTSup 9; Leiden: Brill, 1963) 118–26; Benedikt Otzen, "Traditions and Structures of Isaiah XXIV–XXVII," *VT* 24 (1974) 196–206.

Some scholars have argued on form-critical grounds that eschatological poems and lyrical poetry should be separated into two groups.[19] This is true but arbitrary and gives insufficient attention to the poetic pattern and vigor brought to light by stylistic criticism (see W. Millar's metrical analysis). A more convincing criterion for analysis is the distinction between poetic strophes and the prose of passages bounded by the phrase "in that day." Even this criterion fails in that so often "prose" borders on the verge of poetry, and further, these passages for the most part are inseparable from the tissue and marrow of the whole literary work.

I skirt the whole question of the genesis of the Isaiah Apocalypse and satisfy myself with the recognition that in its final form these four chapters display an overall structural unity.[20] The unit is composed of four poems, which may be outlined as follows:

1. Isa 24:1–20: the first poem, introduced by *hinnēh*, announces Yahweh's impending display of wrath (judgment), which threatens to reduce the earth to precreation chaos (cf. Jer 4:23–28), because its inhabitants have violated the laws of 'the everlasting covenant' (*běrît* *ʿôlām*).

2. Isa 24:21–25:12: the second is introduced with an "in-that-day" cliché and concludes with another "in-that-day" oracle (25:9–12). The subject of this poem is Yahweh's enthronement on Zion as cosmic king and judge, who in a victory banquet "at this mountain" offers security and peace to Israel and the nations.

3. The third poem opens with a song, introduced with the eschatological formula "in that day" (26:1–6), and—following the analysis given above (also W. Millar)—concludes with the "in-that-day" passage about the eschatological conquest of the Serpent (27:1). Here the question of theodicy is raised, and the people are assured that Yahweh will soon come to break the grip of evil, including the threat of death.

4. The fourth poem also opens with a song (Song of the Vineyard) introduced by the eschatological formula "in that day" (27:2–5) and concludes with two "in-that-day" oracles. Here the theme is the eschatological reversal of Yahweh's wrath against the vineyard Israel and the return of the dispersed people to Zion.

19. J. Lindblom, *Die Jesaja-Apokalypse: Jesaja 24–27* (Lunds Universiteit Årskrift, n.s. 1/34/3; Lund: C. W. K. Gleerup, 1938).

20. The Moab passage, 25:10b–12, is suspect to some scholars; but note that "on this mountain" refers back to 25:6 and 24:23.

Whatever prehistory the Isaiah Apocalypse may have had, these four poems display an overall unity and dynamic. Indeed, when read in their present form and sequence, the effect is almost overpowering, especially in current times, when the return of the earth to chaos is an existential possibility. The mythical motif of the slaying of the serpent Leviathan fits nicely into the literary whole. From the outset the theme is Yahweh's judgment, which threatens to return the earth to chaos:

> Now the Lord is about to lay waste the earth,
>   and make it desolate,
> And he will twist its surface
>   and scatter its inhabitants.
>
> Isa 24:1, NRSV

The poet draws upon the Priestly primeval history, which moves from creation-out-of-chaos to the near return to precreation chaos, owing to "violence" (*ḥāmās*).[21] The "inhabitants of the earth" have broken the laws of the Noachic *bĕrît ʿôlām* based on reverence for the life (*nepeš ḥayyâ*), both animal and human, that God has created.

> The earth lies polluted under its inhabitants,
> for they have transgressed law,
>   violated the statutes,
>   broken the everlasting covenant.
> Therefore a curse devours the earth,
>   and its inhabitants suffer for their guilt;
> therefore the inhabitants of the earth dwindled,
>   and few people are left.
>
> Isa 24:5–6, NRSV

In the manner of literary *inclusio*, the poem ends by returning to the chaos theme announced at the beginning:

> For the windows of heaven are opened,
>   and the foundations of the earth tremble.
> The earth is utterly broken,
>   the earth is torn asunder,
>   the earth is violently shaken.
> The earth staggers like a drunkard.
>   it sways like a hut;

21. See Anderson, "Creation and the Noachic Covenant," in *The Cry of the Environment and the Rebuilding of Christian Creation Tradition* (ed. P. Joranson and K. Butigan; Santa Fe, N. Mex.: Bear & Co., 1984). Also in *From Creation to New Creation* (Philadelphia: Augsburg/Fortress, 1994).

> its transgression lies heavy upon it,
> and it falls and will not rise again.
>
> Isa 24:18b–20, NRSV

In this poetic context, Yahweh is the Divine Warrior who comes to conquer the sinister powers in human history that cause oppression and death.

Along with the theme of the *Chaoskampf,* a second motif is developed contrapuntally, namely, the typological contrast between two cities. One is called variously "the city of chaos" (24:10), "the fortified city" (25:2; 27:10), "the lofty city" (26:5); the other city is "the strong city" into which the righteous enter, according to the processional psalm in 26:1–6, and which, according to another song, is a stronghold for the poor and oppressed (25:1–5). The former city is left unnamed; it may have been Babylon, or it could be any city which is a center of oppressive power. Marie-Louise Henry rightly observes that the description of the destroyed city, reminiscent of the fall of Babylon, is stylized and portrays "something typical, something of universal validity."[22] The latter city is clearly identified as Zion, situated in "the midst of the earth" (Isa 24:13; cf. Ps. 74:12), the *omphalos* or *axis mundi,* Zion is the city where creation began and where the new age, the new creation, will start—as in the eschatological poem that opens the book of Isaiah concerning the ultimate pilgrimage of all peoples to the elevated Mountain of Zion (Isa 2:1–4). Apocalyptic (or protoapocalyptic) thought is universal in outlook, but it never surrenders the centrality of Zion or the vindication of God's people.

The Isaiah Apocalypse in Canonical Context

I turn finally to the question of the place of the Isaiah Apocalypse (which highlights the chaos myth) within the canonical context of the book of Isaiah. This question has been largely ignored by earlier commentators. Walther Eichrodt, for instance, in his two-volume commentary, *Der Heilige in Israel* (Isaiah 1–12) and *Der Herr der Geschichte* (Isaiah 13–23, 28–39), completely omitted these chapters, for he was concerned with the original prophecy of Isaiah of Jerusalem.[23] Eliminating chapters from the discussion is unnecessary, however, for even though these two chapters were not composed by

---

22. Marie-Louise Henry, *Glaubenskrise und Glaubensbewährung in den Dichtungen der Jesajaapokalypse* (BWANT 5/6; Stuttgart: Kohlhammer, 1967) 20–34.

23. Walther Eichrodt, *Der Heilige in Israel: Jesaja 1–12* (Die Botschaft des Alten Testaments, Erläuterungen alttestamentlicher Schriften 17/1; Stuttgart: Calwer, 1960); idem, *Der Herr der Geschichte: Jesaja 13–23* (17/2; Stuttgart: Calwer, 1967).

Isaiah, they belong to the Zion theological tradition in which the eighth-century prophet stood.

It is impossible to treat here the large issue of the theological unity of the book of Isaiah as a whole and the movement from prophecy to apocalyptic that can be traced within the book. My own view, set forth in various essays,[24] is that the final form of the book exhibits an apocalyptic rereading of the Isaianic tradition. This apocalyptic *relecture* is made evident in a number of ways: (1) the eschatological editing of chaps. 2–32 [33], which are punctuated with "in that day" refrains; (2) the insertion of the Isaiah apocalypse into the heart of the basic Isaiah collection in chaps. 1–33, thereby providing a context for understanding the oracles against the nations; (3) the placement of "the little apocalypse" (chaps. 34–35) before the poems of Second Isaiah, thereby providing a transition from prophetic to apocalyptic perspective; and last, (4) the addition of the so-called Third Isaiah, which reflects the apocalyptic or protoapocalyptic view of the early years of the Restoration. Viewed in this canonical context, the Isaiah Apocalypse of chaps. 24–27 has an important function in the total composition.

What happened in this movement from prophecy to apocalypse was that Israel's interpreters grappled with the radical power of evil at a different level—some would say at a more profound level—than the prophets who preached repentance and spelled out the consequences of covenant infidelity. The notion that evil is wrongdoing for which the people are responsible was tried in the balance of suffering and found wanting. People are often not just the perpetrators of evil, but the victims of it. Evil manifests itself as an insidious, perhaps we should say "demonic," power in history. It manifests itself typically as a colossal military power that sweeps inexorably over small peoples, as Habakkuk perceived Babylonian imperialism to be (Hab 1:2–2:5). It manifests itself in structures of power that crush the poor and helpless in society. In short, evil manifests itself as "violence"—the theme of Habakkuk's lament (Hab 1:2) and the motive for the Great Flood (Gen 6:11).

The question with which apocalyptic wrestles is not how the human heart can be changed (the question of *šûb* or repentance), but rather how history

---

24. See Anderson, "The Apocalyptic Rendering of the Isaiah Tradition," in *The Social World of Formative Christianity and Judaism: Essays in Tribute to Howard Clark Kee* (ed. Jacob Neusner et al.; Philadelphia: Augsberg Fortress, 1988) 17–38; " 'God With Us'—in Judgment and in Mercy: The Editorial Structure of Isaiah 5–10 (11)," in *Canon Theology and Old Testament Interpretation: Essays in Honor of Brevard S. Childs* (ed. Gene M. Tucker, David L. Petersen, and Robert R. Wilson; Philadelphia: Augsburg Fortress, 1988) 230–45; "The Holy One of Israel," in *Justice and the Holy: Essays in Honor of Walter Harrelson* (ed. Douglas A. Knight and Peter J. Paris; Atlanta: Scholars, 1989) 3–19.

can be exorcized of the demonic evil that holds terrible sway and even threatens the sovereignty of God. In answer to questions of theodicy or laments of "how long, O Lord?" apocalyptic writers stir the imagination with the vision of the imminent advent of God in power to overcome the tyranny of evil or, in the language of the myth, to slay Leviathan the fleeing, twisting serpent. The theme of victory over the Serpent is picked up in the Apocalypse of John, which speaks of the seven-headed monster (Rev 12:3), identified with Satan (12:9), who emerges out of the sea (Rev 13:1; cf. 21:1).

Brevard Childs is right, in my judgment, in observing that the canonical placement of the Apocalypse of Isaiah after Isaiah's oracles against the nations—and, we may add, just before Isaiah's message about God's "strange work" in chaps. 28–30—enables the reader to interpret the prophetic message in a transhistorical setting.[25] Babylon is not just a political power, but a symbol of a sinister force of evil that corrupts human history, and the same is true of other nations that take part in the great power game. Moreover, Jerusalem is not just a Palestinian city victimized in the power struggle, but rather a symbol of the City of God, the *axis mundi*, where the power of God's kingdom and the power of evil clash. In the visionary's religious imagination, the outcome of the battle is sure: God will ultimately—indeed, will soon—overcome the forces of evil concentrated in "the city of chaos" and symbolized by Leviathan, and will free human beings from captivity to evil and even from the fear of death that shadows military aggression. The Israelite people are a paradigm of all poor and helpless victims of evil everywhere; they too are invited to Zion, the center of the earth, where God's kingly power is manifest. This fortified city is the theme of the Psalm of Thanksgiving, occasioned by the destruction of "the city of chaos" or "the fortified city":

> For you have been a refuge to the poor,
> a refuge to the needy in their distress,
> a shelter from the rainstorm and a shade from the heat.
>
> Isa 25:4, NRSV

25. Brevard S. Childs (*Introduction to the Old Testament as Scripture* [Philadelphia: Fortress, 1979] 330–33), on "the theological shaping of First Isaiah," observes: "The redactional connection between chs. 13 and 24 point to Babylon's representative role among the nations, which function is not to be lost by an over-historicizing of the material" (p. 332).

Two Unifying Female Images in the Book of Isaiah

Katheryn Pfisterer Darr

Introduction

F EMALE IMAGERY APPEARS FREQUENTLY in Isaiah. Through various metaphors and related tropes, Isaiah's authors referred to women's experiences and to behavior stereotypically ascribed to women in order to communicate in powerful and persuasive ways.

Because female imagery abounds in Isaiah, biblical scholars interested in such tropes have been drawn to at least portions of the book. Thus far, most studies tend to treat only the Deutero- and Trito-Isaian materials.[1] As a result,

Author's Note: This essay, completed four years ago, reflects an early stage in my investigation of recurring female metaphors and related tropes in Isaiah. Although I remain convinced by the arguments advanced here, my research and thinking have progressed beyond this initial foray. Readers wishing further to pursue recurring female (and child) imagery in Isaiah should consult my book *Isaiah's Vision and the Family of God* (Louisville: Westminster/John Knox, 1994).

1. See, for example, P. Trible, *God and the Rhetoric of Sexuality* (OBT 2; Philadelphia: Fortress, 1978) 50–56, 60–68; M. Gruber, "The Motherhood of God in Second Isaiah," *RB* 90 (1983) 351–59; L. L. Bronner, "Gynomorphic Imagery in Exilic Isaiah (40–66)," *Dor leDor* 12 (1983–84) 71–83; J. J. Schmitt, "The Motherhood of God and Zion as Mother," *RB* 92 (1985) 557–69.

In the years since this essay was completed, however, several articles treating female imagery in Isaiah as a whole have appeared. See especially B. G. Webb, "Zion in Transformation: A Literary Approach to Isaiah," in *The Bible in Three Dimensions: Essays in Honor of Forty Years of Biblical Studies in the University of Sheffield* (JSOTSup 87; ed. D. J. A. Clines et al.; Sheffield: JSOT Press, 1992) 65–84.

broader questions about the functions and significance of female imagery throughout the work as a whole are neglected. In what follows, I shall discuss two recurring female images contributing both to the coherence and to the thematic development of Isaiah.[2] Because my analysis is synchronic rather than diachronic, I shall not pursue questions concerning the author, date, or redaction history of passages to which I refer.

Construing Metaphors and Similes

Old Testament scholars seeking definitions for *metaphor* and *simile* must look beyond their own discipline. Although figurative language appears frequently in Hebrew Scripture, it has not been the object of ongoing investigation and debate within the field.[3] While form criticism has facilitated the classification of fables, allegories, parables, etc.; and contemporary studies of Hebrew verse have illumined many formal characteristics of biblical poetry,[4] the nature and functions of metaphoric thought and speech have often been neglected.

Metaphor

Some exegetes apparently subscribe to a "substitution theory" of metaphor.[5] They either dismiss imagery as mere embellishment, a fancy way of

---

2. M. A. Sweeney summarizes evidence for the "redactional unity" of Isaiah and traces some of its thematic developments in *Isaiah 1–4 and the Post-Exilic Understanding of the Isaianic Tradition* (BZAW 171; Berlin: de Gruyter, 1988).

3. After surveying existing studies of biblical imagery, Kirsten Nielsen also concludes that figurative language has commanded only limited interest in Old Testament studies (*There is Hope for a Tree: The Tree as Metaphor in Isaiah* [JSOTSup 65; Sheffield: JSOT Press, 1989] 25–35). The situation differs in NT studies, of course, because of intense interest in Jesus' parables.

Since the completion of this essay, several studies of biblical metaphors have appeared, including M. Brettler, ed., *God is King: Understanding an Israelite Metaphor* (JSOTSup 76; Sheffield: JSOT Press, 1989); P. W. Macky, *The Centrality of Metaphors to Biblical Thought: A Method for Interpreting the Bible* (Studies in the Bible and Early Christianity 19; Lewiston, N.Y.: Mellen, 1990); J. Glambush, *Jerusalem in the Book of Ezekiel: The City as Yahweh's Wife* (SBLDS 130; Atlanta: Scholars Press, 1992).

4. Of course, figurative language is not restricted to poetic contexts. My point is simply that formal characteristics of biblical poetry (e.g., parallelism, meter) have received far more scrutiny than has imagery. P. D. Miller calls for greater attention to the function of imagery within biblical poetry in "Meter, Parallelism, and Tropes: The Search for Poetic Style" (*JSOT* 28 [1984] 99–106).

5. J. M. Soskice summarizes substitution theories of metaphor in *Metaphor and Religious Language* (Oxford: Clarendon, 1985) 24–26.

---

saying something that can be replaced by a literal expression without loss of cognitive content, or they simply decode it, focusing not upon the imagery itself, but rather upon what lies behind it. In either case, they ignore Northrop Frye's urging to "consider the possibility that metaphor is not an incidental ornament of biblical language, but one of its controlling modes of thought."[6]

Other commentators stress the affective impact of figurative language, that is, its ability to elicit from the hearer or reader a strong emotional response.[7] Such an approach accords with certain emotive theories that define metaphor as the result of deviant word usage. According to these theories, a phrase like "biting comment" lacks cognitive content because it conveys no *literal* meaning (comments cannot bite). Precisely for that reason, however, the emotive impact of the phrase is intensified.[8]

My own understanding of metaphor, influenced by that of I. A. Richards and Janet Martin Soskice, holds that the most interesting metaphors are neither ornamental substitutions for literal speech, nor simply emotive. Rather, they embody fresh insights attainable only through those metaphors.

In *The Philosophy of Rhetoric*, Richards wrote that "when we use a metaphor we have two thoughts of different things active together and supported by a single word or phrase, whose meaning is a resultant of their interaction."[9] When Isa 40:6–8 asserts that "all flesh is grass" (an "A-is-a-B" form of metaphor), for example, the metaphor's "tenor," that is, its underlying meaning (in this case, the frailty and transience of human life), results from the reader's "interanimation" of associations surrounding terms in its vehicle, the utterance itself.[10]

A number of theorists acknowledge their indebtedness to Richards, including philosopher Max Black and Soskice, a theologian. As Soskice points out, however, Black erred when he equated Richards's "tenor" and "vehicle" with his own "two-subjects" view of metaphor ("a metaphor's cognitive content results from the interaction of associated commonplaces surrounding a *principal* subject and a *subsidiary* one" [emphasis mine]).[11] Soskice, who defines

---

6. Northrop Frye, *The Great Code* (New York: Harcourt, Brace, Jovanovich, 1982) 23.

7. J. Lindblom emphasized the emotional impact of metaphor and other tropes in *The Servant Songs in Deutero-Isaiah* (Lund: C. W. K. Gleerup, 1951) 75–93.

8. A summary of emotive theories of metaphor appears in Monroe C. Beardsley, *Aesthetics: Problems in the Philosophy of Criticism* (New York: Harcourt, Brace, 1958) 134–35 (see also pp. 119–22) and Soskice, *Metaphor*, 26–31.

9. *The Philosophy of Rhetoric* (Oxford: Oxford University Press, 1939) 93.

10. Richards coined the tenor/vehicle terminology employed here.

11. J. M. Soskice, "Metaphor," in *Models and Metaphors: Studies in Language and Philosophy* (Ithaca: Cornell University Press, 1962) 41.

metaphor as "that figure of speech whereby we speak about one thing in terms which are seen to be suggestive of another,"[12] recognizes that metaphors have only one subject, the tenor, which the vehicle conveys. Note, for example, the following lines:

> A stubborn and unconquerable flame
> creeps in his veins and drinks the streams of life.[13]

Here, she observes, thoughts of the tenor—a burning fever—are communicated through the interanimation of words in the vehicle. Note that the tenor is nowhere explicitly stated, further refutation of Black's claim that two distinct subjects are present in any metaphor.

To avoid slipping into a two-subjects view of metaphor, we shall abandon Richards's elegant "tenor" and "vehicle" terminology for the admittedly more cumbersome vocabulary used by J. David Sapir in "The Anatomy of Metaphor."[14] Sapir identifies three aspects of metaphor: the "topic" (i.e., "what we are talking about or referring to when we use the metaphor" [= Richards's "vehicle"]); its "continuous term(s)" (those implying the topic and vice versa; in our Isaian example, the continuous term is "flesh"); and its discontinuous term(s)," for example, "grass." Adopting Sapir's terminology permits greater precision.

Simile

A formal distinction exists between metaphor and simile, the mark of simile being the presence of *like* or *as*. Many critics deny simile the impact of metaphor.[15] But the reader encountering Isa 40:6b, "all flesh is grass, and all its beauty is like the flower of the field," will probably conclude that both the initial metaphor and the following simile function in essentially identical ways. Soskice distinguishes between two types of similes: "Modelling similes," like interactive metaphors, "use a [reasonably well-known] subject . . . to explain or provide schematization for a state of affairs which is beyond our full

---

12. Soskice, *Metaphor*, 15.

13. Cited by Soskice, *Metaphor*, 45, from Richards, *Philosophy*, 102.

14. J. David Sapir, "The Anatomy of Metaphor," in *The Social Use of Metaphor* (ed. J. David Sapir and J. Christopher Crocker; Philadelphia: University of Pennsylvania Press, 1977) 7.

15. We need not, in this context, pursue philosophical debates concerning the "truth" of simile vs. the "truth" of metaphor.

grasp." "Illustrative similes," by contrast, simply point to similarities between two entities. The former, Soskice observes, function well if one "wishes to produce an exploratory schema," the latter when precision is the goal.[16]

Both metaphor and simile must be construed, and their deftness judged, *contextually.*[17] Wayne Booth makes precisely this point:

> What any metaphor *says* or *means* or *does* will always be to some degree alterable by altering its context. Every metaphor . . . could be made to communicate various shades of meaning; each of them could even be made, by employing the easy turns of irony, to say the reverse of what it seems to say. . . . It follows that whether any metaphor is judged to be *good* is inescapably dependent on its context: what surrounds it in the text, spoken or written, and who speaks it to whom for what purpose.[18]

Read in isolation, a reader might plausibly construe "all flesh is grass, and all its beauty is like the flower of the field" in various ways, such as part of a larger poem celebrating youth's freshness and beauty. Read contextually, however, the tropes' meanings are clear: like grass, people wither; like flowers, they quickly fade.

In addition to highlighting the importance of context for metaphorical construal, the above illustration points to yet another significant distinction between certain metaphors and similes, and others: the presence or absence of explicit secondary predicates. By "secondary predicate," we mean "the complex of concepts, assumptions and ideas that, correctly or incorrectly, but usually, is linked to the secondary subject and can be derived from it."[19] *Implicit* secondary predicates do not specify those associations crucial for a given simile's (or metaphor's) construal, but *explicit* secondary predicates do. Anticipating the discussion to follow, the explicit secondary predicate of the simile in Isa 42:14b ("Like a travailing woman I shall *shout*, I shall *gasp* and *pant*"; emphasis mine) directs its audience to those aspects of a travailing woman's behavior that are crucial to the simile's topic, that is, God's power and impending salvific acts. While acknowledging the grammatical distinction between metaphor and simile, then, we maintain that certain similes are like metaphors

16. Soskice, *Metaphor*, 60.

17. Soskice also recognizes the importance of context for metaphorical construal, and it is integral to the construction of her "interanimation" theory (*Metaphor*, 43–96). See also Nielsen, *Hope for a Tree*, 48–53.

18. Wayne Booth, "Afterthoughts on Metaphor" IV: "Ten Literal 'Theses'," in *On Metaphor* (ed. S. Sacks; Chicago: University of Chicago Press, 1979) 173–74.

19. M. S. Kjärgaard, *Metaphor and Parable* (Leiden: Brill, 1986) 84–105, esp. 86. Note his use of Black's "two subjects" language.

(and vice versa) when they specify those associations with the discontinuous terms that are especially appropos to the trope's interpretation.[20]

Ancient Israel's prophets and poets appear not to have placed a premium on innovation, as would a modern critic. True, some tropes would seem to be novel (though the extant texts are surely only a slice of ancient Israel's literary creations). But alongside ostensibly fresh imagery, one finds numerous recurring images possessing what Philip Wheelwright has called "ancestral vitality."[21] Such images enriched their new contexts because they brought with them meanings and associations from earlier sources. Finally, Israel's authors appear sometimes to have borrowed familiar imagery but adapted it in striking ways. Such is the case, I shall argue, with the two female tropes in the discussion that follows.

Female Imagery in the Book of Isaiah

Isaiah contains both literal references to women and female imagery. Among its literal references, females often are cited because of their ability to conceive and bear children: a young woman will give birth to a son and call his name "Immanuel" (7:10–17); a certain prophetess and Isaiah share a child whose God-given name, Maher-shalal-hash-baz, makes him a living "word" to the people (8:1–4); Israel's ancestral mother appears within an exhortation: "Look to Abraham your father, and to Sarah who bore you" (51:2a). Elsewhere, the "daughters of Zion" are condemned for their pride, complacency, and devotion to comfort. The prophet details their future humiliation (3:16–26), warning that the devastating effects of Yahweh's judgment will be especially disastrous for females: "Seven women shall take hold of one man in that day saying, 'We shall eat our own bread and wear our own clothes, only let us be called by your name; take away our reproach'" (4:1).[22]

---

20. In *Metaphor* (pp. 58–61), Soskice acknowledges that so-called "modelling similes" function in ways virtually identical to metaphors, but she does not acknowledge that certain metaphors function in ways virtually identical to illustrative similes. Soskice is loathe to allow her "interanimation theory" to lapse into a comparison view of metaphor. Nevertheless, some metaphors perform primarily a comparative function.

21. Philip Wheelwright, *Metaphor and Reality* (Bloomington: Indiana University Press, 1962) 65, 85, 98, and *passim*. Wheelwright's discussion of ancestral vitality appears primarily within a description of symbols, which are "relatively stable and repeatable" (p. 92). Although distinctions between metaphor and symbol are both legitimate and important (in biblical as well as nonbiblical literature), contemporary discussions of symbol also provide helpful insights and concepts for studying recurring metaphors in biblical texts as well.

22. Unless otherwise indicated, biblical passages are from the NRSV.

The number of *literal* references to females in Isaiah pales compared to the numerous times that female *imagery* appears in the scroll. The frequency of female tropes in Isaiah largely results from the ancient Near Eastern practice of personifying cities as females and speaking of surrounding settlements, or inhabitants of the city itself, as her daughters.[23] In Isaiah 23, for example, the Phoenician city of Sidon is depicted as a woman whose offspring have perished, leaving her childless. The poet castigates her, but then assumes her female persona so that she appears to voice her own grief:[24]

> Be ashamed, O Sidon, for the sea has spoken,
> the fortress of the sea, saying:
> "I have neither labored, nor given birth,
> I have neither reared young men
> nor brought up young women."
>
> Isa 23:4

Similarly, Jerusalem (a central concern of the book from beginning to end) is personified as a bride, mother, wayward wife, childless widow, etc. Isa 54:1–6, for example, depicts Jerusalem as a bereaved woman whose husband, Yahweh, miraculously restores her children. So full of offspring does she become that her tent fairly bursts at the seams (see also 49:19–21).

As the preceding examples suggest, women's ability to conceive, be in labor with, and bear children is central to much of the female imagery in Isaiah. On the one hand, this ability fundamentally distinguishes male from female; on the other hand, ancient Near Eastern women were valued to no small extent for their ability to produce children, preferably sons. As we have seen, female metaphors and similes can bear other than maternal connotations. When, for example, the prophet condemns fellow Judeans, saying, "My people—children are their oppressors, and women rule over them" (Isa 3:12), he employs both "children" and "women" metaphorically to criticize the community's leadership for its ignorance, inexperience, and naiveté.[25]

---

23. See Aloysius Fitzgerald, "The Mythological Background for the Presentation of Jerusalem as a Queen and False Worship as Adultery in the OT," *CBQ* 34 (1972) 403–16; Chayim Cohen, "The 'Widowed' City," *JANESCU* 5 (1973) 75–81; Barbara Bakke Kaiser, "Poet as 'Female Impersonator': The Image of Daughter Zion as Speaker in Biblical Poems of Suffering," *JR* 67 (1987) 164–82.

24. In addition to the article by Kaiser cited above, see William Lanahan, "The Speaking Voice in the Book of Lamentations," *JBL* 93 (1974) 41–49, and the discussion of persona in Timothy Polk's *The Prophetic Persona: Jeremiah and the Language of the Self* (JSOTSup 32; Sheffield: JSOT Press, 1984).

25. The NRSV follows the MT (נָשִׁים); however, the LXX reads נֹשִׁים 'creditors'. The translators of the LXX understood 3:12a to mean, "O my people, your exactors strip you, and creditors rule over you."

When he proclaims, "in that day the Egyptians will be like women, and tremble with fear before the hand which Yahweh Sebaoth shakes over them" (19:16), he foretells a time when weakness will incapacitate the Egyptian men.[26] Nevertheless, women's procreative ability is the ground whence grows a variety of female metaphors and similes. Two such tropes recur at points throughout Isaiah. Each moves from stereotypical meaning to fresh connotation, and each contributes to a major theme running throughout the book: the contrast between human impotence and divine omnipotence.

The Travailing-Woman Simile

Our first female image, expressed by a limited variety of Hebrew expressions, can be translated "like a travailing woman," or "like a woman in labor."[27] This simile was not unique to Israel; it appears in other ancient Near Eastern texts as well. In the Akkadian epic of Gilgamesh, for example, we read:

> The gods were frightened by the deluge,
> And, shrinking back, they ascended to the heaven of Anu.
> The gods cowered like dogs
>   Crouched against the outer wall.
> Ishtar cried out like a woman in travail,
> The sweet-voiced mistress of the [gods] moans aloud:
> "The olden days are alas turned to clay,
> Because I bespoke evil in the assembly of the gods."[28]

As in this text, so also in Hebrew Scripture, the travailing-woman simile functions to illumine behavior in some sense resembling the demeanor of women giving birth. Analysis of passages containing this simile reveals that such behavior normally describes "the anguish of the times" and not the emergence of new life and hope.[29] Consider, for example, Ps 48:5–7, where the

---

26. See also Nah 3:13 ("Behold, your people have become women in your midst") and Jer 50:35–38. Delbert Hillers discusses the theme of warriors become women in *Treaty-Curses and the Old Testament Prophets* (BibOr 16; Rome: Pontifical Biblical Institute, 1964) 66–68; see also William L. Holladay, "Jer. xxxi 22B Reconsidered: 'The Woman Encompasses the Man,'" *VT* 16 (1966) 237.

27. כיולדה appears in Isa 13:8, 42:14; Jer 6:24, 22:23, 30:6, 49:24, 50:43; Mic 4:9, 10; Ps 48:7. Both כחולה and כמבכירה appear in Jer 4:31. In Jer 13:21 the simile is כמו אשת לדה. Isa 21:3 has כציריר יולדה.

28. Tablet 11, lines 113–19 in "The Epic of Gilgamesh," translated by E. A. Speiser in *ANET* (3d ed.; ed. James B. Pritchard; Princeton: Princeton University Press, 1969) 94.

29. See Bernhard W. Anderson, " 'The Lord Has Created Something New': A Stylistic Study of Jer 31:15–22," *CBQ* 40 (1978) 463–78, esp. p. 468.

poet expresses the simile's topic (the reaction of foreign rulers beholding Jerusalem, God's inviolable city) through its discontinuous terms, a description of a woman in travail and the anguished demeanor characteristically associated with labor pains. Because this simile includes an explicit secondary predicate, the poet's audience is unlikely to ask, "To what do the kings give birth?" New life is not the issue here, and that association is suppressed. In similar fashion, Jer 6:23–24 employs the simile to describe the fear and dismay experienced by Zion's citizenry in the face of approaching enemy warriors. These two texts, and the others cited as well, demonstrate that the "travailing-woman" simile routinely functioned within the Hebrew Bible to describe the behavior of people who were not *actually* giving birth to anything (literally or figuratively), but whose desperate circumstances led to deportment similar to that of women in labor.

Having identified the stereotypical connotations associated with this simile, we turn to two Isaian passages in which it appears. Both texts are part of lengthy oracles concerning Babylon. The first, Isaiah 13, combines geographically specific scenes with descriptions of cosmic upheaval to portray terrifying events that will transpire on the Day of Yahweh.

> Wail, for the day of the Lord is near;
>> it will come like destruction from the Almighty!
> Therefore all hands will be feeble,
>> and every human heart will melt,
>> and they will be dismayed.
> Pangs and agony will seize them;
>> they will be in anguish like a woman in travail.
> They will look aghast at one another;
>> their faces will be aflame.
>
> Isa 13:6–8

In this passage, כיולדה describes the reaction of persons witnessing that day when divinely consecrated warriors will triumph over the world's wicked and arrogant inhabitants. Predictably there is no suggestion that their labor-like behavior will be "productive" in either a literal or a metaphorical sense. Rather, the simile bears those conventional connotations identified above. Commentators disagree over the precise identity of those so afflicted (some arguing that vv. 7–8 describe the Judean response to advancing Babylonian troops, and others insisting that the Babylonians themselves are panic-stricken).[30] Without question,

---

30. R. E. Clements accepts the former view, seeing in vv. 6–8 a description of the destruction of Jerusalem by the Babylonians in 587 B.C.E. (*Isaiah 1–39* [NCB; Grand Rapids: Eerdmans, 1980] 134–35). Sweeney (*Isaiah 1–4*, 44–46) understands all of 13:1–22

however, the author(s) of this chapter anticipate a time when Yahweh's power will triumph over the proud and wicked, reducing their haughtiness to terror.

In a second passage, the difficult "oracle concerning the wilderness of the sea" (Isa 21:1–10), the image of a woman in labor again functions (ironically) to illuminate the behavior of an anguish-filled person—in this case the prophet himself, to whom Yahweh has revealed the carnage awaiting Babylon's people. Again, the travailing woman simile conforms to conventional usage, depicting human weakness in the face of tremendous military power—power Yahweh claims to control.[31]

Given its connotations, it would not be surprising if the travailing-woman simile were never employed to describe Yahweh's demeanor anywhere in the Hebrew Bible. Surely no biblical author would ascribe to the God of Israel the panic this simile connotes! Yet the image is used of Yahweh in a third passage, Isa 42:14. Is the Lord also victim of incapacitating terror?

As in Isa 13:7–8 and 21:3–4, the travailing-woman simile in Isa 42:14 is surrounded by military imagery. It is preceded in v. 13 by Yahweh going forth like a warrior, shrieking a war cry and gaining victory over foes; and it is followed by Yahweh leading the redeemed on an exodus-like victory march. While forms of this simile function in chaps. 13 and 21 to describe the *reaction* of persons perceiving the threat posed by "Yahweh and the weapons of his indignation" (13:5), however, the image in 42:14 describes *Yahweh's own behavior*. In the only place in the Hebrew Bible where this simile applies to Israel's God, Yahweh says:

> I have long kept silent;
>   I have been mute; I have restrained myself.
> Like a travailing woman I will blow;
>   I will both gasp and pant.
> I will desiccate mountains and hills,
>   and all their vegetation I will wither;
> I will change rivers into islands,
>   and dry up pools.
>
>   Isa 42:14–15[32]

---

as directed against Babylon. Otto Kaiser suggests that not only Babylon, but also a number of other cities, are in view; the day of Yahweh entails world-wide judgment (*Isaiah 13–39* [OTL; Philadelphia: Westminster, 1974] 6–16).

31. Note that this travailing woman simile incorporates the recurring Isaian themes of deafness and blindness.

32. This translation is my own. My fuller discussion of the way the travailing-woman simile functions within Isa 42:10–17 appears in "Like Warrior, like Woman: Destruction and Deliverance in Isaiah 42:10–17," *CBQ* 49 (1987) 560–71.

Here the simile's conventional meaning has been transformed radically. Stripped of its stereotypical connotations, it describes neither panic nor fear, but rather God's powerful behavior and its awesome effects. The poet has discerned within the exaggerated breaths characteristic of women in labor a striking image for conveying a sense of the force of the breath of God. "Yahweh goes forth like a warrior, shouting a war cry, and demonstrates prowess over foes. Yahweh gasps and pants like a woman in travail, and the breath of God desiccates the earth."[33]

If the first two Isaian references to behavior resembling that of a travailing woman did not violate readers' expectations, ascription of this behavior to Yahweh in 42:14 cannot have failed to do so. Surely the simile's conventional connotations of paralyzing panic made it seem an inappropriate rhetorical device for describing Yahweh's demeanor. Yet some Judeans may have found the analogy apt in light of Ephraim's defeat by the Assyrians, Judah's years of vassalage, Jerusalem's demise at the hands of Babylon, years of exile in an alien land, and the trying conditions endured by repatriates in the years following 538 B.C.E.

Isaiah's authors and redactors cannot be counted among such doubters, however. Throughout the tumultuous centuries when the collection was produced and shaped, its creators continually affirmed faith in the power and sovereignty of their God, despite the demise of virtually every earthly institution believed to testify to that power—the Davidic kingship, Solomon's temple, indeed Jerusalem herself. Their unshakeable faith left its mark throughout the scroll in proclamations that the victorious warrior and cosmic king of Zion controls the nations and ultimately will punish oppressors, in their insistence that beyond the strange act of Yahweh's judgment upon Israel lies restoration and renewal, and in their claim that *events are not always as they seem.* At any moment, the earth's mighty rulers can be swept away by the slightest breath from the mouth of God (40:24); the despised and persecuted become instruments for deep healing and reconciliation among their revilers (52:13–53:12). Old images of human terror and pain are transformed into bold new images through which Yahweh's unparalleled power is discerned afresh.

The Inability to Bring to Birth and Its Miraculous Reversal

At first glance a fourth passage, Isa 26:17–18, appears also to belong with those texts in which the simile "like a travailing woman" describes the behavior of

---

33. Ibid., 570.

terror-stricken human beings. In v. 17, supplicants employ the image of a woman with child to describe their own distress:

> Like a woman with child (כמו הרה),
> who writhes and cries out in her pangs,
> when she is near her time,
> so were we because of you, O Lord.
>
> Isa 26:17

In the following verse, however, travail imagery does what other examples of our simile never do. It moves beyond a depiction of labor-like behavior to consider the issue (or in this case, the lack thereof) of birth pangs:

> We were with child; we writhed.
> but we gave birth only to wind.
> We have won no victories on earth,
> and no one is born to inhabit the world.
>
> Isa 26:18

Though they labor to the point of utter exhaustion, human beings are unable to "give birth," that is, to bring about the salvation they seek. Such an accomplishment lies beyond human resources; only God can perform that task.

Some eleven chapters later, the image of a pregnant female lacking the strength to bring to birth appears for a second time. King Hezekiah invokes it to describe Jerusalem's desperate straits (37:3).[34] Hearing of the verbal assault by which the Rabshakeh has sought to undermine the people's confidence in Jerusalem's leaders and, indeed, in their God, Hezekiah sends a message to Isaiah. His words, a metaphorical proverb, describe the crisis facing Jerusalem and her inhabitants:

> Thus says Hezekiah:
> "This day is a day of distress, of chastisement, and of contempt;
> Babes are positioned for birth but there is no strength to deliver."
>
> Isa 37:3[35] (author's translation)

---

34. On the transitional or bridging function of Isaiah 36–39, see P. R. Ackroyd, "Isaiah 36–39: Structure and Function," *Von Kanaan bis Kerala: Festschrift für Prof. Mag. Dr. Dr. J. P. M. van der Ploeg, O. P. zur Vollendung des siebzigsten Lebensjahres am 4. Juli 1979* (ed. W. C. Delsman, et al.; AOAT 211; Kevelaer: Butzon und Bercker, 1982) 3–21; "The Death of Hezekiah: A Pointer to the Future?" *De la Tôrah au Messie: Etudes d'exégèse et d'herméneutique bibliques offertes à Henri Cazelles pour ses 25 années d'enseignement à l'Institut Catholique de Paris (Octobre 1979)* (ed. M. Carrez, J. Doné, and P. Grelot; Paris: Desclée, 1981) 219–26; and Sweeney, *Isaiah 1–4*, 12–17.

35. When the editors of the JPSV footnote the proverb and paraphrase "I.e., the situation is desperate and we are at a loss," they illustrate Carol Newsom's observation ("A Maker

Hezekiah's proverb did not express an idea unique to ancient Israel. In the Hittite myth about the disappearance of Telepinus, we read:

> Telepinus walked away and took grain, (fertile) breeze, . . . and satiation to the country, the meadow, the *steppes*. Telepinus went and lost himself in the *steppe*; *fatigue* overcame him. So grain (and) spelt thrive no longer. So cattle, sheep and man no longer breed. And *even those with young cannot bring them forth* (lines 10–15).[36]

Here is the same notion expressed in Hezekiah's proverb, though it functions differently in the two texts. In the Hittite myth, the inability to bring to birth appears as part of a literal depiction of famine and its consequent weakness. In Isa 37:3, however, it functions as a metaphorical description of the plight confronting Jerusalem's inhabitants.

Jerusalem survives the Assyrian threat, beyond Assyria lies destruction and exile at Babylonian hands.[37] Descriptions of the ruined, depopulated city—a widow, childless and despised—appear throughout Isaiah 40–66, as do unqualified assertions that the devastation of Jerusalem is part of Yahweh's plan for Israel and the nations, but not her ultimate lot: beyond divine judgment and wrath lie forgiveness, reconciliation, restoration—and the transformation of Hezekiah's piteous proverb. Again, the process of giving birth serves to describe the people's situation. But how different is the imagery's function in this context!

> Before she was in labor she gave birth;
> before her pain came upon her
> she was delivered of a son.
> Who has heard of such a thing?
> Who has seen such things?
> Shall a land be born in one day?
> Shall a nation be delivered in one moment?
> Yet as soon as Zion was in labor
> she delivered her sons.
> Shall I open the womb (אשביר)
> and not deliver (אוליד)?
> says the Lord;

---

of Metaphors: Ezekiel's Oracles Against Tyre," *Int* 38 [1984] 152): "If one tries to paraphrase a metaphor, what is lost is more than just a certain effect. What is lost is part of the meaning itself, the insight which the metaphor alone can give."

36. "The Telepinus Myth," translated by Albrecht Goetze in *ANET* (3d ed.; Princeton: Princeton University Press, 1969) 126.

37. Recall that Jerusalem's fate—its plunder by the Babylonians and the deportation of its royal house—is "foretold" by Isaiah in 39:5–7.

Shall I, the one who delivers (המוליד),
   shut the womb?
  says your God.

Isa 66:7–9

This promise of Yahweh, with its lexical correspondence to Hezekiah's anguished message to Isaiah in 37:3b, reveals the obverse of human powerlessness and pain. Human beings are unable to bring about salvation and renewed life, but Yahweh can and will do so in miraculous fashion.

Summary

This article focuses upon female imagery within Isaiah, a lengthy scroll containing numerous references both to human women and to female imagery of various types. Jerusalem's fate is a central concern at every level within the Isaianic tradition, and her personification as a woman accounts in significant measure for the plethora of female images throughout the book. Two female images warrant special attention, however: the woman in travail and the inability to bring to birth, with its miraculous reversal. Both appear at least three times, spanning major sections of the work. Each image shifts from stereotypical meaning to fresh connotations. In so doing, each alerts readers to new perceptions of Yahweh's sovereignty, affirming divine power instead of paralyzing fear, and divine innovation when human impotence threatens to obviate hope.

A Prophetic Vision of an Alternative Community: A Reading of Isaiah 40–55

Ann Johnston

❧

T HE TASK OF ISRAEL'S PROPHETS was not only to give expression to the judgment of God on the life and actions of the community, especially as it violated covenant and disavowed covenant community, but also to image alternatives, especially for a people whose hopelessness had deprived them of creative imagination. Such was the task of the prophet of the sixth century B.C.E. in the Judean refugee camp in Babylon. The terror and devastation of war, the deportations of 597, 587, and 582, the catastrophic destruction of the city of Jerusalem, and the pillaging and burning of the land left the people of Judah in a state of desolation and despair poignantly depicted in Lamentations:

> All her people groan
> as they search for bread;
> they trade their treasures for food
> to revive their strength.
> "Look, O Lord, and behold,
> for I am despised."
>
> Lam 1:11

Deutero-Isaiah, or the anonymous prophet of the sixth century, was a prophet in the full sense of that word—called to judge and called to image hope—but the weight of that task lay primarily in the call to image redemption and re-creation. This call was directed to a people who considered themselves abandoned by God as a consequence of their failure to keep covenant and to respond to the prophetic call to return (שׁוּב), to turn bodily around to meet their God again in face-to-face relationship.

This anonymous prophet was needed to speak peace and wholeness in the wake of the stinging denunciations of Ezekiel:

> Because the land is full of bloody crimes and the city is full of violence, I will bring the worst of the nations to take possession of their houses; I will put an end to their proud might, and their holy places shall be profaned. When anguish comes they will seek peace but there shall be none. Disaster comes upon disaster, rumor follows rumor; they seek a vision from the prophet, but the law perishes from the priest, and counsel from the elders. The king mourns, the prince is wrapped in despair, and the hands of the people of the land are palsied with terror. According to their way I will do to them, and according to their own judgments I will judge them; and they shall know that I am the Lord. (Ezek 7:23–27)

To the elders assembled around this prophet the word of the Lord was addressed:

> These men have taken their idols into their hearts and set the stumbling block of their iniquity before their faces; should I let myself be inquired of at all by them . . . anyone who separates himself from me taking his idols into his heart and putting the stumbling block of his iniquity before his face and yet comes to the prophet to inquire for himself, I YHWH will answer him myself . . . [I will] cut him off from the midst of my people; and you shall know that I am the Lord. (Ezek 14:3, 7–8)

Someone was needed to reach into the profound depths of the national and personal despair depicted by the prophetic voices of Lamentations in order to call the people forth to life. Someone was needed to jolt them into a new and creative way of interpreting their life and, in fact, to help them deal with their distorted views of reality, their lives, their identity, their godly task and calling, and even their God. Election had become for them exemption, and promise, one-sided privilege.

The community gathered in the POW camp in Babylon spent its days questioning:

Who is YHWH our God?
Is YHWH God?
Who are we?
Who are we in relation to this deity?
Have we returned ourselves once more to a slavery comparable to
    that of pre-Exodus Egypt?

Constant critical examination of their traditions, their calling forth from slavery, the reasons for their existence, the sources of their identity, their ritual celebration of the acts of God in history, and the meaning of their existence as expressed in worship and in prayer—these elements defined and circumscribed the crucial task of survival that lay ahead of them during this period. Furthermore, all of this had to be accomplished in the oppressive and humiliating environs of Babylon, among a people whose taunting voices often overpowered the voices of those singing YHWH's praises (Psalm 137). Israel lived in what seemed to her to be a godless land; forms and structures and religious ideals had been demolished or even worse, made insignificant. In the words of John Bright:

> The old national cultic community was broken and Israel was left for the moment an agglomeration of uprooted and beaten individuals, by no external mark any longer a people. The marvel is that her history did not end altogether. Nevertheless, Israel both survived the calamity and forming a new community out of the wreckage of the old, resumed her life as a people. Her faith, disciplined and strengthened, likewise survived and gradually found the direction that it would follow through all the centuries to come. In the exile and beyond it, Judaism was born.[1]

Two figures were instrumental in re-visioning community for Israel. Ezekiel depicted a priestly community centered on the temple and the legal fulfillment of Israel's cultic ritual and practice, a people called to cultic holiness and purity. Ezekiel and the priestly group drew up guidelines for this priestly community, guidelines that would guard them from the unholiness and contamination of the surrounding world, would separate "the holy" from "the common," the Jew from the world in which Judaism was to live.

Deutero-Isaiah imaged a "servant community" called to serve one another in suffering and compassion, ministering to a world beyond the confines of Judah and Jerusalem, bonded to a living God. Rising from the midst of the disciples of Isaiah of Jerusalem, known as the למודים (50:4, 54:14)[2] or 'those who are taught', this poetic voice broke through the darkness of their despair with images of a creation God, a Mother God giving birth, accompanied by the pains of a new exodus. And, just as the first exodus act, upon leaving Egyptian bondage, had created YHWH's Israel, so this new exodus act would create Israel anew, bonding Israel and YHWH in an ever-fruitful relationship and a union so vital that Israel would need "to enlarge the space of her tents" (Isa 54:2) to contain her members.

---

1. John Bright, *A History of Israel* (3d ed.; Philadelphia: Westminster, 1981), 343.

2. The term למודים is first found in the Isaiah material in 8:16. Here Isaiah of Jerusalem entrusts his teaching and testimony to those who have faithfully listened to the word and who hope in that word. This seems to mark the beginning of the Isaianic community, the "servants of YHWH."

This prophet not only gave voice to the judgment of God concerning the idolatries of their lives but, beyond that, imaged an alternative vision of a YHWH-centered community for whom the human desire for power and prestige, for control and the use of others for their own greed, for solidarity and world-renown would give way to YHWH's values of service to the poor and oppressed, caring for the downtrodden and despised, humility rather than prestige, faith in God rather than human control, sharing as opposed to the accumulation of wealth and the acquisition of material possessions, and even of accepting rejection of one's kinsfolk, if that be the consequence of compassion and inclusion.

Each of these visions would take existential shape in the time of return and restoration, but as the priestly community gained the upper hand, the servant community would become an apocalyptic minority who understood their suffering as having its fulfillment and purpose only in a time beyond history, when YHWH would gain the victory over the forces of evil.[3] This community would face rejection even by their own people for the values that their countercultural choices would embody. The great Isaiah Scroll contains this imaged alternative community and the rebirth of Israel in chapters 40–55 and shaped by the person tradition has named Deutero-Isaiah. I propose to examine this text from the historical-cultural horizon of the community of that day and through the lenses of the chosen patterns of rhetoric in which the prophet has embodied and encoded this message. The imaging proceeds, not in linear fashion, but rather calls the hearer/reader to focus on the heart of the matter and the central message by "framing" that central image with successive and ever-widening inclusios, much as a stone dropped in water produces successive encircling rings that move outward until they disappear in a wider whole.[4] In this way the imaged reality is integrated into past and future.

It is precisely this way of imaging that Deutero-Isaiah has used in formulating and shaping a message for the community in exile. The message had the power to stir a community out of its lethargy and inertia and carry it across a desert in a new exodus ending in the birth of an alternative community.

---

3. Paul D. Hanson, *The Dawn of Apocalyptic: The Historical and Sociological Roots of Jewish Apocalyptic Eschatology* (rev. ed.; Philadelphia: Fortress, 1979). Hanson makes a very clear case for this reconstruction of the sociocultural split in the community during the period of restoration.

4. James Muilenberg deals at length with the rhetorical patterns and devices that are integral to the meaning and message of the Hebrew language and literary composition. See "Form Criticism and Beyond," *JBL* 88 (1969) 1–18; "A Study of Hebrew Rhetoric: Repetition and Style," *Congress Volume* (VTSup 1; Leiden: Brill, 1953) 97–111.

The priestly leaders during the exile had reframed for the community all of its images of God, of creation, of being called into existence, of being elected to a task and the mission described in the priestly edition of the Pentateuch with the Exodus Act and the God of the Exodus at the center. They had outlined the prescriptive legislation that defined the binding of a consecrated and holy people to a holy God. The book of Leviticus, especially the Holiness Code of Leviticus 17–26 and Ezekiel 40–48 are good examples of this legislation. These commands were in the language they were accustomed to hearing from their priestly teachers and priestly legislators.

Deutero-Isaiah, however, conveyed God's message in new forms and new rhetoric. Using the old, sacred images of the redemptive, creative Exodus Act, this prophet pictured God and a revitalized program embodying a new exodus, new creation, new birth, and a new and binding commitment between a community and a liberating God. In this vision YHWH's relationship was not intended to enslave but to free, not to demand but to call forth, not to confine but to invigorate and animate. The call and the task were both grounded in the old but so expanded and enlarged as to be overwhelming:

> I am YHWH, your Holy One,
> the Creator of Israel. . . .
> who makes a way in the sea,
> a path in the mighty waters,
> who brings forth chariot and horse,
> army and warrior;
> they lie down, they cannot rise
> they are extinguished, quenched like a wick:
> "Remember not the former things
> nor consider the things of old.
> Behold I am doing a new thing. . . .
> I give water in the wilderness,
> rivers in the desert,
> to give drink to my chosen people,
> the people whom I formed (יצר)[5] for myself
> that they might declare my praise.
> Isa 43:15–17, 19–21

> It is too light a thing that you should be my servant
> to raise up the tribes of Jacob
> and to restore the preserved of Israel;
> I will give you as a light to the nations,
> that my salvation may reach to the ends of the earth.
> Isa 49:6

5. יצר 'to shape or form or mold', as a potter shapes the clay on the wheel. The verb is used in the Yahwist creation account.

I wish to draw attention here to one other characteristic aspect of Hebrew rhetoric significant to an understanding of this body of material as it was addressed to and heard by the community in exile. There is an easy movement back and forth between the use of a term denoting an individual in the singular sense and the use of that same term to indicate an association of individuals as a social unit or corporate personality. This oscillation or fluidity of reference is intensely meaningful. This is seen in particular in Deutero-Isaiah's use of the term 'servant' עבד. The servant is both the individual Israelite and corporate Israel, but this doubling is not just a way of speaking; it is intended to convey a psychosocial truth well understood in the Semitic society of that day: the individual is responsible for the community and the community for the individual. The individual has the power to affect community; in turn the community has a shaping and identifying effect on the individual. The two cannot be separated. The community envisaged by the prophet was to be corporately bound to YHWH, and every individual within that community to bear the responsibility for living the God-relationship that bonded them to one another in community.

I turn now to the shape of the text as a whole. The full message to the community lies not in the individual units but in the structured arrangement of the whole (see chart on p. 151). The core image (44:21–45:19) is centered and then framed by successive pairs of images moving outward from this central core and pointing inward to its dynamic message: YHWH alone is a living, creating, redeeming God. The successive inclusios contrast and compare, expand and magnify, detail and delineate the work of this God and the implications for Israel and for the universe. This holistic way of rhetorical patterning heightens and deepens the central thought. The genius of Deutero-Isaiah lies in the power to use this form and structure both within individual units and within the compass of the whole.

One God alone is a living, creating God: YHWH, the Holy One of Israel. The central image portrays that God as forming and shaping Israel (יצר: 44:21, 44:24, 45:9, 45:18) into a living being and a lifegiving community. The same God who creates the heavens and the earth re-creates Israel and calls her to live in עבד-relationship with her God. The same verbs found in the creation accounts are found here:

> to shape like a potter   יצר
> to stretch out the heavens   נטה
> to spread out the earth   רקע
> to make, to create   ברא
> to make, to do   עשה

40:1–31   *a* Imaging a living Creator God who gives strength to the weary and power to the faint. Stirring up <u>new life</u>.

41:1–13   *b* Israel/Jacob, <u>chosen servant</u>; YHWH speaks: "I will strengthen, help, uphold with my victorious right hand."

41:14–42:9   *c* Imaging the <u>life-giving activity</u> of YHWH, God of Israel, in terms of water, new growth, new justice . . . that you may be a light to <u>the nations</u>.

42:10–44:8   *d* YHWH has <u>formed</u> Israel in the womb; she is brought to birth in Exodus and Wilderness images; born to belong to YHWH and to witness to YHWH (repeated use of יצר).

44:9–20   *e* Polemic against the worship of "non-gods"—these gods have to be fashioned (יצר) by human hands . . . "shall I fall down before a block of wood?"

44:21–45:19   *f* YHWH forms Israel again (יצר 44:21, 44:24, 45:9, 45:18).

45:20–47:15   *e′* Polemic against the "wooden gods" that human beings carry around; YHWH makes, bears, carries, saves.

48:1–49:26   *d′* YHWH calls Israel forth from the womb in a new birth as servant of YHWH, not just for Jacob's salvation but that YHWH's salvation may reach to the ends of the earth. Israel <u>formed</u> (יצר) to be servant.

50:1–52:12   *c′* Imaging <u>the redemptive activity</u> of YHWH turning rebellious Israel back to YHWH with an ear open to hear, in order that YHWH's people may bring deliverance for <u>all peoples</u>.

52:13–53:12   *b′* "<u>My servant</u>" shall be raised up from this state of dejection and rejection, suffering and humiliation, which has brought us back into right relation with God again and hence into new and life-giving relationship.

54:1–55:13   *a′* Imaging the fruitfulness of the reestablished relationship with ". . . your Maker who is your husband," whose compassion and forgiveness has brought you together again—for the <u>life of the world</u>.

Cyrus is envisioned as being called forth by the hand of God for the work of creative liberation. Israel's central task is to make this living, life-giving God known throughout the universe (45:6).

In contrast to this living God are the gods of Babylon who are described as "non-gods," carved wooden images, wood that is a god one day and fuel the next. There on either side of the central core are the extended prophetic denunciations of idolatry (*e*: 44:9–20 and *e′*: 45:20–47:15), not in the vitriolic voices of earlier prophets, but in satirical statements describing the foolishness of turning to "non-gods" for the work of God, to wooden gods made by human hands and carved by their Babylonian captors! YHWH, the living God, addresses Israel:

> I have made, I will bear,
> I will carry, I will deliver.
> Isa 46:4b

In the succeeding *d* and *d′* segments birth imagery is used. In the first (42:10–44:8) YHWH is imaged as a woman in labor, crying out in the joyous anguish of bringing forth new life (42:14). Jacob/Israel, formed and created in the first Exodus (43:1–2), has not been abandoned by God; the dispersed are gathered anew (43:5–7) to be both servant and chosen one (43:10).

The imagery in the *d′* passage (48:1–49:26) again has its center in the formation of Israel in the womb of God (49:1, 49:5). God, the nursing mother, could never forget them (49:14–15). The purposes of this rebirth of Israel are clearly stated as being far beyond the original conception. This rebirth of Israel is not for the sake of Israel alone and her continued existence:

> It is too light a thing that you should be my servant
> to raise up the tribes of Jacob
> to restore the re-formed of Israel;
> I will give you as a light to the nations,
> that my salvation may reach to the end of the earth.
> Isa 49:6

Israel's ministry to herself alone would be narcissistic. She is called beyond that, called to be salvific in the lives of others.

This ministry, again described in segment *c* (41:14–42:9) demands a fidelity to an ever-deepening relationship both with one another and with a God who is real, alive and conversational. YHWH seeks to revivify the lives of the poor and the needy (41:17–20) and in turn gives that same Spirit to Israel, who as servant of YHWH will seek the cause of justice and right (42:2–4). Israel, as individual and as community, is called to a deeper knowing of YHWH through living in covenanted relationship; only in this lived union with her God will she be a light to the nations (42:6) and free herself from slavery to sin and idolatry (42:7–9).

In the *inclusio* passage *c′* (50:1–52:12), the redemptive activity of YHWH in Israel's history is imaged. Israel is called to look at the full history of the nation's life and calling and to recognize and acknowledge the divine action in their lives. A redeeming God, cause of all being, has continually rescued them from annihilation and obliteration and calls them to bear witness to this salvific action:

> The Lord has bared his holy arm
> before the eyes of all the nations;
> and all the ends of the earth shall see
> the salvation of our God.
>
> Isa 52:10

In *b* and *b′* Israel's calling is placed in the context of the universe. She is called to bear witness to a living God in the midst of an idolatrous world (*b*: 41:1–13). The hand of God has raised her and sustains her. *B′* consists of what is known as "the fourth servant song," 52:13–53:12. But, as heard by the community of the exile, with its original intent, it can be seen as the call of the community to accept their suffering as a service to others and the giving of life for one another in order that the nations of the earth might know God's compassion and mercy and God's desire to give life through suffering. The servant community, especially as they became a rejected, defeated minority in restoration Israel, would come to know suffering not as a way of life but as a way to give life. They experienced the power of suffering to bring them to question the meaning of existence, to look for "course-correction" in lives moving away from God. They perceived the call to reestablish the relationships of a community called to be in covenant with one another and with God.

Finally, forming the outer and framing *inclusio* are the two passages *a* and *a′*. These speak of what the time of exile has meant in the re-creation and rebirth of Israel. The life-giving and creating God (40:12–17) is held up against the workman's idol (40:18–20). Those who wait for the living God and hope in the life-giving God and not in lifeless idols, will be strengthened for the task that lies ahead (40:28–31).

Reaching round to meet this passage is the final segment 54:1–55:13. The image is of the barren woman, the Israel of time past, who now in fruitful union with her God gives birth to more offspring than the tent of Israel can contain:

> Enlarge the place of your tent,
> and let the curtains of your habitations be stretched out;
> hold not back, lengthen your cords
> and strengthen your stakes.
> For you will spread abroad to the right and to the left,
> and your descendants will possess the nations
> and will people the desolate cities.
>
> Isa 54:2–3

YHWH's work of re-creation cannot be contained within Israel. When the maker of the universe is "your husband" (54:4), the whole earth is changed, as changed as the earth was after the flood (54:9–10). The compassion of God again encompasses and embraces both Israel and the universe in this vision of the alternative community of "Servants of the Lord" (54:17–55:5). This community of servants is called to return to their God not in pride but simply as God's own, seeking mercy and pardon: servants who have entered into the mind and heart of God; servants who have received the word of God into their lives that God might accomplish his redemptive purpose for the universe (55:6–11). Joy and peace in the midst of pain will be the sign of God's presence (55:12–13).

Deutero-Isaiah has described all the pain and suffering and messiness of Israel's present life in the refugee camps of Babylon but in transforming terms, terms that proclaim the power of YHWH's word to effect change. His word turns rebellion and stubborn resistance into humility and receptiveness to the action and power of the Spirit in prayer. Those who have been deaf and blind and resistant will have open ears, seeing eyes; "iron foreheads" will be turned to flesh. Out of the questioning, searching, struggling, anguished cries, anger, disillusionment, and recognition of a misconstrued calling will come a humbled remnant, a servant community. The suffering, shame, and humiliation of a people are seen as the work of a Potter-God, re-shaping Israel, bringing reconstruction, regeneration, and rebirth. This strand of Judaism will temporarily become disenfranchised and powerless in the social reconstruction of the restoration community. During this time, the hierocratic leaders of the Zadokite priestly family will win in the power struggle for domination and control.[6] But as this alternative visionary community of the Isaiah tradition becomes the alienated and rejected minority, their reconstruction of Israel's historical task and calling will resurface in the form of visions of the apocalyptic victory of YHWH over the forces of evil in the endtime beyond history.

---

6. This thesis is most fully developed in the previously cited work by Hanson, *The Dawn of Apocalyptic*. See in particular pp. 61–77.

The "Fortresses of Rehoboam": Another Look

T. R. Hobbs

S ECOND CHRONICLES 11:5–12 RECORDS the building of what appears to be a system of fortifications by Rehoboam, son of Solomon, after the secession of the northern tribes. A standard translation of the passage is that of the RSV:

> Rehoboam dwelt in Jerusalem, and he built cities for defense in Judah. He built Bethlehem, Etam, Tekoa, Beth-zur, Soco, Adullam, Gath, Mareshah, Ziph, Adoraim, Lachish, Azekah, Zorah, Aijalon, and Hebron, fortified cities which are in Judah and Benjamin. He made the fortresses strong, and put commanders in them, and stores of food, oil, and wine. And he put shields and spears in all the cities, and made them very strong. So he held Judah and Benjamin.

Such a translation is by no means perfect but does reflect the generally accepted interpretation of the passage as a reference to a plan for the defence of Judah in case of attack. The anticipated attack is identified as the invasion of Shishak of Egypt, mentioned in 2 Chr 12:2–12.[1] The invasion took place in 925 B.C.E.[2] Details vary, but the interpretations fall into two camps, those

---

1. H. Donner, "The Separate States of Israel and Judah," in *Israelite and Judaean History* (ed. J. H. Hayes and J. M. Miller; Philadelphia: Westminster, 1977) 381–434.
2. *Contra* W. F. Albright, "Chronology of the Divided Monarchy in Israel," *BASOR* 100 (1945) 16–22. See instead S. J. DeVries, "Chronology, Old Testament," *IDB* 1.580–99 and *IDBSup*, 161–65.

who see the building program as an anticipation of the invasion (a minority), and those who see it as a reaction to the invasion (the majority).

On closer analysis it is clear that the task of interpreting this passage contains several problems. In this study it is my intention to deal with the following issues:

Historical problems. The question here is: does the evidence support the thesis of the building of a *defensive system of fortresses* in Judah at this particular time? I believe that it does not. Two other possibilities may then be explored: (1) that the list was misplaced by the Chronicler and belongs to another, more suitable reign; (2) that the passage has the correct historical context but does not refer to a defensive system.

Geographical problems. Another question that can be asked concerning this passage is whether geographical distribution of the sites makes sense as a *defensive system.* The evidence would suggest that it does not.

Translation problems. And finally, I wish to explore the question: do the words of the passage signify the building of a *defensive system?* A proper understanding of the vocabulary, particularly the word *māṣôr*, demonstrates that they do not.

Historical Matters

Of the writers who take one of the two views on the relationship of the city-list to the invasion of Shishak, I offer only a representative sample. Some historical reconstructions become quite fanciful and imaginative. Orlinsky states that Rehoboam ". . . made a *feverish attempt* to strengthen his own defenses [but] . . . These efforts proved of no avail when Shishak's army began to march. The fortified cities of Judah fell one after the other."[3] Martin Noth, although with much more reserve, also suggests that the system was established in anticipation of the invasion of Shishak. According to him, the main evidence for this is the excessive attention paid to the western border of Judah overlooking the "Via Maris," the direct route to Egypt.[4]

The biblical text is not clear whether the invasion came before or after Rehoboam's building activity, but there are many writers who see the activity as

3. H. M. Orlinsky, *Ancient Israel* (Ithaca, N.Y.: Cornell University Press, 1960) 79–80.
4. M. Noth, *The History of Israel* (London: A & C Black, 1960) 238–40.

a reaction to the invasion. According to Aharoni, this view would explain the list as being the locations of the western line of defence, generally at the inner (eastern) ends of the valleys of the Shephelah. The possible exception to this is the city of Gath. If Tell es-Safit is meant, then the western border certainly "bulged" at this point. However, an alternative site is Moresheth-Gath (Tell el-Judeideh), which location would straighten the hypothetical line considerably.[5] Herrmann clearly sees the program as a reaction to the invasion,[6] whereas Bright is a little less clear.[7] Whether the building activity is seen as before, or after the invasion but directly related to it, problems emerge.

If one theorizes, as some do, that the building activity was done in anticipation of the invasion, then advance knowledge of the invasion on the part of the Judean king is presupposed. However, no indication of such advance knowledge is found in the sources. In fact, Shishak's invasion route avoided many of the sites mentioned, thus suggesting that Shishak's intelligence included the countermeasures taken by Rehoboam. These views are possible, of course, but lack clear support, and actually a convincing case can be made against this reconstruction because, according to Shishak's own city-list,[8] he attacked cities that were *better* fortified than the ones in the biblical list. His strategy was apparently to circumvent the internal cities of Judah and to concentrate on capturing, even for a brief time, the major sites along the main trading routes. Rehoboam's intelligence of the Egyptian's intentions was at best quite defective, and his supposed measures against the invasion ineffective.

If, on the other hand, the system of fortifications was established as a reaction to the invasion—and this is the majority opinion—then the inadequacies of the Judean king as a military strategist become even more apparent. He chose to strengthen those cities that Shishak decided to avoid. This is not simply a case of bolting the stable door after the horse has fled, but of bolting the wrong door! The link between the building activity and the invasion of Shishak is a precarious one.

5. Y. Aharoni, *The Land of the Bible: A Historical Geography* (Philadelphia: Westminster, 1979) 330.

6. S. Herrmann, *The History of Israel in Old Testament Times* (London: SCM Press, 1982) 197–98.

7. J. Bright, *A History of Israel* (3d ed.; Philadelphia: Westminster, 1980), 233.

8. B. Mazar, "The Campaign of Pharaoh Shishak to Palestine," *Volume du Congrès Strasbourg, 1956* (VTSup 4; Leiden: Brill, 1957) 57–66. The article was revised and republished in *The Early Biblical Period: Historical Essays* (Jerusalem: Israel Exploration Society, 1986) 139–50. Mazar suggested that the list be read boustrophedon, reading one line from left to right and the next from right to left.

Archaeological and Historical Matters

To support the hypothesis that the town list is that of a system of defence one must answer two questions satisfactorily. (1) Is there evidence for a large building program of the kind imagined in this period? The nature of this evidence would be archaeological, from Iron Age IIA. (2) Was the "defensive system" a good one? In other words, would it have defended Judah? The answer to both questions is negative.

The archaeological data, which have been well-rehearsed by previous writers,[9] are quite disappointing to those who regard the city-list as part of a large defensive system for Judah. Adoraim, Adullah, Etam, Gath (Tell es-Safit), Socoh, Ziph, and Zorah have not been excavated, only surveyed. There is little at the sites to suggest large early Iron Age fortresses. Of the remaining sites, Bethlehem has offered no extensive Iron Age materials; Beth-zur provides evidence of a small fort from Iron I, but nothing of import from Iron IIA apart from a few dwellings built *outside* the existing fort—all of this is clear evidence that the threat of invasion did not loom large in the minds of the inhabitants. Hebron (Tell er-Rumeideh) contains houses from Iron IIA but no fort. The excavations at Mareshah evidence mainly Hellenistic remains, and no Iron Age material has been found, although the site would have been occupied at the time of Shishak. Lachish (Tell ed-Duweir) contains extensive fortifications from Iron IIB and after but nothing of note from the twelfth to tenth centuries B.C.E. The remaining site, Azekah, alone contains evidence of fortification from the early divided monarchy. However, the original excavations by Bliss and MacAlister deserve reexamination and newer excavations. For the period of Rehoboam's reign (Iron IIA), the archaeological data do not support the hypothesis that the building program of Rehoboam as described in 2 Chr 11:5–12 had anything to do with a well-planned defensive system of fortresses.

I turn now to the question of the geographical appropriateness of the list, if it in fact represents a system of defensive fortresses designed to protect Judah during the reign of Rehoboam. At best, the system was badly designed. This fact is well-disguised in the map with a highly selective road system of Iron Age Judah that appears in Aharoni's historical geography.[10]

---

9. Most recently by N. Naᵓaman, "Hezekiah's Fortified Cities and the *lmlk* Stamps," *BASOR* 261 (1986) 5–24. Some of the details of Naᵓaman's work have been challenged by Y. Garfinkel, "2 Chr 11:5–10 Fortified City List and the *lmlk* Stamps," *BASOR* 271 (1988) 69–73.

10. Aharoni, *Land of the Bible*, 331.

Land communication between centers of population during the early period of the monarchy depended entirely on natural phenomena. Availability of food and water en route was essential, not only for small traveling groups moving between cities and towns, but also for a large army on the march. Natural physical barriers, such as swamps and forests, were avoided. Moving inland from the coastal plain, travelers would find that the wide, fertile valleys of the Shephelah provided an excellent means of movement. When the route began its ascent to the central hill country, valleys, which now became steep-sided and dangerous, were avoided and continuous ridges were sought to expedite travel and keep the traveler safe from surprise attack. Of course it was possible to traverse any kind of terrain when necessary, but I am describing the well-worn, customary paths chosen for efficiency. Roads were not permanent, nor were they constructed, as in later times, but custom was strong and if a road did not connect two points with a straight line, it sought the safest link.

Fortresses were built along such roads to guard the local population, to serve as taxation centers, and to keep watch on any who might pose a threat. Solomon's building program, which included Hazor, Megiddo, Gezer, and the Beth-horons, was intended to protect the royal interests along the "Via Maris." Tracing the lines of communication of this period is a matter of tracing the safest links between centers of population, bearing in mind the factors mentioned above. Campaign lists of ancient kings, Shishak's included, are of great help in finding these links. In areas traveled less by kings and large armies and more by those who left only incidental records of their travels, tracing roads is an exercise in the art of the possible and probable. It was apparently not until the years of the exile and early postexilic period that roads were *constructed* through initially unsuitable terrain (Isa 40:1–8).[11]

With these things in mind, it is revealing to see what the supposed defensive system of Rehoboam did *not* do. It is one thing to demonstrate that the sites mentioned in the city-list were on major internal roadways. In fact, one would hardly expect it to be otherwise since cities are, by their very nature, centers of population along lines of communication. But it is another thing to demonstrate that a comprehensive defense system of Judah at a given time in history covered all the possible entries into the interior of that country. The gaps within the system are much more revealing of either the incompetence of the designer of the system, or of the different purpose for which the system was designed.

---

11. On the road system in early Israel see Aharoni, *Land of the Bible*, 43–63; D. A. Dorsey, *Roads and Highways of Ancient Israel* (Baltimore: Johns Hopkins University Press, 1991).

If the city-list in 2 Chronicles 11 is to be seen as a defense system, then, in spite of the location of many of the sites along important roads, and in spite of the apparent "depth" of the sites, there are some serious gaps to be noted. The map shows that many of the sites are centrally located. With the possible exception of Gath (Tell es-Safit), the western sites are along the inner (eastern) reaches of the Shephelah valleys. There is a cluster of sites on the central divide, and one or two on either side. Missing are any sites in the Negev, any sites in the Southeast (such as Eshtemoa, Carmel, Maon), or any sites in the Judean desert (such as Jericho). Also missing are important cities such as Gezer and the Beth-horons, and—most significantly—any sites along the northern border between Judah and Israel. These gaps are serious and must now be examined in more detail.

1. An extensive gap is found in the southern end of the system between Lachish (Tell ed-Duweir) and Adoraim. Surprisingly, Tell Eton (Eglon?) and Tell Beit Mirsim are left undefended, and the road that links the two sites provides a good entry into the inner Shephelah, allowing the circumvention of Lachish and Mareshah, isolating them from the rest of the system.

2. The lack of attention to Gezer and the Beth-horons by Rehoboam opened a gap in the defenses of the north and allowed easy access to the northern approaches to Jerusalem. The north is the direction from which Jerusalem is most vulnerable. This gap also left isolated the northern cities of the Shephelah, such as Aijalon and Zorah, especially in light of the lack of defense of the Sorek Valley. With Timnah (Tell Batash), Beth-shemesh (ʿAin Shems), and Ekron (Tell Miqne) undefended, an approach through the vulnerable Sorek Valley would have cut the Shephelah in two.

In light of this inadequate southern defense, G. W. Ahlström has proposed that Tell ed-Duweir not be identified with Lachish and that Lachish be relocated at Tell Eton.[12] This would certainly close one of the gaps on the southwestern border. Ahlström further argues that the reference to Lachish in Lachish Letter IV suggests that the destination of the letter, found at Tell ed-Duweir, was not Lachish itself, but some other site. Yadin has effectively dealt with this matter in a recent article.[13] Because of a detailed comparison of the

---

12. G. W. Ahlström, "Is Tell ed-Duweir Ancient Lachish?" *PEQ* 112 (1980) 7–9.
13. Y. Yadin, "The Lachish Letters: Originals or Copies and Drafts?" *Biblical Archaeology in the Land of Israel* (Washington: Biblical Archaeology Society, 1984) 79–86.

site with the Lachish inscription of Sennacherib, the current excavators of Tell ed-Duweir, under David Ussishkin, are convinced of the identification of their site as Lachish.[14] Further, Ahlström's motivation for moving Lachish to Tell Eton is his assumption that the list in 2 Chr 11:5–12 refers to an extensive *defense* system of fortresses, an assumption that remains unproven.

Another way of dealing with these gaps is proposed by Gichon and Herzog.[15] For them, the "terror campaign" of Shishak was ineffective and served only to strengthen the resolve of the local Judeans. It produced "a nationwide upsurge of spirit and a strengthening of the will to hold out against hostile coercion."[16] They suggest that the defense was developed in depth and supported by a reserve of soldiers, modeled it seems on the current staffing of the modern Israeli Defense Force. Using Jerusalem as a link in a chain, this reserve "could move on interior lines to aid any threatened sector or to issue forward through any of the defended approaches and wrest the initiative from the enemy by means of pre-emptive attack, a simultaneous movement, or an offensive counter-action."[17] This reconstruction is as anachronistic as it is imaginative and is totally without support in the sources. Its most serious weakness is that Gichon and Herzog appear to want to be able to have their cake and eat it at the same time. According to them, this defense system was an example of brilliant strategy, yet, judging by the results of Shishak's campaign, was at the same time a dismal failure.

If the system was defensive, then the gaps in the north of Judah are much more serious and cannot be explained away lightly. Because of its water supply, the Gihon spring, the capital of Judah, Jerusalem, is located at a particularly vulnerable spot. It is east of the main route along the central mountain range, and of all the hills in the immediate vicinity, it is situated on the lowest. After the expansion of the city under Solomon, which included a sizeable acropolis, the situation was eased, but not completely alleviated.

To the north of Jerusalem the land continues to rise until it reaches the plateau on which are found the ancient sites of Bethel, Gibeon, Gibeah, Mizpah, Beeroth, and others. Possession of these sites and control of this plateau by an

14. D. Ussishkin, *The Conquest of Lachish by Sennacherib* (Tel Aviv: Institute of Archaeology, 1982). See also the important criticisms of G. I. Davies ("Tell ed-Duweir = Ancient Lachish: A Response to G. W. Ahlström," *PEQ* 114 [1982] 25–28).

15. M. Gichon and M. Herzog, *Battles of the Bible* (London: Weidenfeld & Nicholson, 1977) 134–41.

16. Gichon and Herzog, *Battles of the Bible*, 134.

17. Ibid. See also M. Gichon, "The System of Fortification of the Kingdom of Judah," *The Military History of the Land of Israel in the Biblical Period* (ed. J. Liver; Jerusalem: Maaracoth, 1977) 410–25.

enemy presented a very real threat to the city. It gave an attacker a distinct advantage, since it gave him room to deploy his army, to lodge reserves and supplies, offered an adequate water supply, and provided adequate timber for the construction of siege engines and ramparts. In the words of George Adam Smith, this area was "the most accessible frontier of Judah."[18] The strategic importance of this region is fully appreciated in the account of Joshua's alliance with Gibeon in Joshua 9 and the hasty reaction of the king of Jerusalem. In later history, Philistines (1 Samuel 4), Assyrians (Isa 10:28ff.), Seleucids (1 Macc 7:45), and Romans (Josephus *J.W.* 2.540–55) all appreciated its strategic importance, as did the Israeli army in 1967.[19] 2 Chr 12:15 refers to the constant wars between Rehoboam and his northern neighbor throughout his reign. The background to these conflicts is the struggle for control of this important plateau. *Not* to reinforce the northern border displayed a measure of shortsightedness on the part of Rehoboam that was inexcusable. This shortsightedness becomes all the more puzzling in the light of many scholars' assessments of Rehoboam as a brilliant military strategist.[20] No amount of goodwill toward the north, often created by commentators to account for this oversight, can compensate for this piece of military incompetence. Geographically, as a defense system the city-list in 2 Chronicles 11 is woefully inadequate.

Textual Dislocation

The recognition of these problems has led V. Fritz and others to resurrect an older theory of the composition of the books of Chronicles.[21] The theory, first proposed by E. Junge in 1938, suggests that the list in 2 Chr 11:5–12 was redactionally inserted and had its origin not in the time of Rehoboam, but during the reign of another king.[22] Fritz suggests as an alternative the time of Josiah, bolstering his argument with the fact that the archaeological data offer no support for the traditional reading of the biblical material. He also suggests that the term translated 'fortress' (Heb. *māṣôr*) was a postexilic

18. G. A. Smith, *Historical Geography of the Holy Land* (reprinted; London: Collins-Fontana, 1966) 198. This edition is based on the 25th edition of 1931.
19. See H. Herzog, *The Arab-Israeli Wars* (London: Methuen, 1982) 167–77.
20. So Gichon and Herzog, *Battles of the Bible.*
21. V. Fritz, "The List of Rehoboam's Fortresses in 2 Chr 11:5–12—a Document from the Time of Josiah," *Aharoni Volume* (Eretz-Israel 15; Jerusalem: Israel Exploration Society, 1981) 46–53.
22. E. Junge, *Die Wiederaufbau des Heereswesens des Reiches Juda unter Josia* (BWANT 75; Stuttgart: Kohlhammer, 1938). This oft-cited volume was unavailable to me.

term. Noting that the Shephelah received inordinate attention in the defense plan and that this was an area through which many invaders came later in the monarchy, Fritz concludes that it is unlikely that Rehoboam was the builder of this system. According to his theory, the list was relocated because of the literary-theological agenda of the Chronicler. The original setting must have been the reign of Josiah; hence the undue attention to the Shephelah and the undefended northern border, both of which enabled Josiah to move into the north to conduct his extensive reforms there.

One immediate difficulty with Fritz's relocation of the list is that it is Chronicles (2 Chr 34:6), not Kings, that offers information on the furthest reaches of the Josianic reform. It is hardly likely that the chronicler would deliberately confuse the issue by inserting the reference to the list at the point of the reign of Rehoboam. Leaving it in its supposed original context, the reign of Josiah, would have provided an explanation for the chronicler's additions to Josiah's northern reforms. Relocating it during the reign of Rehoboam removes information from the chronicler's account of the reign of Josiah and introduces confusion to the account of the reign of Rehoboam. In this scheme the Chronicler is presented as being as clumsy an editor as Rehoboam was a strategist. The invasion of Shishak is not mentioned in the narrative until the following chapter, so the intended link is by no means clear. However, it helps to remember that the base of Fritz's reasoning is that the list represents a *defensive system* of fortresses.

To assign the list to the reign of Josiah solves nothing. Moving the list does not explain why it was eventually misplaced or why Josiah would have selected these sites for fortification. The reason could not have been to provide the defensive perimeter envisioned by traditional interpreters of the list, since at the time of Josiah most of those sites were already well within his borders. Furthermore, the southern border of Judah extended farther south than Ziph during Josiah's reign.[23] The only rationale for the dislocation would be to preserve the notion of a defensive system of fortresses, and even that is not supportable, as I have shown.

More recently, Nadav Na²aman has suggested on similar grounds that the list be dated to the time of Hezekiah.[24] He argues that "the list of cities as an

---

23. The Israelite citadel at Arad dates originally from the 10th century B.C.E. (Iron Age IIA), and the fortifications at Beer-Sheba were built first in the 10th century B.C.E. (Stratum V) and destroyed in the 9th century B.C.E. (Stratum IV) after the period with which we are dealing. See Aharoni, "Arad," *EAEHL* 1.82–85, 162–68, and his more complete study *Arad Inscriptions* (Jerusalem: Israel Exploration Society, 1981).

24. Na²aman, "Hezekiah's Fortified Cities."

independent document has long been recognised."[25] Furthermore, the circumstances of Rehoboam's reign could not have accommodated the list: neither Rehoboam's ability nor the archaeological evidence can account for it. The most likely setting for the expansion, Naᵓaman argues, is Hezekiah's preparations for the Assyrian invasions of Judah. In my view, the most convincing evidence for this is Naᵓaman's dating of the royal jar-handle stamps at the time of Hezekiah (*lmlk* stamps).

Some of the details of Naᵓaman's theory have been challenged by Y. Garfinkel,[26] particularly his use of the *lmlk* stamps (see below). There are, however, some additional inconsistencies in Naᵓaman's position that I wish to point out. First, the assumption that the list is an "independent document," while in keeping with one longstanding tradition, is not a good starting point unless the reasons for the assumption are carefully examined. As I have shown, the theory goes back at least to E. Junge, and the reasons for the theory are based on his understanding of the list as representing an extensive fortification-defense system for Judah. Once this presupposition is challenged or set aside, the need to find extensive supporting archaeological data from the time of Rehoboam (Iron Age IIA) lessens. So also does the need to link the list with extensive remains from another reign.

Second, in spite of a tentative acknowledgment of this fact, Naᵓaman himself slips into the same trap. First he states (in agreement with my hypothesis) that:

> The cities mentioned in the list were inhabited by civilian populations, although they functioned as administrative military centers in which garrisons were stationed and food and armor stored. *They certainly were not fortresses and were not necessarily located on the borders of the kingdom.*[27]

But he nevertheless goes on to insist that large remains should be found from Rehoboam's reign and that Rehoboam had the administrative and fiscal ability "to carry out such an extensive fortification project." He then back-pedals by stating, "whether . . . Rehoboam would have been able to enforce an extensive levy to fortify the 15 towns is doubtful."[28] This argument depends too heavily on the assumption that the list represents an extensive fortification project. And that assumption, I contend, has not yet been proven.

The MT of 2 Chr 11:5–12 reads as follows:

25. Ibid., 5.
26. Garfinkel, "2 Chr 11:5–10," 69–73.
27. Naᵓaman, "Hezekiah's Fortified Cities," 6; emphasis mine.
28. Ibid., 7.

וַיֵּשֶׁב רְחַבְעָם בִּירוּשָׁלָ͏ִם וַיִּבֶן עָרִים לְמָצוֹר בִּיהוּדָה: וַיִּבֶן אֶת־בֵּית־לֶחֶם
וְאֶת־עֵיטָם וְאֶת־תְּקוֹעַ: וְאֶת־בֵּית־צוּר וְאֶת־שׂוֹכוֹ וְאֶת־עֲדֻלָּם: וְאֶת־גַּת
וְאֶת־מָרֵשָׁה וְאֶת־זִיף: וְאֶת־אֲדוֹרַיִם וְאֶת־לָכִישׁ וְאֶת־עֲזֵקָה: וְאֶת־צָרְעָה
וְאֶת־אַיָּלוֹן וְאֶת־חֶבְרוֹן אֲשֶׁר בִּיהוּדָה וּבְבִנְיָמִן עָרֵי מְצֻרוֹת: וַיְחַזֵּק
אֶת־הַמְּצֻרוֹת וַיִּתֵּן בָּהֶם נְגִידִים וְאֹצְרוֹת מַאֲכָל וְשֶׁמֶן וָיָיִן: וּבְכָל־עִיר וָעִיר
צִנּוֹת וּרְמָחִים וַיְחַזְּקֵם לְהַרְבֵּה מְאֹד וַיְהִי־לוֹ יְהוּדָה וּבִנְיָמִן:

The English versions consistently translate the passage as though the cities were built for the defense of Judah, although the AV offers the interesting translation of *māṣôr* as 'fenced'. The final comment in v. 12 receives slightly different treatment by the AV, reading, "having Judah and Benjamin on his side." The RSV offers "so he held Judah and Benjamin," and the Anchor Bible suggests, "thus Judah and Benjamin were retained by him." The NEB is similar, "Thus he retained possession of Judah and Benjamin." The question is, however, against what did Rehoboam *retain* Judah and Benjamin? The suggestion that this activity had something to do with the invasion of Shishak breaks the logical sequence of the narrative because the invasion is not mentioned until the following chapter. To deal more fully with this question I return to the meaning of the term *māṣôr*, the term understood in the general semantic range of 'defense'.

The term *māṣôr* occurs thirty-two times in the Hebrew Bible in a number of different contexts. Etymologically the word is derived from *ṣûr*, which BDB translates as 'confine, bind, besiege'. The noun *māṣôr* does not refer to that which 'defends' but 'besieges, confines or binds'. The related term *mĕṣûrāh* is translated as a 'rampart' erected against a city under siege. The term retains this meaning in Deuteronomy, Psalms, 2 Kings, and the prophets and is translated accordingly. It is only in 2 Chronicles that the term is translated differently. There it is consistently rendered 'fortifications', a translation that is in our estimation quite unnecessary. Fritz's judgment that the term *māṣôr* 'fortress' is postexilic involves the best of circular arguments and is unconvincing. In fact, the chronicler did know of the term with the meaning 'siege', since he *added* it to the Kings account of the Assyrian attack on Jerusalem (2 Chr 32:10). Further, where the chronicler wrote unambiguously of a 'fortress', he used the more standard term *mibṣār* and the related term *bĕṣûrāh* (2 Chr 17:1, 24). There is therefore no reason to change the meaning of *māṣôr* in Chronicles to 'fortress'. If the more common meaning of *māṣôr* as something which 'confines, besieges or binds' is retained in 2 Chr 11:5–12— a translation that is quite consistent with its appearance elsewhere—a different picture of Rehoboam's activity emerges. The cities of the list were cities built for *constraint*, and this is the method by which he retained Judah and

Benjamin. According to the narrative of 2 Chronicles 11, the building of the cities followed the secession of the northern tribes, and it is against this background that the city-list should be seen. We now examine this historical context in more detail.

Preceding Events

In 2 Chronicles 10 the northern tribes broke away from the south and eventually formed a kingdom of their own. An important reason for this secession was the system of forced labor that Solomon and Rehoboam imposed on the entire population. A delegation of the people petitioned Rehoboam on the matter of forced labor but was unsuccessful, since the king refused to concede anything. The story may be summed up as follows:

> *2 Chr 10:1–15.* The assembly at Shechem is convened for the anointing of Rehoboam as king over the North as well as the South. The question of forced labor (Heb. *mas*) is raised.

> *2 Chr 10:6–11.* Rehoboam consults the elders (elected officials and representatives of the older tribal organization) and the "young men" (Heb. *yĕlādîm*, court appointees representing the new order) on the matter and accepts the advice of the latter, thus increasing the burden.

> *2 Chr 10:12–16.* The northern tribes reject the covenant with the king and secede from the house of David.

> *2 Chr 10:17–19.* There is a brief attempt to regain control of the North, but it results in the death of a Judean official and a hasty retreat of the king to Jerusalem.

In the following chapter the king musters an army to invade the North, but on the advice of the prophet Shemaiah, the army refuses to march against Jeroboam (11:1–4). The king returns to Jerusalem and while there embarks on his program of strengthening the cities mentioned in the city-list. At the same time, Levites, refugees from the North, come south to resettle. It is important to note that the secession of the North, the abortive invasion, and the building program are all part of the same narrative sequence. The building program is peculiar to the Chronicler's account of the beginning of Rehoboam's reign. Further, the Chronicler did not choose to link the program with the invasion of Shishak, but saw it as the climax of the process of secession.

It is in this broader context that Rehoboam "retained possession of Judah and Benjamin" and not the context of an outside threat. The building followed the refusal of his army (on the advice of a prophet) to invade the North. The cities were cities of *constraint* in the territories of Judah and Benjamin and were designed as a means of *internal security*, rather than as a system of defense against outside attack. This hypothesis can be strengthened further.

In order to complete the supposed defense system of 2 Chr 11:5–12, it has been suggested that the Levitical cities ought to be added to the list (see Joshua 21 and 1 Chronicles 6).[29] But there are problems with this theory. First, the Levitical cities were spread throughout the entire country, including the Transjordan, and were not restricted to Judah. It is therefore difficult to see what relevance they would have had to the defense of Judah. It is also unlikely that the purpose for the building of these cities was to provide places of refuge for the Levites in the South. Second, the tribe of Dan figures in the Levitical city-list, but it is clear that by this time the border between Dan and Judah had been dissolved. Third, there is some overlap in the lists—for example, Hebron and Aijalon appear in both—which would suggest that the list in 2 Chr 11:5–12 was intended for something independent from the Levitical city-lists.

There are some city-lists in the Old Testament that are important to the list in 2 Chr 11:5–12. They are the list of cities of Judah in Josh 15:30–62 and the supplementary list in 1 Chronicles 4. The latter is a list of cities occupied by returning exiles. Following Alt's original study of the Judean districts,[30] Cross and Wright[31] have suggested that the list in Joshua 15 can be subdivided into political districts. They also argue that an original list, dated from the time of David, was expanded by subsequent Judean kings as circumstances permitted. A complete list of the Judean districts is found in Appendix 1.

When this list of administrative districts from Joshua 15 is compared with the list in 2 Chr 11:5–12, one can see that Districts II, III, IV, VI, VII, VIII, and IX overlap with the cities in 2 Chronicles 11. Omitted are District I, the Negev; District II, the south central highlands; District XI, the area northeast of Jerusalem; and District XII, the Judean Desert.

---

29. See Aharoni, *The Land of the Bible*, 332; Z. Kallai-Kleinmann, "Town Lists of Judah, Simeon, Benjamin and Dan," *VT* 8 (1958) 134–60. Kallai-Kleinmann ignores the overlap of Aijalon and Hebron.

30. A. Alt, "Israels Gaue unter Josias," *PJ* 21 (1925) 100–116.

31. F. M. Cross and G. E. Wright, "The Boundary and Province Lists of the Kingdom of Judah," *JBL* 65 (1956) 202–26. See also Y. Aharoni, "The Province Lists of Judah," *VT* 9 (1959) 225–46, and Kallai-Kleinmann, "Town Lists," 134–60.

The facts manifested in these lists are consistent with what is known from other contexts about Rehoboam's reign. District XI, the area northeast of Jerusalem, according to 2 Chr 13:1–7 was not in the hands of the Judean kings until the reign of Rehoboam's successor, Abijah. District XII, the Judean Desert, has yielded Iron-Age pottery, but only from the later monarchy, the ninth to sixth centuries B.C.E. These finds suggest that royal Judean expansion into this region began in earnest only during the reign of Jehoshaphat at the earliest.[32]

Further investigation is required to determine the reason for the exclusion of District I (the Negev) from the 2 Chronicles 11 city-list, though I believe that this problem does not present a serious challenge to my hypothesis. Two matters require comment. First is the question of whether conditions in the Negev in the tenth century B.C.E. were consistent with the intent of the city-list in 2 Chr 11:5–12, as understood in this paper. The studies that have been conducted in the Negev confirm the suspicion that in the tenth century B.C.E. the Negev was in no condition to support large-scale, lucrative agricultural activity. The region lacked adequate rainfall, and the soil was generally unsuitable for large-scale agriculture. The average annual rainfall in the Negev has been calculated at 50–150 mm., with a cyclical variation over a period of about fifty years. Shanan and his associates conclude that this would not have been sufficient to support large-scale agriculture.[33] In addition to the relatively poor rainfall, the nature of the soil was such that surplus agriculture—to provide goods for Rehoboam and his court—was impossible.

Studies in the growth and fluctuation of the population in the region help to fill out this picture.[34] Aharoni's 1958 study confirmed that at the beginning of the monarchy (tenth century B.C.E.) the population of the Negev was "a semi-nomadic population in the process of settling."[35] Unique in the Negev at this time was the central city of Beer-sheba. The later years of the monarchy, the eighth and seventh centuries B.C.E., were characterized by a pattern "absolutely different from the Negeb in the tenth century."[36] The reason for this difference was the concerted effort of later kings to develop the

32. Cross and Wright, "Boundary and Province Lists," 223–24. Subsequent surveys have revealed nothing to alter this viewpoint. See Y. Aharoni, *The Archaeology of the Land of Israel* (Philadelphia: Westminster, 1982) 251.

33. Y. Aharoni et al., "The Ancient Desert Agriculture of the Negev: An Israelite Agricultural Settlement at Ramat Matred," *IEJ* 10 (1960) 23–36, 97–111.

34. See S. A. Rosen, "Demographic Trends in the Negev Highlands," *BASOR* 266 (1987) 45–58.

35. Y. Aharoni, "The Negeb of Judah," *IEJ* 8 (1958) 26–38, quotation from p. 32.

36. Aharoni, "The Negeb of Judah," 33.

region into a large southern administrative district, with the main population being the inhabitants of the string of border fortresses, a kind of *limes judaica*.[37] Shishak's list of captured sites contains approximately seventy names from the Negev, including two Arads. This may indicate that the region was much more widely settled than I have indicated here. However, it has been acknowledged that the ancient population density of the region is notoriously difficult to estimate. Apart from one or two fortresses, there is no indication archaeologically as to the size of these settlements (often called agricultural settlements), nor is there much indication that they were under the control of the Judean monarch. In fact, since many of them are in the southern Negev, this is unlikely. The income from the Negev was not from agriculture alone but also from effective control of trade routes, an important characteristic of the region until the time of the Nabateans. A microcosm of Negev life can be seen at the site of Ramat Matred,[38] which was built initially in the tenth century but abandoned shortly afterward. In the early monarchy the Negev would hardly have been in a position to support Rehoboam's plans. The local population at this time was well scattered. The desert fortresses built by later kings were staffed by military personnel and their families or, as in the case of the late monarchy, by Greek mercenaries.[39]

It is clear then that the major habitations in each of the central Judean administrative districts were covered by the program and that the list of those covered is consistent with what is known of Rehoboam's administrative control from other sources. Cross and Wright have also argued that the districts into which Rehoboam sent his sons as governors (2 Chr 11:23) must have existed prior to Rehoboam's reign, from an earlier division during the time of David.[40] The absence of Judah from Solomon's taxable districts is a fact also consistent with my hypothesis, since it appears that Judah was *already* divided into districts at this time. Also to be noted is the lack of administrative centers in the border districts. The cities mentioned in 2 Chr 11:5–12 controlled the most productive and heavily populated districts of Judah and were ideally suited for purposes of internal security rather than national defense against a hostile neighbor.

37. Y. Aharoni, "Forerunners of the Limes: Iron Age Fortresses in the Negev," *IEJ* 17 (1967) 1–17.
38. Aharoni et al., "Ancient Desert Agriculture," 23–36, 97–111.
39. A point which Y. Aharoni confirmed in his interpretation of the Arad ostraca. See Aharoni, *Arad Inscriptions*.
40. Cross and Wright, "Boundary and Province Lists," 225.

The *lmlk* Jar-Handles

Two additional items of interest provide support for the theory that Reho-boam's cities were built for the purpose of internal security. They are (1) the distribution of the so-called "royal jar-handles" in Judah, and (2) the changing administrative roles within the Judean court at this time, reflected in the social conflicts recorded in 2 Chronicles 10.

Nadav Naᵓaman has brought into the discussion of the city-list in 2 Chr 11:5–12 the collection of "royal jar-handles" found throughout Judah bearing the seal impression "*lmlk*" '(belonging) to the king'.[41] It is Naᵓaman's argument that the distribution of the jar-handles and the cataloging of cities coincided during the reign of Hezekiah and confirm his suspicion that the city-list describes the building and administrative activities of Hezekiah in preparation for the Assyrian invasion. Naᵓaman accepts the widely-held belief that the storage jars were found at administrative centers of the Judean monarchy. Three points of investigation are important. The first task is to determine the correlation between the city-list and the discovery of the storage jars—that is, to determine whether the jar-handles were found at all of the sites. The second involves the general distribution of the storage jar handles—that is, whether they were found at other sites. The third problem is to determine whether there is a link between the city-list and the jar handles containing names of cities.

Naᵓaman notes that of the fifteen cities mentioned in the list, six have yielded royal jar handles (Bethlehem, Beth-zur, Gath, Mareshah, Lachish, and Azekah), of which only the last five have been excavated. The absence of jar handles from the other sites is "understandable" in the light of their unexcavated state.

Naᵓaman also notes that of the four cities named on some of the jar handles—Hebron, Ziph, Socoh, and Mamshit—three are on the list. The identification of the fourth is unknown. He also notes that there is a close congruence between the general distribution of jar handles in Judah and the city-list. Few jar handles have been found in the southernmost part of the Shephelah or in the Negev, despite extensive excavations in those regions. He links this phenomenon with Hezekiah's preparations, because the southern Shephelah and the Negev were outside Sennacherib's anticipated line of approach. In general the distribution of the jar handles, the city-list in 2 Chr 11:5–12, and the congruence between the two suit Hezekiah's reign best.

---

41. Naᵓaman, "Hezekiah's Fortified Cities."

This theory has been carefully evaluated and challenged by Y. Garfinkel.[42] Garfinkel has pointed out that the evidence on the jar handles was used very selectively by Naᵓaman and that up-to-date figures on the distribution of jar handles differ considerably from Naᵓaman's. In Garfinkel's estimation, the argumentation used by Naᵓaman could result in "any historical conclusion in relation to any city-list in the Bible."[43] Of the forty-three sites at which royal jar handles were found, only eight correspond to sites in the 2 Chr 11:5–12 city-list, and these account for only 38% of the jar handles discovered. Even apart from the other serious historical problems identified by Garfinkel, this evidence is hardly a solid basis for identifying the list as being from the time of Hezekiah.

If the jar handles have any relevance to the city-list, it is probably in connection with three of the four sites mentioned on some of them. Hebron (Tell er-Rumeideh), Socoh (Khirbet Abbad), and Ziph all appear in the list. If, as some argue, the jar handles represent a royal taxation system,[44] then these sites might well be early administrative centers for the collection of the taxes. This idea, though tempting, is speculative. However, Avraham Malamat[45] has offered a careful analysis of the "organs of statecraft" at the time of the early United Monarchy, an analysis that throws light on the role of these administrative centers in the developing political structure of the monarchy. Malamat's thesis is well-known, and I present it in outline only.

Following the pattern established by David (2 Sam 5:1–3), the northern tribes were joined to the southern tribes on the basis of a mutual covenant. David's covenant was with the elders of Israel, thus "the rule of the Judaean kings over the northern tribes [was] conditional upon a covenantal agreement between the king and his future subjects."[46] This covenant was also renewed for the South at a time of crisis in the succession (see 2 Kings 12). The precise terminology of these covenant agreements is important. An assembly (Heb. *qāhal*) of elders was gathered to negotiate the covenant. Under this scheme, the assembly "felt it their prerogative to stipulate the conditions for the covenant renewal leading to the enthronement itself."[47] As the account of the

---

42. Garfinkel, "2 Chr 11:5–10," 69–73.

43. Ibid., 71.

44. See D. Diringer, "Royal Jar-Handle Stamps," *BA* 12 (1949) 70–85, and the more recent study of A. F. Rainey, "Wine From the Royal Vineyards," *BASOR* 245 (1982) 57–62.

45. A. Malamat, "Organs of Statecraft in the Israelite Monarchy," *BA* 28 (1965) 34–56. See also Malamat's "Kingship and Council in Israel and Sumer," *JNES* 22 (1963) 247–53.

46. Malamat, "Organs of Statecraft," 36.

47. Ibid., 40.

attempted covenant renewal in 2 Chronicles 11 shows, the northern elders did not accept the conditions laid down by Rehoboam and rejected the union. Their reaction was against "the house of David."

The role of the elders in ancient Israelite society has been studied extensively.[48] They appear here as the relic of the disappearing tribal society, were sought for advice, and at times acted in a judicial capacity. The juxtaposition of 'elders' (Heb. *zĕqēnîm*) and 'young men' (Heb. *yĕlādîm*) is not simply a matter of aged wisdom pitted against youthful hotheadedness. The divisions are sociopolitical. The young men, according to Malamat, "were primarily princes, the offspring of Solomon, reared together with their half-brother, Rehoboam," men who "attained high status at the court and most probably held high rank in the military."[49] The term is not restricted to the offspring of Solomon and reappears time and again in the history of the monarchy. They appear as a potential threat to the revolt of Jehu (here named "sons of the king," 2 Kgs 10:1–6). Their threat to the revolt is not simply that they represent possible heirs to the throne but that they have political power. Because of their background and rearing, they represent the same social stratum, political force, and vested interests of the monarch.

Avigad has confirmed this image in his article examining the role of the "king's son."[50] He concludes that the "king's son" is a member of the royal family, and where his role is described, he is responsible for security. In the light of the discussion above, it is clear that his responsibilities stretched further afield. The conclusion of 2 Chronicles 11, translated according to my theory, supports this well:

> and [Rehoboam] dealt wisely, and distributed some of his sons through all the districts of Judah and Benjamin, in all their cities of constraint; and he gave them abundant provisions, and procured wives for them (2 Chr 11:23).

Political and Social Changes

The reconstruction proposed here suits well the picture of the origins and development of the Israelite monarchy emerging from recent historical studies. Premonarchical Israel was an agrarian peasant society organized according to

48. See H. Klengel, "Die Rolle der Ältesten im Kleinasien in Hethiterzeit," *ZA* 57 (1965) 223–36; J. L. McKenzie, "The Elders in the Old Testament," *Bib* 40 (1959) 522–40; H. Reviv, "Elders and Saviours," *OrAnt* 16 (1977) 201–4.
49. Malamat, "Organs of Statecraft," 45.
50. N. Avigad, "Baruch the Scribe and Jerahmeel the King's Son," *BA* 42 (1979) 114–21.

tribes with little centralization of power. Military organization reflected this social structure.[51]

A major precipitating factor in the founding of the monarchy was the social, political, and military threat posed by the Philistines, a threat which the existing order under Samuel was too corrupt and too inadequate to deal with.[52] The Philistines' monopoly in the iron industry and control over the major roads in the central highlands gave them effective control of the local population and betrayed their intention of integrating the tribes back into the city-state system.

A study of the historical accounts of the emerging monarchy reveals that the textual traditions related to the founding of the monarchy are notoriously difficult to unravel. Traditionally, biblical scholars have identified two distinct parties in 1 Samuel 1–12, one in favor of and one against the monarchy.[53] More recent studies have concentrated on the unity of the narrative.[54] The present text may well reflect the ambivalence that accompanied the radical social and political changes within Israel attending the founding of the monarchy.

For the purposes of this study, two things stand out in the account. First, negotiations for a king are carried out between Samuel and the elders of the people. Second, this tradition of negotiation was continued by David in his dealings with Judah and later with Israel, in his rise to power. The result was that the establishment of the monarchy in Israel was accompanied by strong conditions for its continued existence.[55] It appears that these conditions continued to be embraced by the prophetic tradition.

---

51. I have dealt with this correlation between military organization and its "host society," Israel, in "An Experiment in Militarism," *Ascribe to the Lord: Biblical and Other Studies in Memory of Peter C. Craigie* (ed. L. Eslinger and G. Taylor; Sheffield: JSOT Press, 1988) 457–80. See also T. R. Hobbs, *A Time for War: A Study of War in the Old Testament* (Wilmington: Michael Glazier, 1989) 27–69; B. Mazar, "The Military Elite of King David," *VT* 13 (1963) 310–23; and C. Hauer, "The Economics of National Security in Solomonic Israel," *JSOT* 18 (1980) 63–73.

52. The arguments put forward to Samuel by the elders of Israel in 1 Samuel 8 have echoed throughout history whenever a new regime is inaugurated: the old is corrupt or quite incapable of dealing with the new situation. This is even a common theme of the modern Western election campaign!

53. See Bruce C. Birch, *The Rise of the Israelite Monarchy: The Growth and Development of 1 Samuel 7–15* (SBLDS 27; Missoula: Scholars Press, 1976).

54. See L. Eslinger, *Kingship of God in Crisis: A Close Reading of 1 Sam. 1–12* (Sheffield: Almond Press, 1985).

55. I make no judgment about whether a "constitution" was drawn up to set out the conditions of kingship in Israel. For this fascinating suggestion, see Baruch Halpern, *The Constitution of the Monarchy in Israel* (HSM 25; Chico, Cal.; Scholars Press, 1981).

Soon the costs of the move to a centralized form of government under a king became apparent. First Saul, then David and Solomon, increased the size of the bureaucracy needed to run the affairs of state from the center. Land grants were made by kings to their closest associates as rewards for service. Administration of royal estates necessitated a redistribution of labor, which took workers away from small landowners. It was probably the abuse of this system that was behind Samuel's warning in 1 Sam 8:8–10. Another result of the rising monarchy was the growth and development of a standing army, a factor that played a decisive political role in national affairs.

The social and political costs consequent to this move must have been extensive. Subsistence agriculture was replaced by surplus agriculture at a time when much-needed labor was being diverted to the military or other branches of royal service. And changes evident in the army were but a microcosm of changes in the society in general. Social mobility increased, family structures changed, and society became more cosmopolitan. Most serious was the transfer of political, economic, and "cultural" power from the small village to the city.[56] Israelites, it seems, had now become reintegrated into a system they had once fought to overthrow. The main difference was that this system was now Israelite.

In the eyes of most Israelites during the time of the united monarchy, these changes were focused in Jerusalem and the house of David. The most grotesque symbol of change was the forced-labor gang (Heb. *mas*) used increasingly by David, Solomon, and to his peril, Rehoboam.[57] It was this convention that became the subject of negotiations between Rehoboam and the northern tribes, led by Jeroboam, who had had firsthand experience with the destructive system.

Two features of the narrative of Rehoboam's inauspicious ascent to the throne support well the hypothesis presented in this paper. The first is that it was a prophet, Shemaiah, who advised against the northern invasion. The second is that the address of Shemaiah had its desired effect on the southern army: they returned home. This is just another example of protest against the

---

56. The process of urbanization as a sociocultural phenomenon is one requiring extensive study in the Old Testament. For one attempt, see F. S. Frick, *The City in Ancient Israel* (Missoula: Scholars Press, 1977). I have also investigated some aspects of this in "David and the Invention of Tradition" (*A Time for War*, 59–69).

57. On the subject of the labor-gangs, see A. F. Rainey, "Compulsory Labour Gangs in Ancient Israel," *IEJ* 20 (1970) 191–202, and N. Avigad, "Chief of the Corvee," *IEJ* 30 (1980) 170–73. It is quite possible that the Meṣad Ḥashavyahu Inscription betrays an abuse of the system. For the text see John C. L. Gibson, ed., *Textbook of Syrian Semitic Inscriptions* (Oxford: Clarendon, 1971) 1.26–30.

monarchy from within the prophetic tradition. Shemaiah emulated Ahijah of Shiloh (1 Kgs 11:26–40) and anticipated Elisha (2 Kgs 9:1–37). Rehoboam's response to this potential dissent in the South was to tighten his control over the southern population by building the constraint-cities described above.

Historiography

The final matter to be addressed is that of historiography. The problem is stated well by Garfinkel:

> Rehoboam is the only king the Chronicler criticizes (2 Chr 12:14). Nevertheless, Rehoboam, too, is credited with city building. The historiographic question that should be thus asked is . . . why city building should be attributed to Rehoboam.[58]

My interpretation of the city-list in 2 Chr 11:5–10 offers an answer to this question that is consistent with the chronicler's criticisms of Rehoboam. Rehoboam built "cities of constraint" (Heb. *ʿārê lĕmāṣôr*) to control Judah and Benjamin after the secession of the North. He staffed these cities with his own trusted relatives and dependents and thus retained the southern tribes. The other city-builders whom the chronicler mentions, Jehoshaphat (2 Chr 17:12), Uzziah (2 Chr 26:6), Jotham (2 Chr 27:4) and Hezekiah (2 Chr 32:29) embarked on no such controlling programs but were more involved in economic and demographic expansion. The lone exception is Asa, who also built "cities of constraint" (Heb *ʿārê mĕṣûrāh*) (2 Chr 14:5). In spite of the impressions given by the English translations, it is important to note that these cities were not for defense. As the chronicler clearly states, "he had no war in those years."

Summary

The main arguments and conclusions of this study are:

1. The notion that the list of cities in 2 Chr 11:5–12 was a *defense system* is untenable.
2. The building program associated with these sites had little if anything to do with the invasion of Shishak.

58. Garfinkel, "2 Chr 11:5–10," 72.

3. Attempts to read the list as cities of a defensive system are reductionist.
4. The list should be seen, I believe, in the light of and as a consequence of the secession of the northern tribes.
5. The distribution of sites corresponds closely to the political division of Judah into local administrative districts during the early monarchy.
6. The cities were staffed by political appointees (relatives) of the king, who represented a new political order.
7. The appointees' activity, attested elsewhere in the Hebrew Bible, demonstrates that the system was designed for a political/juridical purpose, that is, as a system of internal security following the secession of the North. In this way Rehoboam retained Judah and Benjamin.
8. This interpretation is consistent with the criticism of Rehoboam by the chronicler.

Appendix 1
The Judaean City-List in Joshua 15
[City-names in boldface are those that appear in 2 Chr 11:5–12]

District

I. Kabzeel, Eder, Jagur, Kinah, Dimonah, Adadah, Kedesh, Hazor, Ithnan, Ziph, Telem, Be-aloth, Hazor-hadattah, Kerioth-hezron, Amam, Shema, Moladah, Hazar-gaddah, Heshmon, Beth-pelet, Hazar-shual, Beer-shena, Biziothiah, Baalah, Iim, Ezem, Eltolad, Chesil, Hormah, Ziklag, Madmannah, Sansannah, Lebaoth, Shil-him, Ain, Rimmon.

II. Eshtaol, **Zorah**, Ashnah, Zanoah, En-gannim, Tappuah, Enam, Jarmuth, **Adullam, Socoh, Azekah,** Shaaraim, Adithaim, Gederah, Gederothaim.

III. Zenan, Hadashah, Migdal-gad, Dilean, Mizpeh, Joktheel, **Lachish,** Bozkath, Eglon, Cabbon, Lahmam, Chitlish, Gederoth, Beth-dagon, Naamah, Makkedah.

IV. Libnah, Ether, Ashan, Iphtah, Ashnah, Nezib, Keilah, Achzib, **Mareshah**.

V. Ekron, Ashdod, Gaza, Shamir, Jattir, Socoh, Dannah, Kiriath-sanah (**Debir**), Anab, Eshtemoh, Anim, Goshen, Holon, Giloh.

VI. Arab, Dumah, Eshan, Janim, Beth-tappuah, Aphekah, Humtah, Kiriath-arba (**Hebron**), Zior.

VII. Maon, Carmel, **Ziph**, Juttah, Jezreel, Jokdeam, Zanoah, Kain, Gibeah, Timnah.

VIII. Halhul, **Beth-Zur**, Gedor, Maarath, Beth-anoth, Eltekon.

IX. **Tekoa**, Ephrathah (**Beth-lehem**), Pagor (Pe^{c}or), **Etam**, Karem, Gallim, Bether, Manahath.

X. Kiriath-baal (Kiriath-jearim), Rabbah.

XI. Bath-arabah, Middin, Secacah, Nibshan, City of Salt, En-gedi.

Appendix 2
The List of Levitical Cities

	Joshua 21	*1 Chronicles 6*
<u>Judah and Simeon</u>	Hebron	Hebron
	Libnah	Libnah
	Jattir	Jattir
	Eshtemoa	Eshtemoa
	Holon	Hilen
	Debir	Debir
	Ain	
		Ashan
	Juttah	
	Beth-shemesh	Beth-shemesh
<u>Benjamin</u>	Gibeon	
	Geba	Geba
	Anathoth	Anathoth
	Almon	Alemeth
<u>Ephraim</u>	Shechem	Shechem
	Gezer	Gezer
	Kibzaim	
		Jokmeam
	Beth-horon	Beth-horon
<u>Dan</u>	Eltekeh	
	Gibbethon	
	Aijalon	Aijalon
	Gath-rimmon	Gath-rimmon
<u>Manasseh</u>	Taanach	
		Aner
	Gath-rimmon	
		Bileam (Ibleam)
	Golan	Golan
	Be-eshterah	Ashtaroth

	Joshua 21	*1 Chronicles 6*
<u>Issachar</u>	Kishion	
		Kedesh
	Daberath	Daberath
	Jarmuth	Ramoth
	En-gannim	
		Anem
<u>Asher</u>	Mishal	Mashal
	Abdon	Abdon
	Helkath	
		Hukok
	Rehob	Rehob
<u>Naphtali</u>	Kedesh	Kedesh
	Hammoth-dor	Hammon
	Kartan	Kiriathaim
<u>Zebulun</u>	Jokneam	
	Kartah	
		Tabor
	Dimnah	
		Rimmon
	Nahalal	
<u>Reuben</u>	Bezer	Bezer
	Jahazah	Jahazah
	Kedemoth	Kedemoth
	Mepha-ath	Mepha-ath
<u>Gad</u>	Ramoth-Gilead	Ramoth-Gilead
	Mahanaim	Mahanaim
	Heshbon	Heshbon
	Jaazer	Jaazer

The Lachish Letters and Official Reactions to Prophecies

Simon B. Parker

W HAT IMPACT DID PROPHETS HAVE on the authorities in ancient Israel? The Bible contains several narratives that refer to the reactions of officials to prophetic pronouncements, but the relation of these narratives to normal historical circumstances is a moot question. The only direct historical evidence for such reactions comes from the Lachish letters, excavated at Tell ed-Duweir in 1935 and first published in 1938.[1] So far, the study of the one undisputed reference to a prophet in an undamaged context in a Lachish letter has focused almost entirely on what it tells about prophets and prophecy. In fact, it tells very little about this subject—Pardee speaks of "modest results."[2] If, however, historians were to ask about the response to prophets and prophecies by the officials writing or referred to in the letters, then the collection would prove to be a more revealing historical source.

In addressing this question, I shall first review some aspects of the general circumstances in which the letters were written. Next I shall discuss the language of the key passage in Ostracon III,[3] explore what this passage reveals

1. H. Torczyner, *Lachish I: The Lachish Letters* (London: Oxford University Press, 1938).
2. D. Pardee, "An Overview of Ancient Hebrew Epistolography," *JBL* 97 (1978) 329.
3. I refer to the ostraca by the Roman numerals of the original publication (Torczyner, *Lachish Letters*). Phoenician texts are cited by *KAI* number (*KAI* = H. Donner and W. Röllig, *Kanaanäische und aramäische Inschriften* [3 vols.; Wiesbaden: Harrassowitz, 1964) and Mari texts by *AEM* number (*AEM* = J.-M. Durand, *Archives épistolaires de Mari I/1* (ARM 26; Paris: Editions Recherche sur les Civilisations, 1988).

about the circumstances behind the letter, and compare these with the circumstances revealed by some letters from the Mari archives. Finally, I return to the Lachish letters to consider further possible reflections of official responses to prophetic pronouncements.

Both archeological evidence and the letters themselves indicate that the Lachish letters were written in expectation of the Babylonian invasion that led to the destruction of Jerusalem in 586 B.C.E. In only one letter does the sender identify himself: Hošacyahu sent Letter III. In three letters the addressee is named Yaʾuš: II, III (largely restored), and VI. In all of the letters to which I shall refer (except possibly the fragmentary XVI), the sender refers to the addressee as ʾdny 'my lord'. The sender of II, V, and VI speaks of himself as "a dog"—hence the general belief that the recipient was a high official and that the letters come from subordinates. Since the identification of the site of Tell ed-Duweir as Lachish is certain,[4] it follows that the letters were sent from smaller towns in the vicinity to Lachish, which itself was the greatest fortress of Judah outside Jerusalem. This is the prevailing view of the matter.[5] Recently, however, Yigael Yadin has argued that the ostraca are in fact drafts and/or copies of letters that were sent from Lachish to Jerusalem.[6] It is necessary to respond to Yadin's arguments before proceeding.

First, Yadin argues that the fact that several of the ostraca come from the same pot[7] indicates that they must have been found at the location of the

---

4. See most recently D. Ussishkin, *The Conquest of Lachish by Sennacherib* (Publications of the Institute of Archaeology 6; Tel Aviv: Tel Aviv University, 1982) and the judgment in L. T. Geraty, "Archaeology and the Bible at Hezekiah's Lachish," *Andrews University Seminary Studies* 25 (1987) 27–37. For a recent debate over the identification, see G. W. Ahlström, "Is Tell ed-Duweir Ancient Lachish?" *PEQ* 112 (1980) 7–9; "Tell ed-Duweir: Lachish or Libnah?" *PEQ* 115 (1983) 103–4; "Lachish: Still a Problem," *PEQ* 117 (1985) 97–99); G. I. Davies, "Tell ed-Duweir = Ancient Lachish: A Response to G. W. Ahlström," *PEQ* 114 (1982) 25–28; "Tell ed-Duweir: Not Libnah but Lachish," *PEQ* 117 (1985) 92–96.

5. Donner and Röllig, *KAI*; J. C. L. Gibson, *Textbook of Syrian Semitic Inscriptions*, vol. 1: *Hebrew and Moabite Inscriptions* (Oxford: Clarendon, 1971); A. Lemaire, *Inscriptions Hébraiques, I: Les Ostraca* (Littératures anciennes du Proche Orient 9; Paris: Editions du Cerf, 1977); D. Pardee, *Handbook of Ancient Hebrew Letters* (SBLSBS 15; Chico, Cal.: Scholars Press, 1982).

6. Y. Yadin, "The Lachish Letters: Originals or Copies or Drafts?" in *Recent Archaeology in the Land of Israel* (ed. H. Shanks and B. Mazar; Washington, D.C.: Biblical Archaeology Society/Jerusalem: Israel Exploration Society, 1984) 179–86. Yadin's views have since been promulgated in a more popular forum (O. Borowski, "Yadin Presents New Interpretation of the Famous Lachish Letters," *BAR* 10 [1984] 74–77).

7. Torczyner, *Lachish Letters*, 220.

sender. I contend, however, that if these letters were sent by the same sender to the same recipient in a short period of time,[8] then one would expect to find them together at their destination. Second, Yadin argues that the absence of the names of the senders or recipients in most of the letters indicates that they were merely drafts. This topic demands discussion in a larger context: for instance, many of the Arad letters show no indication of the sender. Suffice it to say that all this correspondence was in a culture in which most people did not write letters. No mail deliverer could have failed to remember who had sent him or to whom, and for this reason it was not necessary to name the sender or recipient. In fact it would have been superfluous for the scribe always meticulously to include such data in the written form of the message.[9]

Yadin argues further that since several of the ostraca deal with the same subject matter, are written in the same style, and contain numerous repetitions, they must be drafts. But the same evidence is found in many cases of such correspondence, notably the El Amarna correspondence from Palestinian towns to Egypt. No one would claim that these are drafts produced in El Amarna! Yadin's observations here are consistent with the traditional view of the origin of the Lachish letters.

Finally, Yadin argues that the reference to "√šmr ʾl the fire-signal(s) of Lachish" in IV clearly indicates that the sender was in Lachish. Yadin cites 1 Sam 26:15–16 (cf. 2 Sam 11:16) as determinative for the meaning of √šmr ʾl here. In 1 Samuel this phrase refers to Abner's "keeping a watchful eye on," "keeping guard over" the king (cf. BDB: "keep watch and ward"). Yadin claims that this clearly implies that in Lachish Ostracon IV the sender was "tending" the beacon of—and therefore was located in—Lachish, rather than "watching for" it (from another town), as in most translations. But if the meaning of √šmr ʾl is akin to "keep a watchful eye on," then Abner's responsibility is no closer to that

---

8. Lemaire, *Inscriptions Hébraïques*, 140–41.

9. Cf. Pardee's comments: "Since the earlier Hebrew correspondence consists almost entirely of messages on ostraca, it is to be assumed that the traditions (probably guided at least in part by space limitations) regulating the form of these somewhat informal letters did not demand that the sender identify himself. . . . Practically speaking, of course, the bearer of the ostracon could [and would!] always reveal the identity of the sender. It would appear, on the other hand, that tradition did demand some explicit address, including the name or the epithet or both of the speaker [surely Pardee means the intended recipient] (notice that at least an epithet is present in the greetings of the four Lachish letters which lack an address)" (Pardee, *Handbook*, 147).

Hošaʿyahu's identification of himself by name as the sender of III is perhaps an indication of the relative importance of this correspondent, who uses a unique formula of address, sends the longest letter in the group, addresses three separate topics, and reproaches his superior for suggesting that he cannot read a letter for himself.

of someone managing fire signals in Lachish than to that of someone keeping a careful eye on Lachish's fire signals from elsewhere.[10]

Yadin also supports his view that the Lachish remains are the sender's copies of the correspondence by claiming that normally papyrus would have been used for letters.[11] In the urgency of the situation in which the Lachish letters were written, however, file copies were undoubtedly the last thing the senders were concerned with, and multiple drafts the last thing they could afford. In another instance, from preexilic Judah, twenty-two letters from Arad written on ostraca (not papyrus) have been found (not to mention the "judicial plea" from Mesad Ḥašabyahu). Does this mean that all of these letters are also drafts/file copies? It seems more likely that, allowing for changes in the supply of and demand for papyrus, sherds were used for short texts and texts of transient value and papyrus for longer texts or texts considered to be of more permanent significance.[12] This accords generally with the evidence of the Aramaic letters on papyrus, parchment, and ostraca of the sixth to fourth centuries B.C.E.[13]

It seems more likely, because of the location of the finds (the city gate), that Lachish was the recipient of the letters rather than the sender. There is no evidence for a city gate's being used as a scriptorium or filing room for drafts/copies. On the other hand, it is plausible that an officer in charge of a fortress would receive messengers and messages at the city gate and that the first room inside the outer gate would be the immediate depository for such missives.[14]

For these reasons, then, I conclude that Yadin has not made a persuasive case, and that there are no grounds for abandoning the general view that the Lachish ostraca were actual letters (not copies) and that they were received by Lachish.

---

10. Thus Pardee translates simply: "We are watching the Lachish (fire-)signals" (Pardee, *Handbook*, 91).

11. Haran's insistence that *spr*, MT *sēper*, always implies the form of a scroll is also highly questionable ("On the Diffusion of Literacy and Schools in Ancient Israel," in *Congress Volume Jerusalem 1986* [VTSup 40; Leiden: Brill, 1988] 90–91 n. 21). The phrase *mĕgillat sēper*, which appears frequently and only in Jeremiah, Ezek 2:9 (i.e., in the late preexilic and early exilic period), and Ps 40:8, may indicate not that a *sēper* is necessarily a scroll, but rather that the otherwise indeterminate form of the *sēper* is in these cases a scroll—in other words, that the form of a *spr* could not at that period be taken for granted!

12. See the discussion in the *editio princeps* (Torczyner, *Lachish Letters*, 16–17); and for further considerations affecting the choice of papyrus or ostracon, see the discussion in E. Wente, *Letters from Ancient Egypt* (SBL Writings from the Ancient World; Atlanta: Scholars Press, 1990) 4–5.

13. Pardee, *Handbook*, 163–64.

14. See Starckey in Torczyner, *Lachish Letters*, 12.

I turn now specifically to Lachish Ostracon III. In this letter, Hošaᶜyahu addresses three topics in three successive sections of the letter:[15] his reading of letters sent to him (lines 4–13); information he has received about the movements and activities of a Judean general (lines 13–18); and a letter that he has received and is now passing on to Yaᵓush (lines 19–21). The third section reads as follows:

wspr ṭbyhw ᶜbd hmlk hbᵓ ᵓl šlm bn ydᶜ mᵓt hnbᵓ lᵓmr hšmr šlḥh ᶜb⟨d⟩k ᵓl ᵓdny

As for the message[16] of Tobiyahu, the servant of the king, which came to Šallum son of Yadduᶜ/Yadaᶜ from the prophet, saying: "Be careful!"—your servant is sending it to my lord.

This apparently straightforward sentence has accrued a vast amount of comment and an amazing variety of interpretations over the decades since the discovery of the letters. It is necessary, therefore, first to justify this translation philologically and to enter into debate with some recent interpretations.

(1) *"The message of Tobiyahu . . . from the prophet."* The compound preposition *mᵓt* was for a long time widely taken to mean 'through, by means of' in this context.[17] But *mᵓt* normally means 'from', referring to the source or origin of the subject.[18] For the sense 'through, by means of', IX:4–7 attests to the use of *byd* with specific reference to the person transmitting the message: *hšb [l] ᶜbdk dbr byd šlmyhw* 'send back word to your servant via Šelemyahu'.[19] The words *mᵓt* and *byd* are both used in these texts with their traditional meanings. There is no justification for assigning them unique or novel uses. The words *mᵓt hnbᵓ* simply mean that ultimately the message of Tobiyahu came "from the prophet."[20]

15. I shall make some observations about the unity of the letter below.

16. I translate *spr* 'message', recognizing that *spr* is the word normally used of a letter, but also that its meaning is broader than that and that a broader meaning is sometimes appropriate in these letters.

17. So Albright, "The Lachish Ostraca," in *ANET* (3d ed.; ed. J. B. Pritchard; Princeton: Princeton University Press, 1969) 321–22; Donner and Röllig, *KAI*; J. Gibson, *TSSI* 1.

18. See J. Hoftijzer, "Frustula Epigraphica Hebraica," in *Scripta Signa Vocis* (J. H. Hospers festschrift; ed. L. J. Vanstiphout et al.; Groningen: Forsten, 1986) 88.

19. Cf. also Arad 16:3–6, 24:13–14 (both partially restored).

20. There is therefore no basis here for talking about the role of the prophet as a letter-carrier, as in D. W. Thomas, *The Prophet in the Lachish Ostraca* (London: Tyndale, 1946); "Again 'The Prophet' in the Lachish Ostraca," *Von Ugarit nach Qumran: Festschrift Otto Eissfeldt* (ed. J. Hempel and L. Rost; Berlin: Töpelmann, 1958) 244–49; and still in J. Blenkinsopp, *A History of Prophecy in Israel* (Philadelphia: Westminster, 1983) 184, 220 n. 31.

Now if the message came from the prophet, why is it referred to as the message "of Tobiyahu"? Lemaire, who rightly rejected the interpretation of *mᵓt* as 'by', saw the prophet as the actual author and sender of the letter and Tobiyahu as either the scribe[21] or the official messenger. Indeed, he suggested that Tobiyahu might have been a secretary performing both roles, somewhat like Baruch's role with respect to Jeremiah; or, in view of Tobiyahu's title, "servant of the king," a messenger like Elasah, who was sent by King Zedekiah to King Nebuchadnezzar, and who also took along Jeremiah's letter to the exiles (Jer 29:1–3).[22]

If indeed Tobiyahu were on other business for the king, he may have delivered a letter for a prophet. Given the differing social status of a "king's servant" and a prophet, however, it is unlikely that he would have served as the prophet's scribe or otherwise done the prophet's bidding.

Pardee also understands the letter to have been sent by the prophet to Šallum, and to be now "for an unexplained reason in the possession of Tobiyahu."[23] His possession of the letter "apparently indicates that the prophet has become involved in political affairs and is being kept under royal observation." More specifically, "the letter had been confiscated in a more or less friendly fashion to enable the royal chancery to keep tabs on the prophet's activities."[24]

But *contra* Lemaire and Pardee, I find that when *spr* is used in the construct case with the following reference to a person, the person is the author of the *spr*. Another example of this grammatical construction is found in Ostracon VI: *ᵓ[t sp]r hmlk [wᵓt] spry hšr[m]*. The *spr hmlk* and *spry hšrm* are letters dictated and sent by the king and officers.[25] Exod 32:32 affords another comparison: *sprk ᵓšr ktbt* 'your record which you have written'. See also Aḥiram 2 (*KAI* 1:2): *ymḥ sprh* 'let his inscription be effaced'.[26]

---

21. So also Hoftijzer, "Frustula Epigraphica," 88.

22. Lemaire, *Inscriptions Hébraïques*, 105, 108–9.

23. The *spr ṭbyhw* is understood as the letter "in the custody of" Tobiyahu (Pardee, *Handbook*, 84–85, 88).

24. Pardee, *Handbook*, 88. Like Pardee (review of *Biblical and Related Studies Presented to Samuel Iwry*, edited by A. Kort and S. Morschauer, *JNES* 49 [1990] 88–94), I do not understand Cross's "the letter at Tobiah" (F. M. Cross Jr., "A Literate Soldier: Lachish Letter III," in *Biblical and Related Studies Presented to Samuel Iwry* [ed. A. Kort and S. Morschauser; Winona Lake, Ind.: Eisenbrauns, 1985] 43) and cannot surmise what lies behind this misprint.

25. See Hoftijzer, "Frustula Epigraphica," 88; apparently also Pardee, *Handbook*, 100.

26. Aḥiram 2 (*KAI* 1:2); J. C. L. Gibson, *Textbook of Syrian Semitic Inscriptions*, vol. 3: *Phoenician Inscriptions* (Oxford: Clarendon, 1982) 14.

"The message of Tobiyahu" is, therefore, the letter that Tobiyahu composed and dictated. In the letter, Tobihayu reported the message of a prophet, who was therefore the ultimate source of the message of the letter. This is why Tobiyahu's letter can be said to have originated with the prophet.[27] The prophet delivered an utterance that came (more or less directly) to the attention of the royal official, Tobiyahu, who decided to send a report of it to those whose situation and actions would be most immediately affected by the message. This is the simplest solution, and as will be seen, accords with what is known from other sources about messages involving prophets.

(2) *"Be careful!"* Hoftijzer argues that the imperative *hšmr* 'be careful' does not represent the message of the original letter or prophecy, but is a comment on it—is "the message accompanying the letter sent to Šallum." In support of this interpretation, Hoftijzer cites VI:3–6, which reads: *šlḥ ʾdny ʾ[t sp]r hmlk [wʾt] spry hšr[m lʾm] r qrʾ nʾ* 'my lord sent the king's message and the officials' messages, saying: "Read!" '[28] But in this passage the essential syntax is: *šlḥ ʾdny . . . lʾmr* 'my lord sent . . . saying'. The subject of both verbs is "my lord." This passage differs from III:19–21, in which the underlying structure is *spr . . . hbʾ . . . lʾmr* 'the message . . . which came . . . saying'. In this case the subject of both verbs is "the message."[29] "The message" does not distinguish between the prophecy quoted in the letter and the surrounding words of the sender. Further, *pace* Hoftijzer, the citation of the gist of the prophecy in III:21 is not a problem. III:19–21 goes to great lengths to specify precisely the message that is being sent along—everything from *spr* to *hšmr* is such a specification. While *spr ṭbyhw* alone might be translated 'the message of Tobiyahu' or 'a message of Tobiyahu', the use of the modifier *hbʾ* 'the one coming' confers definiteness on the original subject (the message). The mention of the theme of the message, *hšmr* 'be careful', is part of this specification.

Furthermore, *hšmr* 'be careful' is a typical prophetic pronouncement. Here it may have been simply the first word of the utterance, as it is of the speech Yahweh directs Isaiah to address to Ahaz in Isa 7:4 and of the message the "man of god" sends to the king of Israel in 2 Kgs 6:9 (see also a divine message sent through a dream in Gen 31:24, cf. 29). In another passage, Jer 17:21, the plural form of *hšmr* is the first word of the speech that Yahweh directs Jeremiah to deliver to the people at the city gates. Again, the first word that God directs Moses

---

27. See Cross, 'at the instance of', which he sees as the "more natural" meaning, "suggesting that the warning originates from the prophet" (Cross, "Literate Soldier," 47).

28. Hoftijzer, "Frustula Epigraphica," 89.

29. Pardee has now criticized Hoftijzer's argument on similar grounds ("Review of *Biblical and Related Studies*," 93).

to tell the people in Exod 19:12 is *hšmrw*. Alternatively, *hšmr* may have been the *key* word of the utterance, as opposed to being merely the *first* word. The plural form is the key word of the first clause in Jer 9:3–4, for instance. Finally, *hšmr* may have been Hošaᶜyahu's summation of the prophetic utterance.

I turn now to considering the circumstances that lay behind this letter. A prophet made a pronouncement, the essential force of which was: "Be careful!" The reader is not told to whom it was addressed. It was either heard directly by, or reported to, Tobiyahu, a high official at court ("the servant of the king"), who sent word of this prophetic message to Šallum, son of Yadaᶜ/Yadduᶜ. The message was then conveyed, by means unknown to us,[30] from Šallum to Hošaᶜyahu, who in turn sent it on to Yaᵓuš, accompanied by the covering letter now under discussion—the sole remaining access to the other letter and its complicated history. Apart from quoting or summarizing the message (*hšmr*), Hošaᶜyahu's letter gives no interpretation or assessment of the prophetic message. The lack of any mention in Ostracon III of the prophet's name, of the god in whose name he was speaking, or of the addressee(s) of the warning may be explained by the fact that the accompanying original letter would have given such additional information as was relevant.

There is more still that may be learned from Letter III. As mentioned above, the entire passage consists essentially of the core sentence "Your servant is sending to my lord this letter." The rest of the passage is a specification of *which* letter—namely the one written by Tobiyahu, the one that came to Šallum, the one from the prophet, the one saying: "Be careful!" This does not read like the introduction of a letter of which the recipient knew nothing. Rather, it presupposes that the addressee (Yaᵓuš) had heard of this particular letter of Tobiyahu's, perhaps because Hošaᶜyahu had already written to him about it. In any case, Hošaᶜyahu's present letter implies that Yaᵓush had requested to see Tobiyahu's letter for himself. Military strategy may well have involved taking into account the precise wording of any message from a prophet or high official. It makes the most sense, then, to conclude that Yaᵓuš, the final recipient, had learned of this letter of Tobiyahu and the prophecy it reported and had written to Hošaᶜyahu, asking to see it firsthand. He may well have specified the message in which he was interested with words comparable to those later used by Hošaᶜyahu: "Send me the message of Tobiyahu, the servant of the king, which came to Šallum son of Yadduᶜ/Yadaᶜ from the prophet, saying: 'Be careful!'"

---

30. Lemaire speculates that it may have been intercepted by Hošaᶜyahu, because he judged it to be dangerous (*Inscriptions Hébraiques*, 109).

It is already known that Ya³ush had written "You don't know how to read a letter!" since Hoša⁽yahu quotes him (lines 8–9) and devotes the first section of III to responding to that charge. This accusation and Hoša⁽yahu's response—'any letter that comes to me, once I have read it, afterwards I can give it back [i.e., repeat it]'—supports the hypothesis that in lines 19–21 the interpretation required is that the letter is a careful reiteration of the request received. It may be that the second section of the letter is also addressing an issue raised by Ya³uš in his previous letter—perhaps an enquiry about Hodawyahu and his men, to which Hoša⁽yahu now responds: 'Your servant received the following information: "General Kanyahu, son of Elnatan, came down on his way to Egypt and sent for Hodawyahu, son of Ahiyahu, and his men and took them off"' (lines 13–18). The unity of the letter would derive in part from its function as a response to the various matters raised in the previous letter from Ya³uš, one received the previous day according to line 6 (³mš). This function is most obvious in section one, fairly clear in section three, and a reasonable hypothesis for section two.

A second unifying factor in the letter is the common theme of communication: Hoša⁽yahu writes to inform (*l*[*h*]*g*[*d*] lines 1–2); he defends his ability to read communications intelligently (section one); he reports that he has been informed of a general's communication of a military draft (section two); and he explains the transmission of a royal official's report of a prophetic message (section three).

A comparable cover letter for a report on a prophecy in the context of a larger sequence of communications is found at Mari. In the body of *AEM* 201, Bakhdi-Lim, prefect of Mari and son-in-law to the king, writes to King Zimri-Lim:

> Akhum the priest has brought me the hair and hem of the prophetess, and a complete report is written in the tablet which Akhum has written to my lord. Now I am sending to my lord the tablet of Akhum and the hair and hem[31] of the prophetess (lines 7–17).

I infer from this that Akhum the priest has addressed to the king a report on a prophecy. He has brought his letter and the prophetess's hair and hem to

---

31. The hair and hem of a prophet(ess) were used when he or she could not be present. If it was necessary to seek further information from the deity, these two personal tokens served to represent the medium to whom the deity had vouchsafed the first revelation. See the discussion in Durand (*AEM*, 40–41); cf. P. A. Kruger, "The Symbolic Significance of the Hem (*kānāf*) in 1 Samuel 15.27," *Text and Context: Old Testament and Semitic Studies for F. C. Fensham* (JSOTSup 48; Sheffield: JSOT, 1988) 107, 113–14 nn. 18–20.

Bakhdi-Lim, who is now forwarding all three to the king. Bakhdi-Lim's own letter is simply a cover letter. It does not itself identify the prophetess or the divine source of the prophecy, because these would appear in the accompanying report.

It so happens that Akhum's original letter is extant[32] and is now published as *AEM* 200. This letter follows the general pattern of official letters reporting a prophecy,[33] but specifically it answers to the description in the letter just quoted. It is addressed to the king by Akhum, who gives the standard full report of the prophecy and concludes by saying that he is conveying the hair and hem of the prophetess to the king.

Two other letters from Mari may be compared. In *AEM* 214 the queen, Šibtu, writes to the king. She first reports that a certain woman prophesied in the temple of the goddess Annunitum, then quotes the prophecy, explaining further:

> The next day, Akhum, the high priest, brought me this information, the hair and the hem. I am sending word to my lord. I have sealed the hair and hem, and am having them brought to my lord (lines 19–28).

In this case Akhum brought an oral report to the queen along with the hair and hem of the prophetess. The queen now sends to the king her own account of the prophecy, adding that Akhum had brought her this information and the hair and hem the day after the prophecy was uttered. She also refers to having sealed the hair and hem and sent them along with her letter. Clearly this will be news to the king, and the news will be secondhand—that is, it will not come in the form of a direct, firsthand report from Akhum.

In *AEM* 235 Akhum is again the witness of a divine revelation, this time in the form of a dream. Kibri-Dagan, the governor of Terqa, writes to the king (lines 7–8): "A man has had a dream and Akhum has repeated it (to me)." He then quotes Akhum's account of the dream (lines 9–15) and continues:

> Akhum repeated this dream of his to me and made me responsible, saying: "Send word to the king." And so I am sending to my lord (lines 16–20).

Again, this is news to the king, and again, it comes to him secondhand. As in the case of Queen Shibtu's letter, Letter 235 includes a quotation of the divine revelation and refers to Akhum as the original source of the information.

The first Mari letter quoted above, Letter 201, contrasts with both of the latter two, 214 and 235. Bakhdi-Lim did not identify the prophetess nor did

32. Durand, *AEM*, 430.
33. See Durand, *AEM*, esp. 377–452.

he quote the revelation. Instead he referred first to Akhum's having brought him the hair and hem of the prophetess and then to Akhum's full report. It is assumed that the king knows which prophetess is in question and what subject is treated in Akhum's report. The king must already have heard of this prophecy, presumably through a letter from Bakhdi-Lim analogous to those of Queen Shibtu and Kibru-Dagan. He then requested from Bakhdi-Lim a firsthand, written report by the original witness, Akhum, and the personal tokens of the prophetess, which had not been included in Bakhdi-Lim's earlier letter. These Akhum has now produced (according to Letter 201) and submitted to the governor of the palace, Bakhdi-Lim.

The sequence of events is: a prophetess pronounces an oracle; Akhum gives an oral report of this to Bakhdi-Lim, who informs the king of it (cf. the letter of Kibri-Dagan, *AEM* 235); the king demands of Bakhdi-Lim a firsthand report and the personal tokens of the prophetess; Akhum then prepares a full, written report for the king (*AEM* 200) and delivers this with the tokens to Bakhdi-Lim, who sends them on to the king with a brief covering letter (*AEM* 201). Thus, Mari *AEM* 201, like Lachish III, is a cover letter for another letter reporting on a prophecy, both of which are being forwarded to a superior who has asked to see the firsthand report.

The importance of seeing an original letter, rather than just hearing about it, is evident from the fact that in other Lachish letters reference is made to the passing on of letters. In V:3–7 the writer is impressed by the fact that his superior has sent him some letters and writes that he is now returning them to his lord:

my ᶜ*bdk klb ky* [*š*] *lḥth* ᵓ*l* ᶜ*bdk* ᵓ[*t*] *hs*[*prm*³⁴ *k*]*z*ᵓ[*t*] *hšb* ᶜ*bdk hsprm* ᵓ*l* ᵓ*dny*

Who is your servant but a dog that you have sent the messages to your servant like this? Your servant is returning the messages to my lord.

In XVIII:1–2 the writer promises that he will send back to his lord the letter his lord had sent to a third party (the larger context is missing):

yšlḥ [ᶜ] *b*[*dk h*]*spr* ᵓ*šr šlḥ* ᵓ*dny* [*l*] ᶜ*zr*[*y*] *hw*

Your servant will send the message which my lord sent to Azaryahu.

In VI:2–5 the sender is again impressed—his lord has referred letters to him from the highest sources in Jerusalem. This time the text is clearer:

34. On the restoration see Pardee, *Handbook*, 97.

---

my ᶜbdk klb ky šlḥ ᵓdny ᵓ[t sp]r hmlk [wᵓt] spry hšr[m lᵓm]r qrᵓ nᵓ

Who is your servant but a dog, that my lord has sent the message of the king and the messages of the officials saying: "Read!"?

In Letter III Hošaᶜyahu was sending the letter of a royal official to Yaᵓuš. Here, in VI, Yaᵓuš (the 'lord') has sent such letters to one of his subordinates. The subordinate responds that the words in the letters are discouraging. The phrase for "discourage" is identical with that found in Jer 38:4, in which the officials (*hśrym*) say of Jeremiah to the king: *ywmt nᵓ ᵓt-hᵓyš hzh ky-ᶜl-kn hwᵓ-mrpᵓ ᵓt-ydy ᵓnšy-hmlḥmh* 'Let this man be put to death because he is discouraging the soldiers'. If Jeremiah and others like him were having this effect in Jerusalem, it seems reasonable to assume a similar interpretation of VI:5–7, as Torczyner has done in his restoration (followed by Gibson):[35]

whnh dbry h[nbᵓ]lᵓ ṭbm lrpt ydyk [wlhš]qt ydy hᵓ [nšm]

Look, the words of the [prophet] are not good, calculated to discourage you [and to make] the m[en let do]wn their guard.

Lemaire and Pardee prefer the restoration *šrm* 'officials' in line 5 in place of 'prophet', assuming that the writer was commenting on the words of the authors of the letters he had been sent. But, if that were the case, why would he comment on the letters of the officers and not on the letter of the king? And why would the officials be writing things that would discourage the commanders and men in the field? On the other hand, it seems plausible that Jeremiah and his ilk should have been charged with discouraging the inhabitants of Jerusalem. Therefore, on the face of the matter, it seems more likely that the letters of the king and his officials referred to the words of a prophet, and that it is to the prophet's words, rather than to the words of the officials, that the author of Letter VI is referring.

If Torczyner's restoration is for these reasons accepted, then the king and officials had reported the words of a prophet—Jeremiah or another of similar persuasion. They were taking the prophet's words seriously—not as the officers of Jer 38:4 took them, calling for the prophet's death—but passing them on for the consideration of the commanders at the front. Hošaᶜyahu disagrees and urges his superior (Yaᵓuš) to write back questioning such policy: *hlᵓ tktb ᵓl[yhm] lᵓ[mr lm]h tᶜsw kzᵓt* 'By all means write to them: "Why are you behaving like this?"' (lines 8–10).

---

35. The restoration of the last word is that of Gibson and Pardee. Note that it accords with the meaning and situation of the Jeremiah passage just cited.

This seems to me to make the most sense of the passage. In drawing conclusions from it relating to the theme of official reactions to prophecies, however, it is only prudent to recall that the reference to *nb⁾* here is entirely restored. Supposing the restoration to be well-founded, the passage may be summarized as follows: Yaᵓuš has received, without benefit of Hošaᶜyahu's mediation, letters from the king himself, as well as several officials, reporting the words of a prophet. Yaᵓuš deems the message of considerable importance and passes the letter on to his subordinate, urging him to read it. The latter also takes the prophet's words very seriously, observing that they are designed to weaken the defences of the country, and urging his superior to write back in protest.

I conclude that Ostracon III is a clear case of official reporting of a prophetic pronouncement and that VI is a second, less-certain case based on a restoration—a restoration which, I would claim, makes the most sense of the text in question.[36] In the first case (III), Tobiyahu, a royal official, has sent a message originating with a prophet, the essence of which is: "Be careful!" This message came to Šallum ben Yadaᶜ/Yadduᶜ. Somehow, presumably through Hošaᶜyahu, Yaᵓuš, apparently the supreme commander in the Lachish area, learned of this message and demanded that Hošaᶜyahu send it to him. Hošaᶜyahu, who had either received Tobiyahu's letter from Šallum earlier, or had hastily procured it after receiving Yaᵓuš's request, now sends it to Yaᵓuš, accompanied by the cover letter, which is the one clue now extant concerning this whole history.

In the second case (VI), Yaᵓuš received messages from the king and officials referring to the words of a prophet (if Torczyner's restoration is accepted) and sent them on with a cover letter to one of his subordinates, telling him to read them. The subordinate wrote back, offering an opinion on them: "Look, the words of the [prophet] are not good, calculated to discourage you [and to make] the m[en let do]wn their guard." He added his own recommendation for action: "By all means write to them: 'Why are you behaving like this?'"

In both cases the words of the prophet are taken seriously by the highest authorities (the king and/or his deputies) and passed on to other officials for their consideration or evaluation. In the first case, in which the thrust of the prophet's message is a general warning, a chain of communications results,

---

36. It should be added for the sake of completeness that there is one other reference to a prophet in the Lachish ostraca, namely in a broken context in XVI:5–6: *s]pr bny* [   ]*hw hnb⁾* ['me]ssage BNY [   ]HW the prophet'. Here too the letter may be referring to a prophet mentioned in another message.

ending with the commander of Lachish. In the other case, in which the prophecy is apparently interpreted as subversive by at least one official among those likely first to face the approaching Babylonian army, the communication ends with the same commander, after having been referred to one of his subordinates.

This study suggests that officials in Israel did take seriously the pronouncements of prophets, whether favorable or not; that they passed on word of prophetic utterances, insisted on securing firsthand reports, and asked for assessments of such reports from their subordinates. For lack of other biblical evidence, it may be helpful in the future to read biblical narratives about official responses to prophecies in light of this historical information.[37]

37. See now also S. B. Parker, "Official Attitudes toward Prophecy at Mari and in Israel," *VT* 43 (1993) 50–68.

The Perception of Shame within the Divine-Human Relationship in Biblical Israel

Lyn M. Bechtel

❧ ⦿ ❧

S HAMING IS SOMETIMES USED by a society as a sanction against an individual, and it may or may not elicit a response of the emotion of shame within the individual. In the Old Testament there are many instances of shaming and an abundance of "shame vocabulary"; yet there is relatively little research available on the Old Testament sanction of shaming. My introductory article, "Shame as a Sanction of Social Control in Biblical Israel,"[1] deals with social, judicial, and political experiences of shame in ancient Israel and forms the foundation for this study, which explores religious perceptions of shaming.

As I mentioned in the first study, the lack of research on shame is due to lack of sensitivity to the use of shaming as a means of social control in our culture and to the fact that people often have assumed that shame and guilt are the same emotional response, treating shame as though it were guilt.[2] Yet linguistically, in Hebrew there is no inherent meaning of "guilt" in the shame vocabulary.[3] Furthemore, in modern psychoanalytic theory and social

---

1. L. M. Bechtel, "Shame as a Sanction of Social Control in Biblical Israel: Judicial, Political, and Social Shaming," *JSOT* 49 (1991) 47–76.

2. The only extensive study of shame is a monograph by M. A. Klopfenstein (*Scham und Schande nach dem Alten Testament* [Zurich: Theologischer Verlag, 1972]), in which he defines shame as a manifestation of guilt.

3. The variety of Hebrew shame words conveys the prevalence of the emotion and sanction of shame. The emotion and sanction are expressed in Hebrew by the following roots: *bwš* 'to shame'; *klm*, *mkk*, and *špl* 'to humiliate, shame, or be low'; *qlh* 'to be dishonored or shamed'; *ḥpr* 'to be shamed, blush'; and *ḥrp*, *qls*, *lᶜg*, and *lys* 'to verbally shame, taunt, mock, or scorn'. The differences in meaning among all these words are slight

---

anthropological theory, shame is considered an emotional response separate from guilt, stemming from different psychological forces, reflecting different patterns of behavior, and functioning in different social situations, even though shame and guilt can often be interrelated. In the existing analysis of biblical shame, there is lack of understanding of the way shaming functions as a major sanction against behavior within society and of the social factors necessary for the society to use shaming as a sanction against behavior.

I refer the reader to my previous article on shame for a full definition of *shame* and *guilt*[4] and briefly summarize my conclusions here. The feeling of shame is a response to failure or inability to live up to internalized ideals, social identifications, and roles inculcated by parents and society, which dictate expectations of what a person "should" be able to do, be, know, or feel. The response of shame has an impact on "who a person is" because shame is a "failure of self." An individual's healthy sense of pride is based on sustaining the expectations. Failure or inadequacy violates pride, and the response to a violation of pride is shame.

In contrast, guilt is a response to a transgression against internalized societal or parental prohibitions or against boundaries that form an internal authority, the conscience. Guilt relates to "what a person does" and is a "failure of doing." It is the act of transgression that causes guilt, not the essence of the individual.

Shame stimulates fear of psychological or physical rejection (lack of belonging), abandonment, expulsion, or loss of social position and relies predominantly on external pressure from an individual or group. Guilt stimulates fear of punishment and relies predominantly on internal pressure.

The work of Mary Douglas on "group" and "grid" is helpful in understanding the kind of social structure that permits the use of the sanction of shame

---

but discernible. Shame words are often accompanied by phrases that express shame on the face (blushing) or shame expressed in the body position (for example, hanging the head in shame) or that show a person has been shamefully reduced to a lower social position in his or her own eyes and in the eyes of the community (for example, Jer 48:39, 2 Sam 10:5, Isa 16:14, Jer 50:12). The main antonym used is *kbd* ('honor or heaviness').

4. G. Piers and M. Singer, *Shame and Guilt* (New York: Norton, 1953); H. M. Lynd, *Shame and the Search for Identity* (New York: Harcourt Brace, 1958); F. Alexander, *Fundamentals of Psychoanalysis* (New York: Norton, 1948); K. Horney, *Neurosis and Human Growth* (New York: Norton, 1950); Gershen Kaufman, *The Psychology of Shame: Theory and Treatment of Shame-based Syndrome* (New York: Springer, 1989); Donald L. Nathanson, *Shame and Pride: Affect, Sex, and the Birth of the Self* (New York and London: Norton, 1992); Lewis B. Smedes, *Shame and Grace: Healing the Shame We Don't Deserve* (San Francisco: Harper, 1993).

or guilt.[5] In a group-oriented society people's main source of identity comes from the group to which they belong. Consequently, the group is capable of exerting great pressure on individuals in order to control their behavior. In "individual-oriented society, people's main source of identity comes from within the self. Internal conscience is capable of exerting great pressure on people in order to control behavior. Since shame relies heavily on external pressure from the group, it functions as a sanction of social control in a predominantly group-oriented society. In that type of society, public opinion and outward appearances influence the behavior of the individual because group rejection means being cut off from the major source of identity, threatening the individual with psychological or physical abandonment. The importance of shame in a given society corresponds to the amount of group-orientation inherent. Since guilt relies heavily on internal pressure from the conscience, it functions as a sanction of social control in a predominantly individual-oriented society.

The difference between shame and guilt is subtle and important. Yet despite the subtle differences, shame and guilt are often interrelated—they may overlap, one may lead to the other, one may conceal the other, or both may be a reaction to the same stimulus.

In studying the social, judicial, and political use of shame in the Old Testament, I have concluded that ancient Israelite social structure was predominantly group-oriented, with a lesser degree of individual-orientation, which means that shame was the major means of social control. Guilt was secondary. The society relied heavily on public opinion, outward appearances, and group pressure to enforce its norms. Violating social norms threatened rejection and abandonment. Part of the socialization process of Israelite society involved developing a sensitivity to group pressure and to shame. Because group membership was essential, one's standing in the community was important, making people status-conscious. It was a society layered by an "honor" hierarchy, with honor increasing status and shame lowering status.

The sanction of shaming functioned primarily (1) as a means of social control that attempted to repress aggressive or undesirable behavior; (2) as an important means of dominating others and manipulating social status; and (3) as a pressure that preserved social cohesion in the community through rejection and creating social distance between deviant members and the group.[6]

---

5. M. Douglas, *Natural Symbols* (New York: Pantheon, 1970).

6. This is consistent with the findings of G. Piers and M. Singer, *Shame and Guilt*; H. Lowenfeld, "Notes on Shamelessness," *Psychoanalytic Quarterly* 45 (1976) 62–72; F. English, "Shame and Social Control," *Transactional Analysis Journal* 5 (1975) 24–28; R. Lowie, *Primitive Society* (New York: Liveright, 1947); Thomas J. Scheff and Suzanne M.

Shaming was an important sanction against an individual's behavior. The coercive power of the sanction was available officially to state and local authorities as a formal sanction (judicial and political shaming) and unofficially to the community as an informal sanction ("street" shaming).

William James has pointed out that religious emotions and perceptions are not separate or distinct from the common storehouse of emotions and perceptions related to social interaction and existence.[7] It is not surprising, therefore, that the social experience of shame in biblical Israel was closely related to and provided the cultural base and interpretive language for religious perceptions of shame.

The Shame of Divine Abandonment

Just as it was common for people in ancient Israel to shame one another as a means of control, it was also not unusual for them to experience God as shaming them. One of the ways in which people felt shamed by God was through divine abandonment. In general in the ancient Near East, people believed that if the gods were displeased with the behavior of their subjects, they would shame them in order to control their behavior, through national defeat or personal misfortune.[8] In battle a nation's god was believed to march at the head of its army, effecting victory with the divine presence or defeat with the divine absence. Thus, when a nation defeated its enemies, it attributed the victory to the superior power of its own god. Its enemies were believed to have been abandoned by their god, who either had been angered at the people or had bowed to the superior power of the victorious god of the enemy.

Psalm 89, a royal psalm, laments national adversity in light of the promises of the Davidic covenant. According to the royal theological viewpoint, it was the responsibility of YHWH to establish the Davidic throne forever (2 Sam 7:12–16; cf. Ps 89:22–25). Though YHWH had made this covenant, YHWH was now perceived as rejecting and abandoning the king, nation, and covenant.

> But now you cast off and reject, you overlook your messiah, you have renounced the covenant with your servant, you have dishonored (*ḥll*) his crown on the

---

Retzinger, *Violence: Shame and Rage in Destructive Conflicts* (Lexington, Mass.: Lexington Books, 1991); and Thomas J. Scheff, "Shame and Conformity: The Difference-Emotion System," *American Sociological Review* 53 (1988) 395–406, within the fields of social anthropology and psychoanalytic theory.

7. W. James, *The Varieties of Religious Experience* (New York: Longmans, 1902) 27–28.

8. See M. Cogan, *Imperialism and Religion: Assyria and Judah in the Eighth and Seventh Centuries B.C.E.* (Missoula, Mont.: Scholars Press, 1974).

---

ground, you have breached all his defenses; you have laid his fortifications in ruins. All who pass by despoil; he has become a shame/taunt (*ḥrph*) to his neighbors. . . . You have broken his scepter and cast his throne down to the ground.[9] You have cut short the days of his youth, you have covered him with shame (*bwš*).[10] How long, YHWH, will you hide? Will your anger burn like fire forever? . . . Where is your *ḥsd* of old, Lord, your faithfulness sworn to David? Remember, Lord, the shaming/ taunting (*ḥrph*) of your servant, that I bear in my bosom all the insults of the peoples, with which your enemies have shamed/taunted (*ḥrp*), YHWH, with which they shamed (*ḥrp*) the footsteps of your messiah (Ps 89:39–42, 45–47, 50–52).[11]

In the psalter, as in Babylonian psalms, the question "how long" within the context of God's casting off and rejecting usually implies "divine abandonment" (cf. Ps 13:1–3, 74:10, 79:5–6, 106:40–42) and is accompanied by a plea for attention. In Psalm 89 YHWH is perceived as having renounced the Davidic covenant, dishonored (*ḥll*) the crown of the king, broken the king's scepter, cast his throne to the ground, cut off the days of his youth (his care-free days), and covered the king with shame (*bwš*). The description of shaming by YHWH sounds similar to the shaming ritual that Babylonian kings underwent during the annual New Year's Festival.[12] The defeat of the Israelite city (Ps 89:40) had also left it weak, defenseless, and vulnerable—a shameful condition—and as a result, the psalmist feels that it is YHWH who has allowed God's enemies to shame/taunt and despoil the defeated king and the people.

It is important to note that the shame of which the king complained was not interpreted as punishment for guilt. *No lack of obedience, guilty conscience, or shameful behavior on the part of the king or nation was acknowledged.* It was simply a matter of divine abandonment. Whether the particular

9. Accepting the reading of the note in BHS.

10. H. Gunkel (*Die Psalmen* [Göttingen: Vandenhoeck & Ruprecht, 1968] 395) and W. O. E. Oesterly (*Psalms* [London: MacMillan, 1939] 399) suggest that *bwš* should be read *śēbâ* 'gray hairs', 'you have covered him with gray hairs'. M. Dahood (*Psalms* [AB 17; Garden City, N.Y.: Doubleday, 1966] 319–20) proposes *yābēš* from *ybš* 'dryness or lack of sexual vigor', 'you have dried up his sexual vigour', thus prohibiting him from having children to perpetuate his throne as the covenant has promised. But there is no need for a change.

11. There is controversy as to the date, setting in history, and structural unity of this psalm. See Gunkel, *Die Psalmen*, 386–96; H. Ringgren, *The Faith of the Psalmist* (Philadelphia: Fortress, 1963) 105; A. Weiser, *The Psalms* (OTL; Philadelphia: Westminster, 1962) 586–87; C. Westermann, *Der Psalter* (Stuttgart: Calwer, 1974) 29–42.

12. J. Ward, "The Literary, Form, and Liturgical Background of Psalm 89," *VT* 11 (1961) 321–39.

shaming acts carried out by YHWH were metaphorical or actual, they were described as shame inducing.

Why was divine abandonment shameful? Abandonment is rejection, rejection not because of what a person had done, but because the person was insignificant or inadequate and did not warrant YHWH's loyalty. According to E. Becker, humanity's greatest fear is fear of insignificance.[13] This concern for significance is reflected throughout Israel's literature. Abandonment stimulated the fear of insignificance, which violated pride and caused shame. When abandonment was combined with national defeat, leaving a nation vulnerable to shameful treatment from all sides, the suffering from shame was doubled.

Psalm 89 actually begins with praise of the *ḥsd* of YHWH that the king will proclaim to all generations, *ḥsd* that the king believes is firm because YHWH has made a covenant with the Davidic kings (89:2–38). After v. 38 this praise and trust in YHWH's faithfulness is contrasted with YHWH's shaming of the king. The king asks, "YHWH, where is your *ḥsd* of old, which you swore to David by your faithfulness?" This apparently misplaced trust in YHWH's *ḥsd* made the king (and nation) look foolish because it was a reversal of their expectations. The king trusted in the protective relationship of God, but in the abandonment this trust was violated. Both the violation of trust and the reversal of expectation caused shame.

God's Covenant Obligation to Protect from Shaming

In contrast to shame stemming from divine abandonment, people in the ancient Near East believed that it was the responsibility of the gods to protect and deliver their subjects from general affliction and shame. YHWH's obligation to protect the people from shaming[14] is never stated directly in any of the covenants but it is assumed, particularly in deuteronomic theology.[15] The obligation is found in Psalm 119, an elaborate acrostic wisdom poem that espouses deuteronomic theology. The assumption is that if people were righteous and obedient to YHWH's way (the statutes of Deuteronomy), they

13. E. Becker, *Escape from Evil* (New York: Free Press, 1975) 1–5.

14. The obligation of protection from shame is also evident in Akkadian petitions and is reflected in Akkadian personal names. The general protection of one's personal god includes protection from shame, e.g., "I [Ishtar] have given you encouragement, I will not let you come to shame." The dread of being shamed is seen in the personal name, *A-ia-ba-aš-i-li* 'O-My-God-May-I-Not-Come-To-Shame', CAD B 5–6 s.v. "*baʾāšu* B."

15. Deuteronomic theology has a strong emphasis on religious obligation, reward, and punishment, which in Israelite social structure is generally characteristic of the middle class.

would prosper and be protected from unwarranted shaming by the community. If they were wicked and turned away from YHWH's way, their behavior would be controlled by shaming imposed by YHWH. The psalmist prays repeatedly that YHWH will protect him from shame because he adheres to YHWH's precepts.

> Confirm to your servant your promise, which is for those who respect you. Turn away the shame (*ḥrph*) which I dread, for your ordinances are good. . . . Let your mercy come to me, that I may live, for I delight in your way. But let the godless be put to shame (*bwš*), because they have subverted me with guile. But I meditate on your precepts. Let those who respect you turn to me, so that they may know your wisdom. May my heart be blameless in your statutes, so that I will not be shamed (*bwš*) (Ps 119:38–39, 77–80; cf. vv. 6, 22, 31, 46, 80, 116).

The psalmist is a person who has experienced shaming and persecution from his contemporaries because of his pious adherence to the statutes of Deuteronomy. His enemies appear to oppose his theological viewpoint. He refers to his enemies as "princes" (v. 23), "godless" (vv. 69, 78, 85, 122), and "wicked evildoers" (vv. 95, 115, 119). The opposition referred to here may have been the adherents of the royal theological viewpoint, usually members of the upper class, who did not believe in the same heavy emphasis on passive trust. Or the "enemies" may simply have been less pious folks ("the ones who wander from your commandments," v. 21). This psalm, like many others, shows that within the Israelite community there were opposing theological viewpoints in conflict with one another.

The psalmist implies that he has been shamed by those opposing his theological viewpoint as a way of changing his pious behavior. Because he has trusted in the deuteronomic promises, these people have tried to make him look foolish by taunting him for his misplaced trust.

> Let your loyalty (*ḥsd*) come to me, YHWH, your salvation according to your promises. Then I will answer those who taunt (*ḥrp*) me, for I trust in your word. Do not take the word of truth from my mouth [completely] for I trust in your commandments. . . . Uphold me according to your promises so that I may live. Let me not be put to shame (*bwš*) for my hope (Ps 119:41–42, 116).

In addition, since the two viewpoints were generally held by two different social classes, his shaming may have been used for purposes of domination and status manipulation. Shaming "puts a person down" into an inferior social position, so it was often used by the upper class to dominate the middle class and to keep them in their place (that is, to prevent the middle class from moving up into the upper class).

God's Shaming of the Opponent
in Face-saving Vindication of the Shamed Faithful

One of the common cries in the Psalms is for the shaming of enemies (for example, Ps 6:10; 40:15; 53:5; 57:3; 70:2; 71:13, 24; 78:66; 83:16–17; 109:28–29). I have already shown that "enemies" were not always foreign powers but often were those who held opposing theological viewpoints within the community. In Psalm 35, a complaint psalm, the psalmist appeals to YHWH to be his "advocate," to vindicate him against those who have shamed him. His language is highly metaphoric, which is characteristic of the lament psalms that deal with shaming, and therefore the precise shaming that the psalmist suffered cannot always be discerned. The psalmist complains that they have "hid their net" and "dug a pit" for his life; they have rejoiced at and gathered around to view his stumbling; they have mocked (*l⁽g*), gnashed the teeth, winked the eye, and opened their mouths wide, saying, "Aha, aha." Cripples (inferior people) and other people he does not know have slandered him; malicious witnesses have risen up against him (Ps 35:7–21). In this case the shaming was done predominantly for status manipulation (see vv. 15 and 26). Now he calls on YHWH for face-saving vindication from this shameful treatment.

> Let them be shamed (*bwš*) and humiliated (*klm*) who seek my life, let them be turned back and disgraced (*ḥpr*) who plan my calamity. . . . Let them be shamed (*bwš*) and disgraced (*ḥpr*) together who rejoice at my calamity! Let them be clothed with shame (*bšt*) and humiliation (*klmh*) who magnify themselves against me! (Ps 35:4, 26–27; cf. 31:18b–19).

Despite the assumption that God will protect the righteous from shame and suffering and clothe the wicked in shame, in actuality the "wicked" are shaming the "righteous."

Karen Horney explains that one of the most prevalent impulses for a shamed person is to take revenge through counter-shaming to "save face" as vindication for humiliation.[16] She stresses the importance of pride and ego in the shaming experience. By "getting back" at the offender, the shamed person's wounded pride is restored and there is a reversal of positions. Horney goes on to say that the inability to "get back" registers as weakness, which incurs further shame. Yet when a person has been humiliated, he/she usually feels so inadequate and insignificant that retaliation is not possible.

16. Horney, *Neurosis and Human Growth*, 103.

The shamed pious psalmists could not strike back because their piety prevented them from taking such inappropriate aggressive action (see Psalm 15, which many scholars feel is a liturgy for admission to the temple and which lists shaming as inappropriate behavior). Consequently, the psalmists relied on YHWH to do their counter-shaming. The understanding that YHWH would carry out this counter-shaming was dependent on the deuteronomic assumption that the righteous will be protected from shaming, but the wicked will be shamed as punishment. In order to motivate YHWH's counter-shaming, there is the implication in vv. 10, 18, 27–28, that by shaming the wicked, God will receive praise and honor from the righteous.

YHWH's Vulnerability to Being Shamed

Shame was not an experience confined to the human community; it was also perceived as a concern of YHWH. YHWH too was vulnerable to shame. YHWH's vulnerability to shame was the counterpart of the praise and honor he deserved (see Ps 61:8, 66:2, 96:7, 145:5; Prov 14:31; Isa 29:13, 43:23). Israel had an obligation to praise and honor YHWH, and they wanted other nations to praise YHWH as well. But when YHWH received honor, YHWH also risked being shamed. Shame arose when people did not recognize or acknowledge YHWH's power or when YHWH was perceived as impotent. God's being shamed was usually manifested as a shameful reputation.

One example of YHWH's vulnerability to shaming may be seen in the material dealing with Sennacherib's campaign against Judah in 701 B.C.E. (2 Kings 18–19). The account comes from two main sources, one historical (2 Kgs 18:13b–16) and one prophetic (18:17–19:37). The prophetic account, which differs from both the historical account and the Assyrian records, seems to be a reformulation of the events in light of deuteronomic theology.[17] Since in the prophetic account (2 Kgs 18:17–19:35) there are two accounts of the Assyrian mission to Hezekiah demanding his surrender and two responses from Isaiah (18:17–19:9a, 36; 19:9b–35) the passage is no doubt a blending of two different deuteronomic traditions among Isaiah's disciples.

In the first prophetic tradition, which probably stems from the time of the actual events, Sennacherib sent a force with his viceroy (Tartan), chief eunuch

17. See Martin Schreiner, "Zur Geschichte der Aussprache des Hebräischen," *ZAW* 6 (1886) 214–21; L. L. Honor, *Sennacherib's Invasion of Palestine* (New York: Columbia University Press, 1926) 45–48; B. Childs, *Isaiah and the Assyrian Crisis* (London: SCM, 1967) 73–103; M. Cogan and H. Tadmor, *II Kings* (AB 11; New York: Doubleday, 1988) 241–44.

(Rabsaris), and chief cupbearer (Rabshakeh) to deliver a message to taunt/shame Hezekiah (18:19–25). In the taunt the Rabshakeh suggested that reliance on either Egypt or YHWH was pointless. Egypt was weak, and YHWH was angry at Hezekiah for destroying the high places (18:22). In fact, YHWH now supported Sennacherib, suggesting divine abandonment of Hezekiah (18:25). Similar taunts before the walls of besieged cities are found in the Nimrud letter ND 2632[18] and in Assyrian royal inscriptions.[19]

There was no response from Hezekiah, so the Rabshakeh turned to the defenders on the walls of the city and shamed YHWH in front of them by questioning YHWH's power, "Who of all the gods of the countries was able to save his land from me, that YHWH should be able to save Jerusalem from me?" (2 Kgs 18:35).

In the second prophetic tradition, which stems from later deuteronomic tradition, the shaming of YHWH was used in an attempt to control or manipulate YHWH's behavior, in the same way that it was used on a social level to manipulate human behavior. Hezekiah addresses YHWH:

> Turn your ear and listen, YHWH, open your eyes and see, YHWH. Hear the words that Sennacherib has sent[20] to shame (*ḥrp*) the living God. . . . But now, YHWH, our God, save us from his hand, so that all the kingdoms of the earth may know that you alone, YHWH, are God (2 Kgs 19:16, 19; cf. 2 Chr 32:17).

The shaming was held up for YHWH to see and hear. Then it was suggested that if YHWH acted and saved Jerusalem "now," YHWH's reputation would change from one of shame to one of honor among YHWH's people and the kingdoms of the earth.

In an oracle delivered by Isaiah,[21] YHWH addresses Sennacherib:

> The maiden daughter of Zion despises you, scorns (*lᶜg*) you; the daughter of Jerusalem wags her head after you. Whom (do you think) you have shamed (*ḥrp*) and reviled and against whom have you raised your voice? You raised your eyes haughtily against the Holy One of Israel. By the hand of your messengers you shamed (*ḥrp*) the Lord [vv. 21–23a]. . . . Because you have raged against me, and your arrogance has come up into my ears, I will put my hook in your nose and my bridle in your mouth, and I will turn you back on the road by which you came [2 Kgs 19:28].

18. H. W. F. Saggs, "The Nimrud Letters, 1952: Part I," *Iraq* 17 (1955) 23–24.
19. C. Cohen, "Neo-Assyrian Elements in the First Speech of the Biblical Rab-saqe," *IOS* 9 (1979) 32–48, and P. Machinist, "Assyria and Its Image in First Isaiah," *JAOS* 103 (1983) 719–37.
20. Read *šlḥ*.
21. The oracle has been expanded secondarily.

Because Sennacherib shamed YHWH, YHWH will now shame Sennacherib. The reference to the hook and bridle alludes to the common Assyrian shaming practice of leading warriors and kings into captivity as though they were domestic animals. For a king to be treated in such a lowly fashion was extremely humiliating. To "turn back on the road by which [he] came" or to retreat in the face of victory added to the humiliation. This second prophetic tradition molded the departure of Sennacherib and the army into a story in which YHWH took control and vindicated his previous shaming. But in reality, the departure of Sennacherib was logical. Hezekiah had surrendered, and Sennacherib had received tribute. There was no reason to continue the attack.

Shaming in Rivalries and Contests for Superiority among Gods

The gods of Canaan and Mesopotamia were perceived as fighting among themselves to enhance their position and rank in the divine world.[22] This pattern of struggle for position reflected a similar pattern in human society, where there was a constant struggle for position and status. In the divine world the question of position and rank was a question of "who is the high god?" It was a question of identity or of which god had achieved the ideal of being most superior and most powerful. Since shame relates to "who" a person or god is and is manifest in a failure to reach an ideal, these contests were arenas that risked shame. A god striving for power, superiority, and honor also risked impotence, inferiority, and shame.

Contests for superiority are seen clearly in the Assyrian policy of capturing and spoiling the images of foreign gods. As mentioned earlier, political battles between nations became battles between the nations' gods. The victory of one nation over the other indicated the superiority and dominance of its gods. To express the superiority of the victorious god, the image of the defeated god was carried off to Assyria and set in a public place in a position of submission before the Assyrian high god, Ashur. It was then concluded that the enemy's god had abandoned the faithful in submission to the superiority of Ashur. The captured images were held hostage until the defeated rulers begged submissively for their return.[23] The entire ritual was one in which the superior, victorious god received honor, and the inferior, defeated god was

22. P. Miller, *The Divine Warrior in Early Israel* (Cambridge: Harvard University Press, 1973) 64.

23. Cogan, *Imperialism and Religion*, 11–12, 27–28, 37, 61; cf. S. Smith, *Babylonian Historical Texts Relating to the Capture and Downfall of Babylon* (London: Methuen, 1924).

shamed by having the god's inability to achieve victory publicly revealed. The ritual functioned psychologically in the struggle for dominance of one nation over another because the honoring of the victorious god boosted the morale of the victors; the shaming of the defeated god destroyed the morale of the defeated nation. The shamed, defeated warriors were less likely to retaliate when they and their god had been shamed.

Socially, ancient Israel was caught up in these struggles for status and significance. Consequently, we would expect to find in Israel's literature similar contests for status and significance involving YHWH and other gods. Scholars have been puzzled by the fact that there are *very few* biblical accounts of divine rivalries. But it must be remembered that these contests dealt with the status of the nations; they were contests for "superiority." Israel was an insignificant nation in the ancient world. She made no major conquests in the world, struggling just to hold onto her own territory. As an insignificant, less powerful nation she was not in a position to win many contests for superiority. It is therefore not surprising to find the majority of the accounts of these contests coming from the cultural and political giants of the age. They, of course, were the ones who won the contests and therefore were interested in recording their victories.

The reason so few of these rivalry accounts exist in the biblical text can be found in the commandment, "There shall not be to you no other gods beside/above/towards[24] my face" (lit. trans. of Exod 20:3 and Deut 5:7). This command no doubt originated from situations in which there were threats from rival deities. The commandment suggests that rival deities were not to be considered equal or superior to YHWH because such thinking threatened YHWH's status as High God. The commandment was necessary because throughout Israel's history there were rival gods to YHWH, gods who became equal or superior to YHWH. The presence of this kind of competition is confirmed by the frequent suggestion that YHWH is a "jealous" God—an attribute uncharacteristic of other great gods of the ancient Near East.[25] "Jealousy" indicates that God's position could be threatened and that God's pride was perceived as vulnerable.

In 1 Sam 5:1–12, an account involving the capture and subsequent return of the ark of YHWH by the Philistines, Miller and Roberts find an incident

---

24. There are a variety of translations that have been suggested in addition to the traditional "beside me." The issue cannot be resolved in terms of Hebrew grammar but must be approached exegetically. The translation should reflect position, not monotheism, as in "no other gods except me."

25. P. Miller, "God and the Gods," *Affirmation* 1/5 (1973) 57.

that resembles the Assyrian practice of capture and spoliation of the images of defeated gods.[26] This Israelite account portrays a contest for superiority between Dagon and YHWH that involves shaming and is interfaced with a tradition that explains why the Ashdodites did not step on the threshold of Dagon's temple.[27] Since the text is part of the deuteronomic tradition, it reflects the deuteronomic theology of honoring the righteous and shaming the wicked enemy (in this case, the enemy is a rival god).

According to the text, the ark, which represented God's presence and power, was captured in battle by the Philistines and taken to Ashdod to the temple of Dagon, where it was placed beside Dagon.

> After the Philistines captured the ark of God and brought it from Ebenezer to Ashdod, the Philistines brought the ark of God into the house of Dagon and placed it beside Dagon. When the Ashdodites arose the next morning, Dagon had fallen on his face to the ground before the ark of YHWH. So they raised up Dagon and set him in his place again. But when they arose the following morning, Dagon had fallen on his face to the ground before the ark of YHWH, and the head of Dagon and both of the palms of his hands were cut off and lying on the threshold; only the back[28] of Dagon remained intact. Therefore, even today the priests of Dagon and everyone entering Dagon's house do not step on the threshold of Dagon in Ashdod (1 Sam 5:1–5).

In battle Dagon had been the superior god, so the Philistines took the equivalent of an image, the ark of YHWH, into captivity. They placed the ark publicly beside the statue of Dagon. It is interesting that the text indicates that the Philistines placed the ark "beside" Dagon, suggesting equality to Dagon, despite the fact that Dagon had just been proven the superior victor. But during the night YHWH shamed Dagon by causing him to lie face down before YHWH. This position was used to humiliate captive kings or warriors by making them feel helpless and defenseless, a way of lowering their status, literally a way of "putting them down." If bowing the head demonstrated submission and often humiliation, then lying facedown on the ground represented ultimate submission and shame. On the second morning, even though Dagon had been set

26. P. Miller and J. Roberts (*The Hand of the Lord: A Reassessment of the "Ark Narrative" of 1 Samuel* [Johns Hopkins Near Eastern Studies; Baltimore: Johns Hopkins University Press, 1977] 42–43) base their investigation on Cogan's study of Assyrian practices.

27. This legend about YHWH shaming Dagon in Dagon's temple (1 Sam 5:1–5) has been combined with one stemming from a plague that swept the Philistine territory while the Ark of God was in captivity there (5:6–7:2).

28. The MT reads, *raq dāgôn niš ʾâr ʿālāyw* 'only Dagon was left to him'. The LXX suggests that the word before Dagon has fallen out. Most scholars, in light of Dan 10:6, restore to *gaw dāgôn* the 'back of Dagon'.

upright in a dominant position, he was again found facedown before the ark of YHWH. This time Dagon's head and palms had been cut off and were lying on the threshold of the temple.[29] The head was a symbol of superiority and the palms of the hands a symbol of physical power.[30] If I am correct in restoring the text to read "only the *back* of Dagon remained intact," then what remained was the inferior part of Dagon. In a face-to-face contest, YHWH shamed Dagon by lowering Dagon's position or status and by removing Dagon's power and superiority, so that only an inferior god was left. On Dagon's turf, YHWH rose from apparent defeat and inferiority to victory and superiority. The legend may have been developed to boost the morale of the Yahwists at a time when Yahwism was threatened by other cults.

It must be remembered that the notion that gods experienced shame was a human idea, and these descriptions of the gods were used for human purposes. The gods were described in terms related to the human psychological need for significance and the ultimate fear of insignificance.

Summary

In ancient Israel shaming appears to have been as much a religious concern as it was a social concern. Just as shame functioned as a means of control, domination, and status manipulation on a social level, it also functioned in a similar way on a religious level. On the one hand, people experienced YHWH's shaming through divine abandonment; on the other hand, they felt that it was the responsibility of YHWH to protect the pious from undeserved shame. YHWH was also called on for face-saving revenge from shame. Shame became an important tie between YHWH and the people, a tie that strengthened rather than weakened the relationship.

It is noteworthy that YHWH was perceived as being vulnerable to shaming. In this predominantly group-oriented society, YHWH was perceived in a strongly anthropomorphic way that allowed YHWH to utilize the prevalent forms of social control of the society and to feel human emotions, to take pride in superiority, and to have that pride violated. To recognize that YHWH was vulnerable to shame is to bring a new dimension to the understanding of Old Testament thinking, which was diametrically opposed to twentieth-century, individual-oriented thinking.

29. In the death of Jezebel there was nothing left to bury except her skull, feet, and the palms of her hands (2 Kgs 9:35).

30. H. W. Wolff, *Anthropology and the Old Testament* (Philadelphia: Fortress, 1974) 49–69.

The Motherhood of God:
The Use of *ḥyl* as God-Language
in the Hebrew Scriptures

Julia A. Foster

❧•☙

IN 1977, SHARON NEUFER EMSWILER WROTE that "one of the best-kept secrets of the church is the fact that the Bible itself sometimes describes God in feminine terms."[1] She recounted a story of a Roman Catholic nun who asked a class of high school girls to look at Deuteronomy 32 and

> find there a feminine image for God. When none of the girls was able to find it, she was puzzled. Then she realized that they were all using the [then] new Jerusalem Bible with the translation: "You forgot the Rock, who begot you, unmindful now of the God who fathered you."

Not being a Hebrew scholar and yet curious to know the derivation of the word or words for "God who fathered you,"

> she found out who had translated that particular section and telephoned him. She asked him whether the original Hebrew reflected the masculine understanding of God as he had translated it, or the feminine, as the other translators indicated. She said: "he just hemmed and hawed and refused to answer my question." But . . . when she insisted long enough, he finally admitted that it was feminine.[2]

1. S. N. Emswiler, *The Ongoing Journey: Women and the Bible* (New York: United Methodist Church, 1977) 119.
2. Ibid., 120. P. Trible has characterized this translation as "inadmissible" (*God and the Rhetoric of Sexuality* [Philadelphia: Fortress, 1978] 70).

Research and discussion during the past two decades ensure that the presence of feminine God-language in the Hebrew scriptures is no longer a "secret."[3] There is, however, no consensus on the significance and appropriate interpretation and employment of these images. While some, like the 1984 General Assembly of the Church of Scotland, upon receiving a report on the "Motherhood of God," resolve "to depart from the matter" without debate,[4] others have produced detailed critiques of the "feminist hermeneutic." John Miller, after citing a number of passages involving feminine words in reference to God, states:

> The point at issue is whether in doing so God is actually thought of *as* mother (and not just mother-*like*). This is excluded by the fact that the texts in question clearly and consistently maintain a paternal-masculine point of reference. Not once in the Bible is God addressed as mother, said to be mother, or referred to with feminine pronouns. On the contrary, gender usage throughout clearly specifies that the root metaphor is masculine-father.[5]

Sakenfeld interprets the same evidence differently:

> This is one of the complications of Hebrew grammar—that the grammatical form whenever God is being referred to will consistently be masculine even though the word may be . . . "to give birth." So there is a discontinuity between the technicality of the grammar and the content of the image. Since Christian theology does not regard that grammatical technicality as evidence that God is male, then we can surely let go of using the pronoun "he" when we deal with such texts.[6]

Clearly, although the "secret" is out, the topic has not been exhausted. Where interpretation is at issue, it is valuable to return frequently to examination of text and language. As a contribution to that enterprise, this paper offers a study of occurrences of the verb *ḥyl* in reference to God in the Hebrew scriptures. This root is of interest because its meaning is so unambigu-

---

3. Summaries of work in this and related areas can be found in, e.g., V. R. Mollenkott, *Women, Men, and the Bible* (rev. ed.; New York: Crossroad, 1989) vii–x; A. E. Zannoni, "Feminine Language for God in the Hebrew Scriptures," *Dialogue & Alliance* 2 (1988) 12; L. A. Mercadante, *The Influence of Gender Imagery for God* (Dissertation, Princeton University, 1986) 1–47.

4. A. E. Lewis, "The Biblical Witness to Our Motherly Father," *Irish Biblical Studies* 7 (1985) 8.

5. J. W. Miller, "Depatriarchalizing God in Biblical Interpretation: A Critique," *CBQ* 48 (1986) 614.

6. K. D. Sakenfeld, "Feminine and Masculine Images of God in Scripture and Translation," *The Word and Words: Beyond Gender in Theological and Liturgical Language* (ed. W. D. Watley; Princeton: COCU, 1983) 55.

ous. While *yld* may refer to either the mother's or father's role in procreation (as in Zech 13:3, "father and mother who bore him") *ḥyl* means distinctively 'to bring forth in pain' or 'to writhe in labor'.[7] During the course of this study, four passages using this stem in reference to God will be discussed. Each of these emphasizes a different aspect of God's motherhood.[8]

God Brings Forth Wisdom: Proverbs 8:22–26

יהוה קָנָנִי רֵאשִׁית דַּרְכּוֹ
קֶדֶם מִפְעָלָיו מֵאָז:

22 The Lord created me at the beginning of his work,
the first of his acts of long ago.

מֵעוֹלָם נִסַּכְתִּי מֵרֹאשׁ
מִקַּדְמֵי־אָרֶץ:

23 Ages ago I was set up, at the first,
before the beginning of the earth.

בְּאֵין־תְּהֹמוֹת חוֹלָלְתִּי
בְּאֵין מַעְיָנוֹת נִכְבַּדֵּי־מָיִם:

24 When there were no depths I was brought forth,
when there were no springs abounding with water.

בְּטֶרֶם הָרִים הָטְבָּעוּ
לִפְנֵי גְבָעוֹת חוֹלָלְתִּי:

25 Before the mountains had been shaped,
before the hills, I was brought forth—

עַד־לֹא עָשָׂה אֶרֶץ וְחוּצוֹת
וְרֹאשׁ עָפְרוֹת תֵּבֵל

26 When he had not yet made earth and fields,
or the world's first bits of soil.[9]

7. A. Bauman, "ḥyl," *TDOT* 4.344–47. The root may be related to a number of others containing radicals *ḥet* and *lamed*; it is sometimes cited as *ḥwl* or *ḥwl/ḥyl*. Following Bauman, *ḥyl* is used in this study.

8. Several authors have pointed out this verb's distinctiveness: K. P. Darr, "Like Warrior, Like Woman: Destruction and Deliverance in Isaiah 42:10–17," *CBQ* 49 (1987) 564–65; D. J. McCarthy, " 'Creation' Motifs in Ancient Hebrew Poetry," *CBQ* 27 (1967) 93; V. R. Mollenkott, *The Divine Feminine: The Biblical Imagery of God as Female* (New York: Crossroad, 1983) 16; Zannoni, "Feminine Language for God," 5. The most extensive treatment of *ḥyl, yld*, and other maternal words used in reference to God is by Trible, *Rhetoric*, 62–68. Neither she nor Bauman, however, specifically identifies all four passages examined here as referring to God.

9. English translations have been taken from the newly published *New Revised Standard Version* (Nashville: Thomas Nelson, 1990). Other English versions examined were KJV, NKJV, RSV, JB, NJB, NEB, NAB, and NIV. PHI/CCAT CD-ROM 1 (Los Altos: Packard Humanities Institute; Philadelphia: Center for Computer Analysis of Texts, 1987) was the source for the following editions of ancient texts: BHS (1967/77); LXX (ed. A. Rahlfs; 1935/1971); Vg (ed. B. Fischer et al.; 1975); Tg. Neof., *Biblia Polyglotta Matritensia, Series IV: Targum Palaestinense in Pentateuch* (ed. A. Díez Macho; Madrid: CSIC, 1980); Tg. Ps.-J., *Targum Pseudo-Jonathan of the Pentateuch* (ed. E. G. Clarke; New York: KTAV, 1984). Other text sources consulted were: A. Sperber, *The Bible in Aramaic* (Leiden: Brill, 1959–1973); B. Grossfeld, *The Targum Onqelos to Deuteronomy* (Aramaic Bible 9; Wilmington: Michael Glazier, 1988); M. L. Klein, *The Fragment Targums of the Pentateuch according to Their Extant Sources* (AnBib 76; Rome: Biblical Institute Press, 1980); B. D. Chilton, *The Isaiah Targum* (Aramaic Bible 11; Wilmington: Michael Glazier, 1987); J. F. Stenning, *The Targum of Isaiah* (Oxford: Clarendon, 1949).

Much attention has been paid to the figure of Wisdom as a female image of the Divine, a "secondary persona of God."[10] The focus here is rather on the image of YHWH as Wisdom's mother. Lang believes that the entire passage may be understood in terms of birth:

> Wisdom says of herself, "I was born (*holalti*)," an expression used to refer to human birth. . . . Two other verbs are used to describe the origin of Wisdom: *qanah* and *nasak*. Although both terms have given commentators considerable headaches, it seems that the most natural interpretation would be to relate these two verbs to the process of birth too.[11]

Lang believes that the name YHWH in v. 22 replaces an original El and speculates that "El's consort, Athirat . . . may indeed be Wisdom's mother. There is another possibility, however. . . . The Greek goddess Athena, for instance, . . . has no mother. In mythical parlance this is represented by saying that Athena sprang from Zeus's forehead."[12]

Whatever the ultimate origins of the portrait of Wisdom, the established text portrays Wisdom as YHWH's firstborn. The LXX, which varies considerably from the MT here,[13] has a single occurrence of an active verb: *gennạ me*. The Vulgate translates the first occurrence with *ego iam concepta eram* and the second with *ego parturiebar*. Terrien, apparently drawing on the Vulgate, finds that

> the poet has placed a threefold stress on the mode by which Wisdom, unlike nature, came into being. Wisdom sings: "Yahweh begot me" (vs. 22a), "I was conceived" (vs. 24a), and "I was brought forth" (vs. 25b).[14]

All the English versions examined (KJV, NKJV, RSV, NRSV, JB, NJB, NEB, NAB, NIV) translate *hwllty* straightforwardly as 'I was brought forth', 'I was born', 'I came to birth'.

In the formation of the MT and in its subsequent translation and interpretation, there is a concern for the safeguarding of the image of Israel's one God, who has no consort and is neither male nor female. While other ancient

10. R. R. Ruether, *Sexism and God-Talk* (Boston: Beacon, 1983) 57.

11. B. Lang, *Wisdom and the Book of Proverbs: An Israelite Goddess Redefined* (New York: Pilgrim, 1986) 63.

12. Ibid., 64.

13. See H. Conzelmann, "The Mother of Wisdom," *The Future of Our Religious Past* (New York: Harper & Row, 1971) 240.

14. S. Terrien, *The Elusive Presence: Toward a New Biblical Theology* (San Francisco: Harper & Row, 1978) 356.

Semitic texts not only portray divine couples, but use "Father and Mother" to refer to the same god or goddess,[15] the MT uses "Father" sparingly and "Mother" not at all.[16] The ancient mythopoetic celebrations of God's creative acts were recast in the MT, and further recast by ancient versions such as the targums and LXX, which generally avoid anthropomorphisms and anthropopathisms.[17]

The employment of *hwllty* in Proverbs 24–25 is an example of a simple and effective anti-anthropomorphic device—the use of the passive voice. Ancient and modern translators alike seem generally comfortable with the imagery of Wisdom somehow "brought forth"; the vivid verb, in passive voice, becomes abstract. In subsequent examples involving active forms of *hyl*, translators have had more difficulty.

God Brings Forth All Creation: Psalm 90:1–2[18]

תְּפִלָּה לְמֹשֶׁה אִישׁ־הָאֱלֹהִים	1	A prayer of Moses, the man of God.
אֲדֹנָי מָעוֹן אַתָּה הָיִיתָ לָּנוּ		Lord, you have been our dwelling place
בְּדֹר וָדֹר:		in all generations.
בְּטֶרֶם הָרִים יֻלָּדוּ	2	Before the mountains were brought forth,
וַתְּחוֹלֵל אֶרֶץ וְתֵבֵל		or ever you had formed the earth and the world,
וּמֵעוֹלָם עַד־עוֹלָם אַתָּה אֵל		from everlasting to everlasting you are God.

Psalm 90, the only Psalm attributed to Moses, has affinities with the passage just examined (Proverbs 8), as well as with Deuteronomy 32 and the Genesis creation narratives.[19] The form *wthwll* may also be read as a *Polal*, paralleling *yldw*; a passive form is reflected in the LXX, *plasthēnai*, both versions of the Vulgate, *parturiretur* (from the Hebrew) and *formaretur* (from the Greek) and most other ancient witnesses.[20] Both verbs are translated in the passive by the JB, NJB, NEB, and NAB. These translations all maintain the basic sense of *hyl*, with renderings such as 'were brought forth', 'came to

15. P. A. H. de Boer, *Fatherhood and Motherhood in Israelite and Judean Piety* (Leiden: Brill, 1974) 15–16, 40.

16. "Father" is used of God "about 15 times" in the MT, according to C. Mangan, *Can We Still Call God "Father"?* (Wilmington: Michael Glazier, 1984) 28.

17. B. M. Metzger, "Versions, Ancient," *IDB* 4.750; E. Tov, "Septuagint," *IDBSup* (ed. Keith Crim et al.; Nashville: Abingdon, 1976) 810.

18. Ps 89:1–2 in the LXX and Vg.

19. C. A. and E. G. Briggs, *A Critical and Exegetical Commentary on the Book of Psalms* (ICC; Edinburgh: Clark, 1907) 2.272.

20. Ibid.

birth'. The NEB renders the meaning particularly clearly with 'earth and world were born in travail'.

Of those versions maintaining the active translation of the verb, most follow KJV with some version of its "thou hadst formed the earth and the world," translating with a more abstract "creation" word: thus RSV, NRSV, NKJV.[21] The NIV preserves the specific sense of *ḥyl*: "You brought forth the earth and the world." Patrick Miller makes the sense even more explicit with his translation, "Before the mountains were born or you had brought forth in labor the earth and the world, from everlasting to everlasting you are God."[22]

God Brings Forth All Individuals and Nations according to the Divine Plan: Isaiah 45:9–11

הוֹי רָב אֶת־יֹצְרוֹ	9	Woe to you who strive with your Maker,
חֶרֶשׂ אֶת־חַרְשֵׂי אֲדָמָה		earthen vessels with the potter!
הֲיֹאמַר חֹמֶר לְיֹצְרוֹ		Does the clay say to the one who fashions it,
מַה־תַּעֲשֶׂה		"What are you making"?
וּפָעָלְךָ אֵין־יָדַיִם לוֹ:		or "Your work has no handles"?
הוֹי אֹמֵר לְאָב	10	Woe to anyone who says to a father,
מַה־תּוֹלִיד		"What are you begetting?"
וּלְאִשָּׁה מַה־תְּחִילִין:		or to a woman, "With what are you in labor?"
כֹּה־אָמַר יהוה	11	Thus says the Lord,
קְדוֹשׁ יִשְׂרָאֵל וְיֹצְרוֹ		the Holy One of Israel, and its Maker:
הָאֹתִיּוֹת שְׁאָלוּנִי עַל־בָּנַי		Will you question me about my children,
וְעַל־פֹּעַל יָדַי תְּצַוֻּנִי		or command me concerning the work of my hands?

Deutero-Isaiah, according to Gruber, contains "the only instances in the Hebrew Bible where God is *explicitly* compared to a mother."[23] Schmitt believes that "When Isa 42:14, 45:10, 49:15, and 66:13 refer to God as a mother . . . those passages and others in Isa 40–66 show that the author was influenced by the idea that Zion is a mother, an idea that was easily transferred to God."[24] For Gruber, an "explicit" comparison seems to be one employing a female noun such as "woman" or "mother." In a different sense, however, the root *ḥyl* is also "explicit" in its distinctive meaning. Furthermore, Schmitt's Zion concept will not fit the present study, since the refer-

21. Note also that the NAB translates *yldw* by 'were begotten'.
22. P. D. Miller, *Interpreting the Psalms* (Philadelphia: Fortress, 1986) 126.
23. M. I. Gruber, "The Motherhood of God in Second Isaiah," *RB* 90 (1983) 351.
24. J. J. Schmitt, "The Motherhood of God and Zion as Mother," *RB* 92 (1985) 557.

ences in the two passages already examined are to ages when the mountains (including Mount Zion) had not yet come into being.

The *Interpreter's Bible* designates Isa 45:9–13 by the heading "Divine Sovereignty over nature and history."[25] The verses examined here, which speak of God as parent/creator of humanity, are contained in a context proclaiming God's rule over all: "I made the earth, and created humankind upon it; it was my hands that stretched out the heavens, and I commanded all their host" (45:12).

In analyzing this passage, it is necessary to point out that there are a number of textual problems. I suggest following the textual emendation of the BHS apparatus, replacing *hwy* with interrogative *ha* at the beginning of Isa 45:9 and 10. The passage then poses three parallel sets of questions, as in the NEB. Naidoff, following this emendation, diagrams the rhetorical structure thus:[26]

v. 9	work of the hands	A
v. 10	procreation	B
v. 11bα	procreation	B_1
v. 11bβ	work of the hands	A_1

Other versions, *Tg. Neb. t^cdn*, LXX *ōdinēseis*, and Vg *parturis*, translate 45:10 literally. Interestingly this is the only instance of the four passages studied in this article where the LXX uses a word specifically denoting the pangs of labor. The Vulgate, however, employs forms of *parturio* in the Proverbs and Psalm texts as well. All the English versions translate the Hebrew words *twlyd* and *thylyn* with some form of "What/why have you begotten?" and "What/why have you brought forth?" or "With what are you in labor/travail?"

One problem that occurs to a person reading this text is that the parallelism between "father" and "woman" seems awkward. The reason for this may have been that the use of the Hebrew word "mother" would have called up an image too close to the mother-worship of the fertility cults. The rather free rendition of the NEB captures the sense of the passage well:

> Will the babe say to his father,
>   "What are you begetting?,"
>   or to his mother,
>   "What are you bringing to
> birth?"

25. *IB* 5.526.
26. B. D. Naidoff, "The Twofold Structure of Isaiah 45, 9–13," *VT* 31 (1981) 183.

God Brings Forth Israel: Deuteronomy 32:18

צוּר יְלָדְךָ תֶּשִׁי   18   You were unmindful of the Rock that bore you;[27]
וַתִּשְׁכַּח אֵל מְחֹלְלֶךָ   you forgot the God who gave you birth.

The Song of Moses, Deut 32:1–43, abounds in imagery of God as parent, creator, sustainer, judge, and savior of Israel. Luyten describes the Song as a "most impressive composition" combining "primeval and eschatological elements":

> The great variety of motifs, the richness of vocabulary, the flamboyant style, the broad spectrum of parallels with all kinds of biblical literature strongly suggest that the song of Moses of Dt 32 is the work of someone who was versed in the law and the prophets, in psalm and wisdom literature, of someone who was a forerunner of the apocalyptists.[28]

This passage is the only one of the four examined that juxtaposes divine names and birth-words. The names and the corresponding verb forms are masculine, but the meanings of the roots *yld* (probably) and *ḥyl* (certainly) are feminine. Both ancient and modern translators have had difficulty with this combination.

Tg. Onq. dealt with this difficulty by translating both verbs with less anthropomorphic terms: "who created you," "who made you." The Palestinian Targums have an expanded translation in which

> the verbal element *mḥllk* "that bore thee" is rendered first by *dy škll ytkwn* "who perfected you" . . . then by words sounding closer to the Hebrew model . . . "and who has made you (with) so many cavities." The last words are understood as plural forms of *meḥillā* "cavity."[29]

Midrashic interpretations included the "cavities" tradition, but the central focus was on the pain experienced by God as parent of faithless children—an anguished pain like that of a male in labor! Both verbs in the passage were understood as referring to birth. Comparison was made by the commentators to Ps 48:7, "Pangs [*ḥyl*], as of a woman in travail."[30] The LXX reads *ton gen-*

---

27. Or 'that begot you'; alternate NRSV reading.

28. J. Luyten, "Primeval and Eschatological Overtones in the Song of Moses," in *Das Deuteronomium* (ed. N. Lohfink; Leuven: Leuven University Press, 1985) 341.

29. S. Segert, "Rendering of Parallelistic Structures in the Targum Neofiti, the Song of Moses," *Salvación en la Palabra* (Madrid: Cristiandad, 1986) 526.

30. H. W. Basser, *Midrashic Interpretations of the Song of Moses* (New York: Peter Lang, 1984) 188–92.

nēsanta se . . . tou trephontos se. The Vulgate reading is *te genuit . . . creatoris tui.*

As noted above, some interpreters have construed the form *yldk* as a *Hiphil* with the meaning 'begot you'. The verse would then follow the pattern of Isa 45:10, with references to divine fatherhood and motherhood in parallel.[31] It seems more likely that de Boer is correct that "the reading *yelādĕkā* 'that bore you' (*Qal*) is unequivocal, and its rendering cannot be mistaken. The rendering 'that begot you,' reading a *Hiphil*, is against the text transmitted to us or assumes a meaning of the *qal* that this form is not carrying."[32]

Clearly, it has always been possible, then, to translate this verse as the NRSV has done. Yet none of the earlier English translations did so. Furthermore, several of them seem to have been uncomfortable with the clear meaning of *mḥllk* and made it more abstract (KJV, "God who formed thee") or male (JB, NKJV, "who fathered you"). It is interesting that the NKJV has here abandoned the parent KJV to follow, apparently, the JB.

The NRSV translation reverses the text/note relation of 'begot' and 'bore' found in the RSV. The NJB, abandoning the "inadmissible" rendition of JB, now reads, "You forgot the Rock who fathered you, the God who made you, you no longer remember." Different as the two versions are, each probably reflects a renewed consideration of the text, perhaps in response to questions raised by the "feminist hermeneutic."

Conclusion

The root *ḥyl,* used to describe God's creative power, has a significant place in the Hebrew Scriptures. Though it appears in only four passages, these four are found in the context of some of the Bible's most powerful and beautiful poetry. All three divisions of the Scriptures are represented. The whole sweep of God's sovereignty is encompassed, from the birth of Wisdom before the beginning of the world to the birth of Israel in the salvation-history of the Exodus.

There are evidences in the texts examined here of concern by the writers that their God-language not be misunderstood. We can be grateful that the biblical writers were not so wary of the Great Mother as to censor out all the

---

31. "Schliesslich wird JHWH im Lied des Mose (Dtn 32,18) als väterlich *und* mütterlich zugleich geschildert"; U. Winter, *Frau und Göttin* (Orbis Biblicus et Orientalis 53; Freiburg: Universitätsverlag, 1983) 536.

32. De Boer, *Fatherhood and Motherhood,* 42.

poetry of the old mythology, but appropriated it for a new use instead. Anti-anthropomorphic concerns further obscured some of these references in the interpretations of the targums and LXX. Jerome's return to the Hebrew restored a closer reading in several instances: the most striking example is found in the contrasting Vulgate translations, 'formed' from Greek and 'to travail' from Hebrew for Ps 90(89):2 (see p. 97).

A factor further influencing Christian reading and translation of these texts has been the dominance of the Father name and image for God in the NT and Christian doctrine. Cross argues that the fatherhood (but not motherhood) of God is not poetic metaphor but strict analogy:

> Yet the importance that God in his Triune Persons be always considered masculine to us human beings is so overwhelming that in *every* case in Scripture the truth of this is rigorously guarded.[33]

In the case of Deut 32:18, it may be that such a viewpoint influenced some translators to observe this principle more "rigorously" than was justified by the text itself. Against such a preference for what is familiar, traditional, and attested by authority as doctrinally correct, a return to the original language of the text can be surprising and illuminating. In studying the text and its language, neglected words and concepts can be recovered. Consciousness of feminine terminology has been raised, so that modern translators do not so easily "lose" this aspect of the biblical heritage.

A note of caution is worthwhile at this point. It is important not to be so zealous in restoring the buried feminine aspect of God that we use language that is simplistic for the complex and dynamic language employed by the Scriptures about God. God begets, bears, molds, speaks. No single image can hold the divine presence. If we follow the biblical pattern we may use many names and images for God—including both Father and Mother.

33. N. Cross, "Those Poor Misquoted Scriptures," *Homiletic & Pastoral Review* 86/10 (July 1986) 58.

ARCHAEOLOGY AND THE BIBLE

Archaeology, Texts, and History-Writing: Toward an Epistemology

William G. Dever

❧

Introduction

I N THIS ESSAY DEDICATED TO THE MEMORY of H. Neil Richardson, who sought to foster a constructive dialogue between biblical studies and archaeology (both in the classroom and in the field), I shall lay the groundwork for what I believe must be the next phase as both disciplines come to maturity.

During the period when Richardson was most active, from ca. 1965–1990, "Biblical archaeology" of the older style gradually gave way to a more professional, more specialized, more "secular" discipline of Syro-Palestinian archaeology. Elsewhere I have charted and applauded the growth of the newer archaeology, suggesting that it will at last bring about the revolution in biblical studies that Albright had confidently predicted.[1] Yet in one fundamental dimension the new archaeology has so far proven as deficient as the old—namely in its failure to address the issue of *epistemology*. It has built a much more adequate foundation in some aspects of theory, but it has not probed deeply

---

1. See, among other treatments, W. G. Dever, "The Impact of the 'New Archaeology' on Syro-Palestinian Archaeology," *BASOR* 242 (1981) 15–19; "Syro-Palestinian and Biblical Archaeology," in *The Hebrew Bible and Its Modern Interpreters* (ed. D. A. Knight and G. M. Tucker; Philadelphia: Fortress, 1985) 31–74; "Impact of the 'New Archaeology,'" in *Benchmarks in Time and Culture: An Introduction to Palestinian Archaeology* (ed. J. F. Drinkard Jr., G. L. Mattingly, and J. M. Miller; Atlanta: Scholars, 1988) 337–52; "Biblical Archaeology: Death and Rebirth?" in the *Congress Volume* (Second International Congress on Biblical Archaeology [forthcoming]) and references there to a wider literature.

---

enough to reach the philosophical and methodological level at which all archaeological and historical inquiry must begin: how is it possible to know *anything* with certitude about the human past? Until this question has been addressed, both disciplines will remain superficial, arcane, and too speculative to have anything of substance to say to each other.[2] I begin with some definitions.

Observations on the Nature of Archaeological and Historical Evidence

To make archaeology and biblical history truly intellectual rather than antiquarian enterprises, we need to think much more profoundly about what we are doing. By this I do not mean simply more attention to "method"—which in our field has usually meant asking how to dig better, how to collect and record more information. Improvements in archaeology at this level are indeed important, and the past two decades have seen remarkable progress. However, technological advances and the proliferation of new material have now brought archaeologists to a critical stage where they must ask: What is the *point*? What are we trying to *learn*?

It might have been better, of course, to have asked these theoretical questions at the outset of the new archaeology. But as Thomas Kuhn has stated in *The Structures of Scientific Revolutions*, theory often follows rather than precedes the practical "shift in paradigm" that he regards as constituting a revolution in most research disciplines.[3] Thus it is indeed "better late than never" to raise these questions. In the discussion that follows I would like to begin by reflecting on terms that all use but seldom bother to define, wrongly assuming that their meaning is self-evident.

---

2. There is virtually no literature on epistemology in our field; but see provisionally Dever, "Of Myths and Methods," *BASOR* 277 (1990) 121–30; "Biblical Archaeology: Death and Rebirth?" (referred to in n. 1 above); "Unresolved Issues: Toward a Synthesis of Archaeological and Textual Reconstruction of Ancient Israel," *The Bible and the Politics of Exegesis: Essays in Honor of Norman K. Gottwald on His Sixty-Fifth Birthday* (eds. D. Jobling, P. Day, and G. Sheppard; Cleveland: Pilgrim, 1991) 195–208. On a plea for dialogue, see Dever, "Biblical Archaeology: Death and Rebirth?" Perhaps the most radical yet stimulating epistemological challenge in general archaeology is found in M. Shanks and C. Tilley, *Re-Constructing Archaeology: Theory and Practice* (Cambridge: Cambridge University Press, 1987).

3. Thomas L. Kuhn, *The Structure of Scientific Revolutions* (2d ed.; Chicago: University of Chicago Press, 1970). For an application of Kuhn's model to our field, see W. G. Dever ("Impact of the 'New Archaeology,'" 337–52).

"Facts"

Archaeology's original fascination for Albright, and I suspect for many of his followers, was that it could serve as an antidote. Archaeology promised new *facts* to offset the speculation of various schools of critical biblical scholarship, which seemed to have reached the limits of useful inquiry. This was what Albright meant when he spoke so confidently of *realia.*[4] But archaeologists must delimit for themselves the facts that are recoverable through archaeology; or, for that matter, define the so-called "facts of history."

By *fact* (derived from Latin *factum*, past participle of the verb *facere*, 'to do') we usually mean those discrete, irreducible, empirically observable things or events whose existence cannot be doubted by reasonable persons. That is, facts (1) are theoretically provable and (2) correspond to reality. In practice, however, facts are merely inferences that each person draws, based not only on observation, but also on our own social conditioning and the intent of our investigation. Even in the natural sciences, this is true and is increasingly recognized; and in all the social sciences, such as archaeology and history, the factor of individual bias is even more operative. Thus, while in theory archaeology does recover objective "facts" from the past—for example, a pot, a stone tool, a figurine, the foundations of a building, perhaps the entire plan of a village, or even a written text—the apprehension of the reality of any of these is always dependent on present, subjective human interpretation. Facts do not speak directly. They may in principle have a concrete existence of their own; but they come to life, empowered to speak to me of the past, only as I am able to incorporate them into my consciousness; this process is obviously an extraordinarily complex matter.

A useful analogy is still the old philosophical puzzle: if a tree falls in the woods and there is no human or animal in hearing range, is there any sound? One must say "No," because *sound*, like *meaning*, is dependent on response, in this case the impact of airwaves set in motion by the crash upon human eardrums or other biological hearing mechanisms. Similarly, facts may be

---

4. A typical early statement of Albright forecast and virtually summed up his life's work: "Archaeological research in Palestine and neighboring lands during the past century has completely transformed our knowledge of the historical and literary background of the Bible. It no longer appears as an absolutely isolated monument of the past, as a phenomenon without relation to its environment. The excessive skepticism shown toward the Bible by important historical schools of the 18th and 19th centuries, certain phases of which will appear periodically, has been progressively discredited. Discovery after discovery has brought increased recognition of the value of the Bible as a source of history" (*The Archaeology of Palestine and the Bible* [New York: Revell, 1935] 137–38).

assumed to "speak," but until meaning—a uniquely human quality—is supplied, there is no message (see below). These inherent limitations of the facts brought to light by archaeology must always be kept in mind.

Are there, then, *no* facts in archaeology? There are, but they are relatively few and generally of minimal significance in themselves. Even these facts, however, must be carefully established as such before becoming admissible evidence. For example, using the list of items above, one might make an assertion that a particular pot is a "wheelmade cooking pot"; but laboratory analysis may show that it was handmade or that it was made for cooking but used for something else. In anther instance, the plan of a building may be used as evidence that it was a "domestic house," not a temple. But it is important to keep in mind that no one can be absolutely sure of this analysis.

The element of subjectivity increases in the case of stratigraphy. It is possible to conclude, using the geological "law of superimposition," that the material in the uppermost of a sectioned series of earth layers is the latest; but further exposure may reveal that the entire series is an inverted fill, and the earliest material is on top. Again, a floor may be said to abut a wall rather than being cut by it, and so is contemporary. But a careful scholar will bear in mind the fact that foundation trenches can be surfaced-over so skillfully by later floors that the earlier purpose of the wall remains undetected.

For all these and other reasons, I suggest that archaeologists ought rarely to use the word *proof,* because the kind of verification that is possible in sciences that investigate the physical world is simply not obtainable for material-culture remains, even though they are also physical objects. "New archaeologists" today do of course formulate and test hypotheses, do seek regularities in the cultural process, and in that sense they may aspire to "scientific" status of a sort. Ultimately, however, they are dealing with human behavior, and behavior cannot be replicated in the laboratory, nor is it predictable.

Thus archaeologists are better off speaking not of "laws" or "proofs" or even of "facts," but rather of various *probabilities,* some of which are better (i.e., more useful) than others. They may also speak of "levels of inference," of which the lower are more certain than the higher. For example, to infer that the structure above is a "house" may be relatively safe; but to conclude that "the family is nuclear" is riskier, that "the social structure is segmentary" is still more risky. What is essential in the necessary process of interpretation is not to deny or minimize the difficulties, but rather to make presuppositions absolutely clear and above all not to claim more than is actually known. This—*knowledge* of what is true—is what the epistemological dilemma is all about.

Before leaving the topic of facts, it is worthwhile distinguishing three *kinds* of facts with which the archaeologist (and biblical historian) works:

(1) artifacts, (2) textual facts, and (3) ecofacts. Artifacts have already been mentioned above, and all who work in the fields of historical archaeology are well acquainted with the necessity for using biblical and extrabiblical texts wherever possible for the illumination of the past. I would point out in passing that these two classes of facts are much more similar than usually thought. Both texts and artifacts symbolically represent a particular perception of reality; both are "encoded messages" that must be decoded, using rational, critical methods as well as empathy; both remain somewhat enigmatic, however skillful and persistent the attempts to penetrate their full meaning.[5] Finally, I would argue simply that both objects and texts *are* artifacts, that is, thought and action frozen in the form of matter, the "material correlates of human behavior." Even the Bible is an artifact, in this case what archaeologists call a "curated artifact," or an item that originally functioned in one social context but has subsequently been reused in other ways and settings. Thus the Bible is what it once was, plus what it has become over the centuries of interpretation as scripture by synagogue and church. This fact must always be kept in mind when biblical texts are used as evidence in archaeological reconstructions.[6]

"Data"

Both archaeologists and historians refer constantly to the basic *data* on which their arguments rest. That is why an archaeological epistomology must begin with a definition of the word *datum*. Etymology suggests that *data* (plural past participle of Latin *dare* 'to give') are those facts that are "given" to us, the bedrock evidence upon which conclusions are based. What is "given" and how it is given, or by whom, are fundamental epistemological questions.

Ordinarily the terms *fact* and *data* are used interchangeably, but I contend that they represent two successive stages of the interpretive process. Archaeological facts in themselves, as has been seen, may possess intrinsic value, but this is not true for meaning, which must be supplied by human beings. In that

5. See further Dever, "Archaeology, Material Culture, and the Early Monarchical Period," in *The Fabric of History: Text, Artifact, and Israel's Past* (ed. D. Edelman; JSOTSup 127; Sheffield: Almond Press, 1991) 103–15; for an independent analogy of the parallels between "reading" artifacts and "reading" texts, see I. Hodder, *Reading the Past: Current Approaches to Interpretation in Archaeology* (Cambridge: Cambridge University Press, 1986) 121–24).

6. See Dever, *Recent Archaeological Discoveries and Biblical Research* (Stroum Lectures; Seattle: University of Washington Press, 1990) 8–11, for further development of this idea.

sense, facts *become* data—that is, useful information—only as interpreted within an intellectual framework that is capable of giving them significance. To put it another way, it is possible to learn about the past, not simply by amassing more and more bits and pieces of disjointed "evidence," but rather by coordinating the pieces of evidence and situating them within a context, relating knowledge to a deliberate quest.

In all disciplines, but particularly in archaeology, the advance of real and lasting knowledge comes not so much from chance discovery (as the popular misunderstanding assumes), but rather from the systematic investigation of specific questions.[7] Thus what is learned depends largely on (1) what is already known, (2) the goals and orientation of the investigation, and (3) the method of inquiry. Simply put, the best answers—true "data"—result from framing appropriate questions. The use of the word *appropriate*, of course, does not imply any value judgment about what the "right" questions are, but a notion of what may be possible, given the nature of the material at one's disposal and the intellectual stage of the discipline at the moment.

All of the foregoing is, of course, what should be intended by the use of the current phrase "research design" in archaeology, but the typical design entails more practical field strategy than it does an adequate theoretical base for the expansion of knowledge.

As Binford and other "new archaeologists" reminded us, limitations of knowledge are more the result of inadequate research design than poor data.[8] The archaeological record can be *much* more efficiently exploited, if only it is better understood what cultural formation processes are[9] and how superior data can be generated from broader and more sophisticated research strategies. Again, it all depends on asking appropriate questions. David Noel Freedman, one of Albright's protégés and a leading biblical scholar, sums up the wrong approach:

---

7. On such "research design," see Dever, "Archaeology in Israel Today: A Summation and Critique" (*Recent Excavations in Israel: Studies in Iron Age Archaeology* [AASOR 49; Winona Lake, Ind.: Eisenbrauns, 1989] 143–52).

8. See L. R. Binford, "A Consideration of Archaeological Research Design," *American Antiquity* 29 (1964) 425–41; *Pursuit of the Past: Decoding the Archaeological Record* (New York: Thames & Hudson, 1983).

9. Cultural formation processes have scarcely been treated at all in the field of archaeology, but see provisionally Dever, "The *Tell*: Microcosm of the Cultural Process," forthcoming in the Gus Van Beek festschrift (ed. B. Magness-Gardiner and J. D. Seger); also A. Rosen, *Cities of Clay: The Geoarchaeology of Tells* (Chicago: University of Chicago Press, 1986); and for wider orientation to the issues, see especially M. B. Schiffer, *Formation Processes of the Archaeological Record* (Albuquerque: University of New Mexico Press, 1987).

Albright's great plan and expectation to set the Bible firmly on the foundation of archaeology buttressed by verifiable data seems to have foundered or at least floundered. After all the digging, done and being done and yet to be done, how much has been accomplished? The fierce debates and arguments about the relevance of archaeology to the Bible and vice versa indicate that many issues remain unresolved. Can anyone say anything with confidence about the patriarchs or the patriarchal age? The fact that skeptical voices now dominate the scene indicates that the Albrightian synthesis has become unglued and we are further from a solution than we ever were. Archaeology has not proved decisive or even greatly helpful in answering the questions most often asked and has failed to prove the historicity of Biblical persons and events, especially in the early periods.[10]

I contend, however, that it was not archaeology that went wrong, but a generation of biblical historians who were *asking the wrong questions*—not wrong in a moral sense, but certainly wrong heuristically. Much of classical "biblical archaeology" was an exercise in futility in that the questions posed were either parochial and so received trivial answers at best, or were basically theological in nature and so received no answers at all. Only as scholars learn to structure questions more appropriate to the archaeological record itself and to socioeconomic history, rather than religious and political history, will archaeology become the powerful interpretive tool that Albright envisioned for reconstructing biblical life and times.

"Context"

Context is another term that is used loosely in biblical archaeology. While recognizing the theoretical importance of context, archaeologists often mean by it little more than the immediate provenience of an object—its locus or stratum, or at most its associated materials. Rarely do they grasp that it is the *total* systemic context that is essential, that is, an ascending hierarchy of find-spot, stratigraphic phase, site-wide chronological horizon, multi-site evolutionary stage, ecological setting, and indeed long-term settlement-history. Lying behind this holistic approach is often General Systems Theory, which assumes that any given archaeological item functions within a larger environmental and sociocultural system, without which it cannot be understood.[11] It

10. These remarks were made at a symposium honoring Albright; see D. N. Freedman, "Remarks Reported by the Editor," *BAR* 11/1 (1985) 6.

11. For an orientation to General Systems Theory and an application to the end of the Early Bronze Age in Syria–Palestine, see Dever, "The Collapse of the Urban Early Bronze Age in Palestine: Toward a Systematic Analysis," *L'urbanization de la Palestine à l'âge du*

is this larger setting that provides significance, for without it, an artifact is torn out of its original context, isolated as a curio, fit for little more than viewing in a museum. It can tell us little of the culture that produced it and was in turn partly shaped by it.

Biblical historians are often just as myopic in using biblical texts, fragmenting sources into verses and verses into still smaller units. Ultimately the critic becomes bogged down in the minutiae of literary analysis and loses sight of the larger picture of Israel's whole life and history. This narrowness of vision is all too prevalent, despite the broadening horizons of such newer approaches as rhetorical and canonical criticism. It is true that from the beginning form criticism stressed the importance of the *Sitz im Leben*, but in practice this tended to mean simply *siting* a text within the literary tradition, not within the larger social and historical context of "real life." There were many times when the broader context could be recovered only through archaeology, but the dialogue between archaeology and biblical studies proved once again to be deficient. Refreshing exceptions can be found, of course: Coote and Whitelam's *Emergence of Israel in Historical Perspective*, for example, takes a settlement-history approach over very long time-spans.[12]

Context has come to the fore anew in archaeology with Ian Hodder's attempt to move beyond the "new archaeology" of the 1970s and 1980s to what he calls "post-processualist" or, preferably, "contextual" archaeology. In *Reading the Past: Current Approaches to Interpretation in Archaeology*, Hodder outlines this approach as a reaction against the materialism and determinism of much recent archaeological theory, stressing rather the role of ideology, of culture, even of the individual in social change. The "new archaeology," with its one-sided focus on "behavior" rather than on "events"—on what was supposed to be the "universal cultural process" rather than on "particularism"—was often inimical to culture-history of the older sort. It was even opposed to history-writing itself as a goal of archaeology. Hodder's "contextual archaeology," on the other hand, places artifacts in the *largest* social and natural context possible, uses a variety of approaches, and includes textual and historical

---

Bronze Ancien (BAR International Series 527; ed. P. Miroschedji; Oxford: British Archaeological Reports, 1989) 225–46; for its application to the Late Bronze/Iron I transition and the origins of early Israel, see Dever, "The Late Bronze–Early Iron Age Horizon in Syria–Palestine: Egyptians, Canaanites, Sea Peoples, and Proto-Israelites," *The Crisis Years: the 12th Century B.C.* (ed. M. Joukowsky and W. A. Ward; Dubuque, Iowa: Kendall Hunt, 1992) 99–110.

12. For a response to R. B. Coote and K. W. Whitelam, *The Emergence of Israel in Historical Perspective* (Sheffield: Almond, 1987), see Dever, "Unresolved Issues."

context. Thus material culture, *with* texts ("*con*text"), can in fact be "read" for the purpose of instruction about the human past. Furthermore, Hodder reminds the reader, "context" includes the intellectual and social milieu within which the *modern* interpreter operates, for this, as much as the original context of artifacts and texts, helps to determine the final meaning assigned to the past.[13]

Archaeology and History: Epistemological Principles

It is fashionable once again to speak of history-writing as a primary goal of archaeology, and for this reason I turn now to the matter of defining the term *history*. Unfortunately, both biblical scholars and archaeologists have neglected historiography until very recently, except for a few scholars such as Thompson, Van Seters, Lemche, Halpern, Garbini, and a few others. Syro-Palestinian archaeologists, historians of a sort, usually manifest a naiveté regarding the nature of history and the task of history-writing. Albright, on the other hand, was familiar with and responded to works of such philosophers of history as Toynbee, Croce, Collingwood, Voeglin, and others, but his followers have shown little such inclination.[14] The current result is highly technical archaeological studies of isolated problems and periods but nothing approaching the full-scale synthetic history of ancient Palestine that today's proficient archaeology is capable of producing. This criticism is true even of the best recent works, such as Helga Weippert's *Palästina in vorhellenistischer Zeit*[15] or Amihai Mazar's *Archaeology of the Land of the Bible, 10,000–586 B.C.E.*[16]

This lamentable deficiency is the direct result of an attenuated notion of history-writing among both archaeologists and biblical scholars. Scholars have produced a bare-bones "political history" based exclusively on select biblical texts and highly visible, monumental archaeological remains such as temples, palaces, and destruction-layers. This "history" has emphasized public events and the deeds of great men, but it largely ignores socioeconomic history, much less the kind of long-term history of the masses that Braudel

13. Hodder, *Reading the Past*, 118–46.

14. See in particular some of W. F. Albright's later works, such as *History, Archaeology, and Christian Humanism* (New York: McGraw-Hill, 1964).

15. Helga Weippert, *Palästina in vorhellenistischer Zeit* (Munich: Beck, 1989).

16. Amihai Mazar, *Archaeology of the Land of the Bible, 10,000–586 B.C.E.* (New York: Doubleday, 1990). For a review of Weippert, see Dever, "Review of H. Weippert, *Palästina in vorhellenistischer Zeit*," *JAOS* 112 (1992) 645–46.

and the *annales* school undertake.[17] Such an elitist history is unsatisfactory on many accounts, not least of which is the modern biblical historian's apparently unconscious (and certainly uncritical) appropriation of the ideological bias of the ancient writers. It is history written "from within," rather than from the perspective of the external evidence now available from the Ancient Near East, both in abundant texts and artifacts. Here again, even the most critical current works, such as Miller and Hayes' *A History of Ancient Israel and Judah*, are a disappointment.[18] Yet progress in this matter is unlikely without a more adequate concept of history and of the historian's task.

At this point I wish to present a methodology for what I foresee to be a more adequate written history of ancient Israel in the future. Since, as I have argued, epistemology is basic, I begin with an appeal for theory.

Archaeology Theory-Building

In his 1977 work *For Theory-Building*, Binford elaborates on one of the original motifs of the "new archaeology" of twenty-five years ago, stressing that archaeology is unlikely to advance further unless this earlier revolution in basic *theory* is carried forward.[19] Unfortunately, the "new archaeology" has come and gone, and most Syro-Palestinian archaeologists have missed the signal for change. To judge from the scant discussion in the literature, the notion of "theory" meets with apathy at best and often with open hostility. American archaeologists, striving to reeducate themselves in newer approaches, have shown some interest in what is usually called "theory and method"; but they have construed *method* to mean simply improved digging and recording techniques, rather than an inquiry that concerns the very intellectual foundations of the discipline. Israelis view the few attempts at theory-building by Americans or archaeologists in other fields with a skepticism revealing only their innocence.[20]

17. See further L. Marfoe, "The Integrative Transformation: Patterns of Sociopolitical Organization in Southern Syria," *BASOR* 234 (1979) 1–42, and Dever, "Impact of the 'New Archaeology,'" 337–52.

18. J. M. Miller and J. H. Hayes, *A History of Ancient Israel and Judah* (Philadelphia: Westminster, 1986). For a further critique, see Dever, "Archaeology, Material Culture, and the Early Monarchical Period."

19. See L. R. Binford, ed., *For Theory-Building in Archaeology: Essays on Faunal Remains, Aquatic Resources, Spatial Analysis, and Systemic Modelling* (New York: Academic, 1977).

20. For an example of this naïveté, see, for instance (among the very *few* analyses of Israeli method and theory), E. Stern, "The Bible and Israeli Archaeology," *Archaeology and*

Both Middle Eastern and American archaeologists fail to understand that "theory" does not mean idle speculation (which our field has indeed seen too much of) but simply *a body of principles that guide research.* The purposes of theory-building are: (1) to make explicit and examine the presuppositions that are brought to research, whether consciously or not; (2) to define a discipline with respect to methods and objectives; (3) to establish a common ground for discussion within a discipline and for dialogue with other disciplines; and (4) to promote the health and advancement of a particular discipline and the branch of knowledge that it represents. I seriously doubt that archaeologists who resist theory really believe these goals are undesirable. And surely it is obvious that such goals will not be achieved automatically.

I contend that the unprofessional standards in "biblical" and Syro-Palestinian archaeology, the failure to keep pace with other branches of archaeology, the endless controversies, the isolation, and the failure to engage in productive dialogue with biblical and historical studies are *all* largely the result of a reluctance to confront basic questions of theory. Syro-Palestinian archaeology will "come of age" only when it addresses the issue of theory, the first consideration in developing an epistemology.[21]

Archaeological Reasoning

A second step in developing an epistemology is reflecting on the nature of the reasoning process of archaeology, as well as the reasoning process of history. It is evident that both disciplines employ critical methods to sift the evidence, whether artifactual or textual, in order to select data that can be judged useful in reconstructing the past. Whatever the principles employed in this initial sifting task, they should be made explicit.

Biblical scholars over the past century have indeed developed explicit methodologies,[22] but archaeologists are far behind. Often the assessment of excavated evidence is based on little more than intuition or on the competence of

---

Biblical Interpretation: Essays in Memory of D. Glenn Rose (ed. L. G. Perdue, L. E. Toombs, and G. L. Johnson; Atlanta: John Knox, 1987) 31–40.

21. See further, Dever, "Archaeology, Syro-Palestinian and Biblical," *The Anchor Bible Dictionary* (New York: Doubleday, 1992) 1.354–67.

22. See, for example, J. Van Seters, *In Search of History: Historiography in the Ancient World and the Origins of Biblical History* (New Haven: Yale University Press, 1983); B. Halpern, *The First Historians: The Hebrew Bible and History* (San Francisco: Harper & Row, 1988); T. L. Thompson, *The Origin Traditions of Ancient Israel* (Sheffield: Almond, 1989).

---

the excavator. Data of varying quality are categorized indiscriminately. Wide-ranging historical and cultural conclusions are drawn from the flimsiest of evidence or based on the cavalier citation of various "authorities." It is true, unfortunately, that archaeology today is so specialized and so esoteric that the nonspecialist (historian or biblical scholar, for instance) is at a loss to know whom or what to trust. For this reason, among others, Syro-Palestinian archaeologists need desperately to *develop a hermeneutic*, preferably one that takes into account a number of parallel methods of interpreting artifacts and texts, as pointed out by Hodder in *Reading the Past.*

One aspect shared by both biblical scholarship and archaeology is a dependence on *analogy* as a fundamental method of argument. It is possible to know the past only by making inferences from artifacts preserved from that past. Inferences, by definition, are observations (one might say "guesses") made by individuals who experience the present world. Only by using analogies—parallels thrown alongside—can one hope to illuminate these enigmatic relics. Without some point of contact, it is impossible to determine the use of objects from the past.[23] This is true of ancient texts as well as ancient objects, since translation is analogy, an attempt to render the images of the text into images familiar to the reader.

The challenge is to find *appropriate* analogues, those offering the most promise yet capable of being tested in some way. Ethnoarchaeology is useful in this regard, particularly in places where unsophisticated modern cultures are still found superimposed, as it were, upon the remains of the ancient world, as in parts of the Middle East.[24] Analogies drawn from life in modern Arab villages or Bedouin society can, with proper controls, be used to illuminate both artifacts and texts, as many studies have shown. What is more, postulates made in this way can be partially tested: those regarding social structure, by modern usage; those regarding individual objects, by replication (a device all too infrequently employed).

Conclusion

The *limitations* of inquiry into the meaning of both artifacts and texts must always be borne in mind by archaeologists, regardless of their method of in-

23. See further M. Salmon, *Philosophy and Archaeology* (New York: Academic, 1982).
24. See, for example, P. J. Watson, *Archaeological Ethnography in Western Iran* (Tucson: University of Arizona Press, 1979); C. Kramer, *Village Ethnoarchaeology: Rural Iran in Archaeological Perspective* (New York: Academic, 1982).

terpretation. It is no coincidence that Wright and de Vaux, leading scholars in Bible and archaeology, wrote articles near the end of their lives on both the capabilities and the limitations of archaeology.[25] All historians deal with possibilities, at best with probabilities, never with certainties. The degree of subjectivity can and should be reduced, but it can never be eliminated. It is possible to hone the tools of textual analysis and archaeology fieldwork to an ever-sharper edge, thus increasing the true data in quantity and quality, but the past will always remain partly elusive. As Hodder says, of his new "postprocessual" or "contextual" archaeology:

> It is characterized by debate and uncertainty about fundamental issues that may have been rarely questioned before in archaeology. It is more an asking of questions than a provision of answers.[26]

25. Thus R. de Vaux, "On Right and Wrong Uses of Archaeology," *Near Eastern Archaeology in the Twentieth Century: Essays in Honor of Nelson Glueck* (ed. J. Sanders; Garden City, N.Y.: Doubleday, 1970) 64–80; G. E. Wright, "What Archaeology Can and Cannot Do," *Biblical Archaeologist* 34 (1971) 70–75.

26. Hodder, *Reading the Past*, 170. Since this essay was completed, biblical scholars have produced several histories of ancient Israel, with significant implications for epistemology, including P. R. Davies, *In Search of "Ancient Israel"* (JSOTSup 148; Sheffield: JSOT Press, 1992); T. L. Thompson, *Early History of the Israelite People from the Written and Archaeological Sources* (Leiden: Brill, 1992); G. W. Ahlström, *The History of Ancient Palestine from the Palaeolithic Period to Alexander's Conquest* (JSOTSup 146; Sheffield: JSOT Press, 1993).

Demographic Aspects of the Problem of the Israelite Settlement

Ilan Sharon

చి.౿

Introduction

THIS WORK IS A DEDUCTIVE EXERCISE, designed to examine the problem of the transition between the Bronze and Iron Ages in Palestine from the viewpoint of *processual archaeology*. It will examine under several theoretical paradigms the role of various social and demographic variables and their interaction in causing cultural change. My contention is that each of the current theories regarding the settlement of the Israelites in Canaan can be expressed as a processual model with a unique configuration of identical variables. Processual models reveal the implicit view of the causes of social change upon which these theories are based. Furthermore, this paper presents a new theory using these same variables and a hitherto unused paleodemographic model.

The variables dealt with in this paper are *population growth*, the *resources* available in a given region, the *social organization* of the human community, and its *technology*. In the first section I show how these variables are thought to interact to cause cultural change in several prevalent social paradigms. In the next section I examine the theories proposed by Bible analysts, historians, and archaeologists to explain the origins of Israel and the conquest of Canaan by the Israelites in terms of the interaction of these variables. In the last section the same variables are restructured into yet another configuration according to a new paleodemographic model, and a theory conforming to this view is outlined.

Paradigms

While a direct connection between research into biblical history and paleo-demography cannot be argued, it is nevertheless true that all thinkers are influenced by the intellectual climate of their times. Major trends in social thought are reflected in both the social and historical sciences. In this section I wish to point out some of the social theories that provided the stimulus to both demographic theory and existing theories about the origin of the Israelites. This short essay is not, of course, an instant guide to social philosophy, and I deal only with those points affecting the four variables of interest to this study—population density, natural resources, technology, and social organization. These variables are factors in any theoretical discussion about the sociological history of Israel. For the purposes of this paper, the various theories can be divided into two categories: previous theories that have now fallen into disfavor and post-war theories.

The *Population Principle* formulated by Malthus[1] and promoted by neo-Malthusian population theories holds that the potential growth of human population always exceeds the carrying capacity of the territory in which it exists, and the rate of population growth is faster than the human possibility of bettering the carrying capacity through technological change. Therefore, any population will in time outgrow its food supply, and this will cause a crisis manifested in hunger, poverty, sickness, or war. These problems will in turn reduce the population again to a size below the carrying capacity of the region. Thus, the population principle sees the exploitation of natural resources in a given technological level as a limiting factor on population size and population density as a cause for the deterioration of social order.

Social Evolution[2] and Darwinism, with which it is intimately connected, see the Malthusian crisis as a primary cause for evolution. Spencer's basic unit is the society, often equated with a nation or an ethnic group. Demographic stress is relieved by a constant search for arable land and other resources. This in turn causes conflict between nations or ethnic groups. The solution to nations' "Malthusian dilemma" is war, in which the weaker nation is conquered or annihilated. Nevertheless, population pressure is the pri-

1. T. R. Malthus, *An Essay on the Principle of Population* (London: J. Johnson, 1798); rept. in E. A. Wrigley and D. Souden, eds., *The Works of Thomas Robert Malthus* (London: William Pickering) vol. 1.

2. H. Spencer, *Principles of Sociology* (London: Williams & Norgate, 1876–1896) vols. 1–3.

mary cause for human progress. The principle of survival of the fittest describes the fact that more advanced peoples will eradicate less advanced peoples or at least impose their culture over them, thus advancing human culture as a whole.

Like Spencer, Marx, the principal founder of *Dialectical Materialism*, saw conflict as a primary tool in shaping social structure.[3] The difference between the two paradigms lies in the definition of the basic social unit. Marx saw the nation as an artificial construct. It is the conflict between classes over the control of the means of production that causes social change. Marxist theory refuses to accept the principle of Malthusian "demographic pressure." Population growth is not seen as an independent variable that necessarily leads to poverty and hunger. It can be controlled in society by a wide variety of methods, most of which have been known and available since ancient times. Their use or lack of use is dictated by law, social norms, and ideology. Poverty and hunger, according to Marxist thought, do not "happen" but are caused by these classes within society who create social laws and norms.

Current Paleodemographic Theories

The social evolutionary approach dominated the historical view of the nineteenth century and the first half of the twentieth, perhaps because it provided an ideological background both to European nationalism and to Western imperialism. Imperialism and the fact that some of the approach's manifestations smack more than a little of racism are also the cause for this theory's rapid fall from favor after the world wars. It still exerts great influence over our thinking today, however, owing to the fact that most of us implicitly view human history as an evolutionary process.

In the post-war years, historians and archaeologists started to consider paleodemography as an independent field of study. It has formulated several theories positing causative connections between population size and cultural change.

Thus far, technological change has not been considered as an independent factor in this discussion. Technological innovation is seen by Childe as the cause for social change.[4] He sees "invention" of agriculture as the cause for the "Neolithic Revolution" and the creation of surplus by the improvement of agricultural technology as the trigger for "Urban Revolution." Childe's theories

3. F. L. Bender, *Karl Marx: The Essential Writings* (Boulder: Westview, 1986) 159–208.
4. V. G. Childe, *What Happened in History* (Harmondsworth: Penguin, 1964) 55–57, 97–102.

combine a belief in unilinear evolution (a result of man's never-ending search for means to better his control over his environment) and Marxist determinism.[5] Progress is effected through intragroup economic pressure (rather than interethnic strife). Technological improvement leads, in his opinion, to a new social/spatial organization. This is manifested first and foremost by an increase in population.

The ecological determinism which led, in Childe's opinion, to the "invention" of agriculture is no longer usually accepted.[6] Of the theories that attempted to correct this lapse, it is only necessary to mention Binford and Flannery's marginal zone hypothesis,[7] which proposes that the impulse to investigate new technologies is manifested in zones where conditions for subsistence are less than optimal. Demographic pressure in the optimal zones pushes population to the marginal zones around it. Necessity leads to technological advancement,[8] and this in turn necessitates changes in social organization.

Boserup's thesis again sees population growth as the cause and social and technological change as effects.[9] She asserts that the knowledge of the existence of new technologies does not necessarily imply their use. Demographic pressure forces society to adopt a more intensive economy in one (or both) of two ways:

1. Technological change: usually the adoption of previously known, but economically less feasible technologies.
2. Social reorganization: usually one which necessitates more investment on behalf of each participant.

These new modes of production become "profitable" only when traditional methods can no longer satisfy society's needs. Under the new system the "carrying capacity" of the region is enhanced, but as a rule it is less congenial to each individual.

---

5. B. G. Trigger, "The Role of Technology in Gordon Childe's Archaeology," *Norwegian Archaeological Review* 19 (1986) 1–14.

6. L. R. Binford, "Post Pliestocene Adaptation," in *New Perspectives in Archaeology* (ed. L. R. Binford and S. Binford; Chicago: Aldine, 1968) 319–21.

7. Ibid., 332–35; K. V. Flannery, "Origins and Ecological Effects of Early Domestication in Iran and the Near East," in *The Domestication and Exploitation of Plants and Animals* (ed. P. J. Ucko and G. W. Dimbleby; London: Duckworth, 1969) 80–81.

8. For a similar idea, see the next paragraph.

9. E. Boserup, *The Conditions of Agricultural Growth* (London: Allen & Unwin, 1965); *Population and Technological Change* (Chicago: University of Chicago Press, 1981).

Current Theories of the Settlement of the Israelites in Canaan

The problem of the settlement of the Israelites in Canaan and the various schools of thought regarding it have been extensively dealt with elsewhere.[10] In this section it is helpful to define the problem in terms of the four variables listed above.

The facts on which there seems to be general agreement are these: In the thirteenth/twelfth centuries B.C.E., Palestine underwent a crisis manifested by a decline in urban culture; the appearance of many small settlements, usually in previously unpopulated regions; and a comprehensive change in material culture. The new culture underwent a process of reurbanization in the eleventh/tenth century, resulting in the crystallizing of a new national entity known by the name Israel. Israel's tradition (albeit written down only several centuries later and transmitted to us after editing and revision) sees its own origin as a process of conquest by tribes of nomads coming from the desert and their settlement in place of the urban Canaanite culture. The same crisis led to the formation of other geopolitical units in Syria–Palestine in the first millennium, such as Edom, Moab, Ammon, Aram, and Philistia. The process of the creation of these units was similar, though there were distinct factors in the formation of each.

From this point on, however, opinion diverges. It is common to group the various theories under three headings:

The *Conquest* theories adhere closely to the biblical narration. They see first a concerted attack of desert nomads on the established Canaanite urban centers, causing the military collapse of Canaanite culture within a short time (no more than about a generation). This initial attack was followed by a longer period of settlement and consolidation, characterized by seminomad habitation. Reurbanization followed the formation of the Israelite monarchic state.

Settlement theories reverse the above order: they see first the infiltration of desert nomads into uninhabited regions between the major Canaanite urban centers. A long period of cohabitation ensued. Local strife may have led to the early demise of some of the lesser Canaanite centers, but on the whole the downfall of the Canaanite culture was a lengthy process, and the conquest of the major centers took place closer to its end.

The *Revolution* theorists argue that the basic process was not one of transhumance. Rather, it was a social change in which the peasants within Canaanite society rid themselves of the ruling classes, forming an egalitarian society.

10. For a recent view, including a full bibliography, see I. Finkelstein, *The Archaeology of the Israelite Settlement* (Jerusalem: Israel Exploration Society, 1988) 295–314.

Ilan Sharon

Israelite Settlement as a Process of Demographic Change

Viewed in the context of demographic theory, the relevant question is not
the ethnic identity of one group or the other, nor is it the reason that a certain group became dominant after the turn of the millennium. The relevant
question is, what caused the collapse of the political and economic system in
Canaan at the end of the Bronze Age?[11] In the next section I examine the
three current schools of thought, with this question in mind.

The *Conquest* hypothesis is a typical Spencerian theory. Motivated by hunger for land and pushed by still more savage tribes from behind, the tribes of
Israel invaded Canaan. The military conflict between these two ethnic units
ended in the annihilation of the Canaanites and the settlement of the Israelites in their stead.[12] The "justification" for the decimation of the Canaanites
is also typically Spencerian:

> From the impartial standpoint of a philosopher of history, it often seems necessary
> that a people of markedly inferior type should vanish before a people of superior po-
> tentialities, since there is a point beyond which racial mixture cannot go without
> disaster ... Thus the Canaanites, with their orgiastic nature worship, their cult of
> fertility ... and sensuous nudity, and their gross mythology, were replaced by Israel,
> with its pastoral simplicity and purity of life, its lofty Monotheism, and its severe
> code of ethics.[13]

The *Revolution* hypothesis is a straightforward Marxist theory, down to the
use of the usual jargon.

> Israel's dawning self-ascription as a people took place ... where peasants and other
> producers and providers of services struggled to take command of the agrarian
> means of production.[14]

---

11. For a similar approach, see A. B. Knapp, "Complexity and Collapse in the North
Jordan Valley," *IEJ* 39 (1989) 129–48; idem, "Response: Independence, Imperialism, and
the Egyptian Factor," *BASOR* 273 (1989) 64–68.

12. See, e.g., B. Mazar, *The World History of the Jewish People: Judges* (Tel Aviv: Mas-
sada, 1971) 79–93.

13. W. F. Albright, *From the Stone Age to Christianity* (Baltimore: Johns Hopkins University Press, 1940) 214.

14. N. K. Gottwald, "The Israelite Settlement as a Social Revolutionary Movement,"
*Biblical Archaeology Today: Proceedings of the International Congress on Biblical Archaeology,
Jerusalem, April 1984* (ed. Avraham Biran et al.; Jerusalem: Israel Exploration Society,
1985) 34–46.

Perhaps the hardest to pigeonhole is the *Settlement* hypothesis. Some of Aharoni's later writings seem to depend on a conceptual model similar to that of V. G. Childe, though this dependency is never quite made explicit.[15] Put in different terminology, such a model might look like this: The adoption of several new technologies (plastered cisterns, hill terracing, deforestation) caused the sedentariness of the population in marginal zones that once supported only a nomadic population. The increase in the "carrying capacity" of such zones resulted in population growth (through immigration of yet more desert nomads), which in time provided opportunity for the Israelites to challenge the Canaanite centers in the plains. The development of new technologies by the hill dwellers rather than by the Canaanite inhabitants of the optimal zones can be explained by the marginal zone hypothesis. The difference between the settlement theory and Childe's model is that in Aharoni's model the "Israelite revolution" is seen basically as a process of displacement of one ethnic group by another. Furthermore, following Childe's attempt to explain away the initial impulse that pushed the Israelites into Canaan's hill regions, Aharoni invoked an old Spencerian gambit—pressure by desert tribes and "land hunger."[16]

Several attempts have been made in recent years to combine the "settlement" and "revolution" hypotheses. Two of these deserve special notice. Finkelstein sees the origin of the new population in the mixing of nomadic groups infiltrating from the east with vagrant elements of the urban Canaanite society. Most of the Israelite population, in his opinion, has its origin in a pastoralist Canaanite subculture that inhabited the central highlands and desert fringes after the end of the Middle Bronze Age. He also stresses natural population growth as a factor aiding the consolidation of the new population. Finkelstein rejects the role of new technologies in the settlement process (see below) but does not offer an alternate causative connection between the different processes taking place at the time.[17]

Callaway develops the settlement theory in the opposite direction.[18] He accepts technological innovation as the cause of the settlement process, but sees this process as an internal development and not as the result of immigration of a foreign ethnic element. In historical terminology, therefore, his

15. Y. Aharoni, *The Archaeology of the Land of Israel* (Philadelphia: Westminster, 1982) 157–62.

16. Ibid., 150, 157–58, 167.

17. Finkelstein, *Archaeology of the Israelite Settlement*, 348.

18. J. A. Callaway, "A New Perspective on the Hill Country Settlement of Canaan in the Iron Age I," *Palestine in the Bronze and Iron Ages: Papers in Honour of Olga Tufnell* (ed. J. N. Tubb; London: Institute of Archaeology, 1985) 40–43.

model should be classified as a "revolution" model. In paleodemographic terms Callaway's model is virtually identical with Childe's paradigm. Stager's three articles in sum propose a similar view.[19]

A Boserupian Model of the Israelite Settlement

In this review of current paleodemographic theories, the only one missing in the discussion of the phenomenon of the Israelite settlement in Canaan is Boserup's thesis. At this point, therefore, it is useful to attempt to construct a model based on her views. To build this model, I use the following assertions:

1. Tribal subsocieties were a permanent phenomenon on the outskirts of Canaanite society.[20] They formed part of the Canaanite economic system and maintained a symbiotic relationship with it. Therefore, they had no discrete material culture.
2. The Late Bronze Age was characterized by a marked fall in the total population in Palestine. This decrease has become evident in all the surveys of all regions of the country.[21] The earlier view of the Late Bronze Age as the apex of Canaanite culture is a good example of the way marginal data of high salience (the existence of a few pieces of fine art or international trade in luxury items) can skew the archaeological picture when it is viewed nonquantitatively.
3. The beginning of the Iron Age was characterized, among other things, by the reversal of this cultural trend and accelerated population growth.[22]

19. L. E. Stager, "The Archaeology of the Family in Ancient Israel," *BASOR* 260 (1985) 1–35; "Merenptah, Israel, and the Sea Peoples," *Avigad Volume* (*Eretz-Israel* 18; Jerusalem: Israel Exploration Society, 1985) 56–64 [Eng.]; " 'Response' to 'Archaeology, History and the Bible—The Israelite Settlement in Canaan': A Case Study," in *Biblical Archaeology Today: Proceedings of the International Congress on Biblical Archaeology, Jerusalem, April 1984* (ed. Avraham Biran et al.; Jerusalem: Israel Exploration Society, 1985) 83–86.

20. Finkelstein, *Archaeology of the Israelite Settlement*, 342–43.

21. R. Gonen, "Urban Canaan in the Late Bronze Period," *BASOR* 253 (1984) 61–73; Y. Portugali, "Theories of Population and Urbanization, and Their Importance for Demographic Research," *Sites, Population and Economy in Ancient Israel* (ed. M. Kochavi, A. Kasher, and S. Bonimovitch; Tel Aviv: Tel Aviv University, 1988 [Heb.]; A. Zertal, "Following the Pottery Trail—Israel Enters Canaan," *BAR* 17/5 (1991) 32–33; Finkelstein, *Archaeology of the Israelite Settlement*, 185–87; A. B. Knapp, "Complexity and Collapse in the Jordan Valley," *IEJ* 39 (1989) 141–45.

22. Finkelstein, *Archaeology of the Israelite Settlement*, 185–87.

The problem I find with both the "conquest" and the "settlement" theories is that there is no archaeological evidence for the existence of nomadic populations in the deserts around Palestine in the Late Bronze Age. Taking into consideration the nomadic campsites found by modern archaeologists from other periods, and given the present state of knowledge of these regions (at least in the Negev, the Sinai, and the Jordanian highlands), I must reject the possibility that "phantom pastoralist" populations[23] of any considerable size did exist in those deserts during that time but have evaded detection. The glaring defect in both these hypotheses is the lack of a pool of manpower to supply an invasion, much less a situation of demographic pressure to motivate one. Finkelstein's suggestion that such a pool be sought in the central hill country has to be rejected on the same grounds.[24] He correctly points out some indications (the existence of cemeteries far from any known urban sites) of the existence of a few nonsedentary people in these regions in the Late Bronze Age, but the estimate that fully one-half of the Canaanite population of these regions were tent-dwelling pastoralists, though none of their sites has been located, is not acceptable. I admit that such a population existed (see above) but maintain that it was very small.

One may find prototypes within the Late Bronze Age culture for almost anything also found later in the Early Iron Age. These prototypes cannot be found in other cultures, and, therefore, the idea of a foreign origin for the Israelite culture is unprovable. What characterizes the Israelites is not a discrete style but restricted borrowing from the Canaanite culture, combined with different settlement and intrasite organization patterns.[25]

Differences within this "pioneering" regional culture of the Late Bronze and Early Iron Ages cannot be categorized according to ethnic distinctives. Some societies that are reasonably identified as Israelite used the famous "collared-rim jars" and some did not. On the other hand, these same jars were found in sites more reasonably identified with other ethnic groups.[26] From this information it can be seen that this material culture does not characterize "a people" in the ethnic sense, but a certain way of life.

The technologies attributed to the Israelite culture were not novel. The existence of various plastered pits before the Iron Age has been documented,

23. Stager, "Archaeology of the Family."

24. Finkelstein, *Archaeology of the Israelite Settlement*, 342–44.

25. A. Mazar, "The Israelite Settlement in Canaan in the Light of Archaeological Excavation," *Biblical Archaeology Today: Proceedings of the International Congress on Biblical Archaeology, Jerusalem, April 1984* (ed. Avraham Biran et al.; Jerusalem: Israel Exploration Society, 1985) 64–69.

26. Ibid., 68–69.

and there is no doubt that the Canaanites possessed the knowledge needed to deforest or terrace the hills had they wanted to do so.[27] Be that as it may, it is farfetched to assume that hill-country terrace agriculture was superior to traditional Canaanite valley cultivation. On the contrary, all the extra effort involved in deforestation, hewing of cisterns and building of dams and terraces must make it more expensive in terms of exertion per unit of crop. This line of argumentation puts one in mind of Binford's and others' criticism of Childe's model (see p. 122 above).[28]

There is one important way in which Boserup's model is different from other theories of social change. Unlike most other theories of human history, Boserup does not see social and technological change as an evolutionary process. Spencer sees the fountainhead for human evolution in man's quest for resources, Marx attributes it to his quest to control means of production, while Childe views it as man's quest for technology. They all share a belief that humanity is progressing. However, all of these theories fail to explain regressional episodes in human history, and the collapse of one second millennium civilization in the eastern Mediterranean is an example of just such a regression. Boserup, on the other hand, sees man's social organization and technology merely as a response to ecological or demographic pressure. "Progress," according to Boserup, is not necessarily unidirectional. Population growth will make an intensive technology and social organization more efficient (though more labor-consuming). By the same logic, a decrease in population below a given level may cause a more extensive economic base (for example, pastoralism augmented by fallow crops) and a simpler (tribal) social organization to be *more efficient* than a market economy and an urban-stratified social organization.

A New Model of Israelite Settlement

Accepting this explanation or a similar one (e.g., Finkelstein's)[29] for the apparent regression of the economy and social organization at the beginning of the Iron Age still leaves a large degree of freedom for defining the mechanics of the Late Bronze Age collapse.

One might argue that the progressively inefficient Canaanite economic system was further irritated by military weakness, which resulted in the Canaan-

27. Finkelstein, *Archaeology of the Israelite Settlement*, 309.
28. Binford, "Post Pliestocene Adaptation," 326–28.
29. Finkelstein, *Archaeology of the Israelite Settlement*, 309.

ite civilization falling prey to leaner, more efficient societies. On the other hand, it is possible to postulate a situation of proletarian revolution against the nonproductive classes that had become redundant in the new economic reality. Such hypotheses lead us back to the "invasion" and "revolution" theories, neither of which explains the main archaeological phenomenon, which is that the finds are not indicative of an "Israelite" takeover of the Canaanite means of production, but of the creation of an alternative production system. This leads me to the next step in developing my own model, which at this point becomes more speculative, since I must now formulate several new working hypotheses:

1. To review, the urban Canaanite society in the Late Bronze Age had a negative demographic balance. A decrease in population enables a society to raise the standard of living without technological advancement or a change in social organization—by discontinuing the use of zones in which the per capita yield is less than that the society considers a minimal standard of living.[30] In this way a society is enabled, in a perverse way, to solve its demographic problems, the result of which is a social equilibrium. One would not then expect revolutionary pressures to develop.

2. The main logical drawback in any "social regression" theory, however, is that one would not expect a society to dissolve its institutions willingly. This is especially true if such actions will lower the average standard of living, as indeed seems to have happened in this case.

3. The last hypothesis needed to draw upon, already mentioned above, is that the rate of population growth can be controlled by society through abstinence (at least by some women during part of their reproductive age), various methods of prophylaxis, abortion, and infanticide. These were in the past often dictated by societal norms, such as the age of marriage, inheritance laws, and use of child labor.[31]

Based on these hypotheses, I contend that the probable kernel around which the new Israelite life-style crystallized was traditional tribal semi-nomadism subsistence in subsocieties on the outskirts of Canaanite civilization. The main driving force of this "revolution" was a differential population growth rate.

Such a society would have been the first to suffer when market economy became restricted due to a reduction in buying power. On the other hand,

30. A. B. Knapp, "Response," 65.
31. F. A. Hassan, *Demographic Archaeology* (New York: Academic Press, 1981) 143–60.

the price it would have had to pay in order to dissolve its dependence on the urban society by lowering the living standards or changing social structure is minimal. It is interesting to theorize how such a society would react when it discovered that economic independence, or even active competition, was a more efficient strategy then the traditional symbiosis.

The first effect would be a change in demographic growth rates. Economic dependence upon an urban community means that the total production of the dependent subsociety is limited by the urban market's demand for its produce. The size of this market therefore imposes an upper limit on demographic growth in the marginal societies. Economic independence would mean that such a society could grow to the limit of the carrying capacity of the region upon which it lives.

A further effect may be a change in the subsistence pattern. The nature of the dependence of the nomad or seminomad on urban society is the exchange of agricultural surplus for supplemental food products and manufactured consumer durables.[32] The demand for agricultural products would be intensified due to population growth, leading to increased sedentization. Cessation of trade with the urban centers, plus increased population, would create a demand for self-manufactured goods, while sedentization offers the opportunity for craftsmen to become full-time providers. The formerly agricultural, nomad society begins to produce manufactured goods, and at this point it becomes archaeologically visible as a distinct material culture.

At this point two communities would exist, sharing the same region. One has a negative demographic balance and is hampered by nonproductive classes. Its social organization compels it to organize itself into large urban aggregates, and it seeks to maintain (or even raise) its high standard of living. These characteristics cause a negative feedback that is "solved" by cutting back the population even further. The other community is growing at maximum rate. A more efficient (under the circumstances) social organization, successful experimentation with new technologies, an austere standard of living—all cause a positive feedback cycle, which encourages further increase of the population. The "carrying capacity" of the same region is defined differently by the two populations living upon it. One thrives and increases under conditions that are less than minimal for another.

It is now necessary to determine whether it is possible that the principle of natural increase can account for the "formation" of the Israelite nation. Several independent assessments estimate that the population of Israel on the eve

---

32. A. M. Khazanov, *Nomads and the Outside World* (Cambridge: Cambridge University Press, 1984) 198–227.

---

of the monarchy was approximately 50,000 people.[33] Assuming that, on the average, every adult woman had three children who reached adulthood (this is within the realm of possibility, as ascertained by ethnographic corollaries)[34] and that half of these are (productive) females, a growth rate of 1.5 per generation can be postulated. At this rate, the population would more than double every two generations. In eight generations (the Iron I Period—from the collapse of Late Bronze Age civilization to the beginning of the monarchy is approximately 200 years) an initial population of 2,000 could grow to 50,000. A growth rate of 1.5 is indeed exceptionally high. However, allowing that all along this process, assimilation of Canaanites into the Israelite society and some immigration of seminomads from surrounding regions did take place, the 1.5 growth rate per generation can actually be lowered.

Next, one must consider whether a mere change in relative productivity is capable of causing such momentous cultural and political upheavals as are posited above. It might be instructive to point out, at this juncture, that recent research indicates that the "population explosion" that ushered in the industrial revolution in the mid-eighteenth century was due, not to a drop in mortality[35] (that did not dramatically change until the middle of the nineteenth century), but to an increase in relative productivity, brought about by a lowering of the average age of marriage for women and a decrease in the number of spinsters and unmarried widows. These norm changes were, in turn, due to economic prosperity and (as industry developed) the efficiency of child labor as a supplementary source of income.[36]

The relations between emerging Israelite culture and the entrenched Canaanites would, under this model, be ambivalent. On the one hand because of economic independence, the Israelites would not have abstained from sacking a Canaanite city or at least seizing its agricultural hinterlands, should the opportunity arise. On the other hand, the fact that these two societies exploited two different ecological "niches" meant that a general confrontation was not inevitable until the end of the process. The violent confrontation with the Canaanites, the destruction of the major centers, and the occupation of the bulk of Canaanite territory probably took place at the same time as the urbanization of the Israelites themselves, the disintegration of their tribal structure, and the beginning of their monarchy. These processes,

---

33. Finkelstein, *Archaeology of the Israelite Settlement*, 332–33; Stager, "Response," 84.

34. Hassan, *Demographic Archaeology*, table 6.8.

35. L. Clarkson, *Death, Disease, and Faminine in Pre-Industrial England* (Dublin: Gill and MacMillan, 1975) 171.

36. G. E. Mingay, *A Social History of the English Countryside* (New York: Routledge, 1990).

interesting both from the point of view of biblical history and of processual archaeology, have not received due attention from scholars. They are, however, outside the scope of this work.

Textual Support

This work has presented the archaeological perspective on the economics of early Israelite settlement patterns. The question now to be entertained is whether the biblical text can support such hypotheses. Although the realm of biblical analysis lies outside my expertise, I wish to point out here the general lines along which defense of my model might be established. It is useful to classify the biblical stories dealing with the origins of Israel:

1. Stories in which communities of seminomads (tent-dwellers) live alongside urban Canaanite society (the narratives of the Patriarchs).
2. Stories of the sojourn in Egypt.
3. Stories of nomads roaming the deserts of Sinai, Negev, and Transjordan (Exodus stories).
4. Stories of wars against the Canaanites (Joshua).
5. Stories of a tribal society inhabiting the highlands of Palestine (Judges).

The invasion theorists claim that, barring minor deviations, the narrative order above reflects the chronological order of events. The settlement theorists argue that the stories are ordered according to editorial convenience, rather than chronologically. While they would agree that the stories of nomads roaming the deserts precede the stories of wars against the Canaanites and stories of inhabiting Palestine, they would posit a temporal overlap between the war stories and the inhabiting stories. In fact, they see the beginning of the inhabitation-of-Canaan stories as actually preceding the war stories.

The model proposed here places the stories of the cohabitation of the seminomads and urban Canaanites (1), the desert sagas (3), the war stories (4), and the inhabiting-the-land stories (5) in positions contemporary to each other. But I would define the first category as more of a reflection of the beginning part of the process and the last two (and especially no. 4) as a reflection of the latter part of the process.

Summary

The model I have proposed in this paper posits two parallel demographic processes that caused the collapse of the Canaanite social system and the consolidation of Israelite culture.

(1) The Canaanite society was in the process of demographic decrease. Such decrease erodes the efficiency of both the urban stratified civilization and the tribal egalitarian society dependent on it. The collapse proceeds from the edges inward as marginal societies find that it is more attractive to disengage themselves from the central economy and develop an alternative production system (and hence material culture).

(2) Independence from the urban economy results in demographic growth in the new culture. The Israelites exploited territories that the Canaanites gave up as underproductive and experimented with technologies that the Canaanites did not utilize because they were too labor-intensive.

These two processes—the gradual collapse of the Canaanite system as marginal societies drifted over to the Israelite camp and the rapid natural reproduction of the Israelites—went on for approximately 200 years, at which time the Israelites reached a demographic (and military) superiority.

Obviously, this model is rather simplistic, if only because it attempts to explain a complex phenomenon in terms of a limited number of variables. It does not, for instance, explain the coincidence of the Canaanite collapse with the collapse of the Aegean and Anatolian civilizations.[37] Nor does this theory explain what triggered the Canaanite demographic decrease. It has been suggested that it was the increasing demands of the Egyptian overlords[38] or internal strife within Canaanite society.[39] It should be noted, however, that a single occurrence of war or pestilence, catastrophic as it must seem in itself, has much smaller effect on long-range demographic trends than even moderate changes in the reproduction rate over a long period.[40]

Perhaps Knapp's suggestion that this was because the Egyptian overlords sapped most surplus, thereby reducing the incentive to produce, and that dependence upon central authority eroded the healthy competition between Canaanite city-states is a better explanation for this phenomenon.[41]

The advantage of this model is that it explains the transition between the Canaanite and Israelite cultures without requiring the infusion of a group of people from an unknown source or theorizing about pressure that pushed nomads from the desert into the Palestinian heartlands. In terms of types of

37. The only theory that offers an explanation of this point is the Spencerian *Conquest* theory, which sees a "Domino effect," whereby the pressure of one ethnic group displaces another, forcing it to conquer the homeland of a third, etc.

38. Gonen, "Urban Canaan," 70.

39. Finkelstein, *Archaeology of the Israelite Settlement*, 342.

40. J. D. Durand, "The Viewpoint of Historical Demography," *Population Growth: Anthropological Implications* (ed. B. Spooner; Cambridge: MIT Press, 1972) 370.

41. Knapp, "Complexity and Collapse," 142–45.

theory, mine falls somewhere between the "settlement" and "revolution" schools, perhaps in close proximity to Finkelstein's model[42] on the side of "settlement" and close to the model proposed by Stager[43] on the "revolutionary" side.

In sum, I do not claim to possess the single key to understanding the origin of Israel. Nor do I claim that the model proposed here is necessarily better in all aspects than earlier proposals. The purpose of these remarks is to stress the fact that, inasmuch as the transition from the Late Bronze Age to the Iron Age in Palestine was accompanied by a process of social change, any theory about the nature of this transition implicitly embodies a conceptual model of what causes societies to change. It is fundamental that any theory must explicitly state its controlling models; that understanding of a problem of cultural change is advanced by defining it in terms of social theory; that causal variables ought to be identified; and that cultural change can then be explained by methods of social research.

42. Finkelstein, *Archaeology of the Israelite Settlement*, 336–51.
43. Stager, "The Archaeology of the Family"; "Merenptah, Israel, and the Sea Peoples"; and "Response."

Notes on the Development of Stamp-Glyptic Art in Palestine during the Assyrian and Persian Periods

E. Stern

❧•☙

D URING THE EXCAVATION of Area B1 at Tel Dor, Israel, directed by H. Neil Richardson, a unique find was uncovered: an imported Assyrian Cylinder Seal made of red granite. The seal is 26 mm. long and has a diameter of 13 mm. A hole 3 mm. in diameter pierces it from side to side. It depicts the King of Assyria struggling with two monsters (fig. 1). Some time later another stamp made of glass and a few coins displaying the same motif but belonging to the later Persian Period were found in other areas at Tel Dor (fig. 7).

In the following discussion I attempt to sum up the history and development of these stamps and others, as well as their significance in understanding the cultural changes that occurred in Palestine during these periods.

Introduction

The conquest of Palestine by the Assyrian armies from 733 B.C.E. to the end of the century opened, for the first time in the history of Palestine, a new era of direct influence from Mesopotamian culture. It is due to this conquest that so much Assyrian influence is evident in the cultural finds: in architecture,

---

Author's note: This paper is dedicated to the memory of H. Neil Richardson, a distinguished scholar, a colleague, and a friend, who for eight years directed the Richdor group in the excavation of Tel Dor.

burial customs, cult objects, pottery vases, and glyptic art.[1] It is clear that this influence had already begun as the result of direct import of items, but during the eighty or so years of Assyrian rule in the country, Assyrian culture was adopted by the Israelites, who also adapted it to their own tastes. When Palestine was later conquered by other Mesopotamian empires, namely Babylon and Persia, this tendency to assimilate increased, and we may confidently assume that during the entire period, which continued for about 400 years (730–330 B.C.), the country was under continuous homogenous cultural influence.

I have recently analyzed the penetration of Mesopotamian burial customs into Palestine during the Assyrian Period, continuing into the Babylonian and Persian Periods.[2] In a separate study I intend to deal with Assyrian "palace-ware," its appearance in the country, and its continued use into the Babylonian and Persian Periods. In this study I concentrate on the art of Assyrian stamp-glyptics as represented in the Palestinian finds within these three periods, its continuity during this era, and its influence on the style of stamps and coins of the time. This study is limited in three ways: (a) only a few typical examples out of all of the finds of this type in Palestine will be used as illustrations; (b) only a few common motifs among many are analyzed; and (c) the discussion is confined to style of motif, leaving the analysis of cultic meaning for another paper.

The Hero Struggling with Two Monsters

The first motif to be dealt with is that of the hero (a king or perhaps a mythological figure) struggling with two monsters. This motif was already well known in Mesopotamian glyptic in the earliest periods. It was derived from the Gilgamesh Epic, where he is depicted grasping two monsters, and arrived in Palestine with the Assyrian conquest. The best known Assyrian example is the cylinder seal discovered in Richardson's area at Tel Dor (fig. 1). The stamp was found in a locus with other finds that included an "Assyrian"

1. See E. Stern, "Israel at the Close of the Period of the Monarchy: An Archaeological Survey," *BA* 38 (1975) 26–54; R. Amiran and I. Dunayevsky, "The Assyrian Open-Court Building and Its Palestinian Derivatives," *BASOR* 149 (1958) 25–32.

2. E. Stern, "Achaemenian Tombs from Shechem," *Levant* 12 (1980) 90–111. Since the publication of this article, more Assyrian-type clay coffins have been uncovered, some in Jerusalem in the excavations of Ketef Hinnom (see G. Barkay display, "Ketef Hinnom Facing Jerusalem's Walls," in the Israel Museum, 1986, and other coffins from Tell El Mazar in Jordan). Also see K. Yassine, *Tell El Mazar I: Cemetery A* (Amman: University of Jordan, 1984).

pottery vase as well as other pottery vessels of the time.[3] It depicts a bearded man in Assyrian dress struggling with two gryphons standing on each side. The gryphons have the shape of horned and winged bulls(?). As is typical, the area between the three figures is filled with fire altars and a pair of fish facing each other at the feet of the king and the gryphons. On both sides of the scene, a schematic branch was added in order to form a border. Another stamp, executed in a similar method but from a later stage, the end of the Babylonian Period or the beginning of the Persian (sixth century B.C.E.), was discovered at Jericho.[4] From the small drawing published in the final report, it is hard to study the details, but it appears that the animals on both sides of the hero are of different types, though both are winged.

While the seals of the Assyrian and Babylonian Periods are still uncommon, this motif became very popular during the later part of the Persian Period, undoubtedly because it was used continually by the empire's officials themselves. The examples that follow were collected from quite a large number of seals and may be classified by shape, origin, and material.

Type A

Some of the local seals (both cylinder and stamp) are almost identical in shape to those discovered in Iran or the major urban centers of the empire. The type of stone used to manufacture the seals is not local; the stamps are of chalcedony, cornelian, agate, jasper, or other minerals not common to this area. I have chosen two examples of this type: one cylinder seal and one stamp seal. The cylinder seal was discovered at Tel el Ḥeir[5] and depicts the king wearing the *kidaris* (the royal crown), holding two winged lions by their necks. The lions are standing upright on one hind leg, kicking the king with the other hind leg (fig. 2). The second is a stamp seal made of agate, discovered by R. A. S. Macalister at Gezer at the beginning of the twentieth century in one of the tombs that he labeled Philistine but which actually should

3. The seal's number is 28029. It was found in Locus no. 2815 in Area B1; A. Gilboa, "The Assyrian Pottery of Tel Dor," an unpublished M.A. Thesis presented to the Institute of Archaeology of the Hebrew University, Jerusalem, 1992.

4. K. M. Kenyon and T. A. Holland, *Excavations at Jericho, vol. 4: The Pottery Type Series and Other Finds* (London: British School of Archaeology in Jerusalem, 1982) 557, fig. 226:7; 558, fig. 201; and cf. analogies there.

5. E. Oren, "Migdol: A New Fortress on the Edge of the Eastern Nile Delta," *BASOR* 256 (1984) 7–44.

be dated to the Persian Period.[6] The agate seal, which was imported from Mesopotamia, depicts the Persian king holding the horns of two standing, winged sphinxes. The king himself is standing on a gryphon, and above him is the emblem of the winged sun-disc in its Assyrian-Persian version (fig. 4).

Another variation of type A (fig. 3) was published by N. Avigad, who describes this stamp as follows:

> The central scene represents a Persian king in combat with two roaring lions, each of which is standing upright on one of its hind legs and kicking with the other. The king wears the billowy Persian garments and is standing on a couchant animal, probably an antelope. Above the scene is represented the winged sun of the Assyrian type, and on the very top, at the edge of the seal, are incised the three 'Pmn', i.e., the name of the seal owner.

Avigad dates the seal to the fifth century B.C.E.[7]

Seal-impressions depicting upright, roaring lions from the Persian Period were also found in Judea at Ramat Raḥel and Gibeon.[8] Originally I considered them to be part of another Assyro-Persian motif, that of the king shooting lions with bow and arrows. After further thought, I have decided that they should probably be classified as belonging to our type A.

Type B

This version of the first motif is known to us mainly from three bullae dating to the fourth century B.C.E. discovered in a cave at Wadi ed-Daliyeh in Samaria to which the citizens of a nearby town had fled in 332 B.C.E. The three seals are identical and are described by F. M. Cross as follows: "The King or hero wearing the 'Kidaris' and Persian dress holds in either hand at arm's length a twisting animal upside down. On the right is a lion; the animal on the left seems also to be a lion" (fig. 5). The scene, which is slightly different from type A, which depicts a hero struggling with two monsters, is also well known among the Achaemenian seal repertoire at Persepolis. In the Wadi ed-Daliyeh cave, a few bullae depicting similar scenes were found attached to a

6. R. A. S. Macalister, *The Excavation of Gezer* (2 vols.; London: John Murray, 1911) 1.292, fig. 153. The seal was found in grave no. 2 of the "Philistine graves," which was also the richest in objects. In the same grave, a cylinder seal was found, which, according to Macalister, had "a conventional Assyrian pattern." Unfortunately, this seal disappeared before being photographed or drawn. The "Philistine graves" are from the Persian Period, as is well known.

7. N. Avigad, "Three Ornamented Hebrew Seals," *IEJ* 4 (1954) 236–37, pl. 21:B:3.

8. See E. Stern, "Seal Impressions in the Achaemenid Style in the Province of Judah," *BASOR* 202 (1971) 6–16.

Fig. 1.

Fig. 2.

Fig. 3.

Fig. 4.

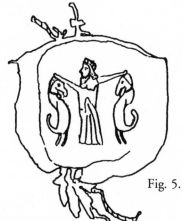

Fig. 5.

preserved papyrus document, and although they were undoubtedly influenced by the Persian motif, none of them has a Persian name, nor are they Persian.[9] In the fourth century B.C.E., these motifs were indeed common among the local inhabitants in general and among the Phoenicians in particular. Seals of this type evidently were mass-produced during this period, and many have turned up in various digs.

Type C

One group of stamps that were mass-produced were conoid stamps, which are distinguished on their upper part by a hole pierced for a thread, allowing the seal to hang around a person's neck. They are made of blue or green glass. Of this type only a single example is presented here, a stamp discovered in the excavations of Samaria.[10] This stamp also shows the king of Persia struggling with two animals, the nature and identification of which are not clear (fig. 6).

Type D

These conoid stamps, although their overall number is quite large, are only a minority of the recently found stamps, which are usually in the shape of scaraboids or scarabs, sometimes made of semiprecious stones, but more often of glass or steatite and blue or green faience. These have been found by the dozens in the coastal sites of the country and were mainly in the service of the Phoenician population. During this period the Phoenicians borrowed from three different sources, and I categorize the stamps accordingly.

The first source was *Persian*: the hero was depicted wearing Persian dress. One example of this type is a glass stamp discovered at Dor.[11] This type of scarab stamp is rare, because heroes from two other traditions are more prominent. The *Egyptian* hero who struggled with an animal was usually the Egyptian-Phoenician god Bes. In the local Phoenician cult he played a decid-

9. F. M. Cross Jr., "The Papyri and Their Historical Implications," in *Discoveries in the Wadi ed-Daliyeh* (AASOR 41; Cambridge, Mass.: American Schools of Oriental Research, 1974) 28–29, pls. 62:17, 36, 51; cf. now also M. I. W. Leith, *Greek and Persian Images in Pre-Alexandrian Samaria* (Cambridge: Harvard University Press, 1990); E. Stern, "A Hoard of Persian Period Bullae from the Vicinity of Samaria," *Mikmanim* 6 (1992) 7–30 [Hebrew].

10. J. W. Crowfoot, G. M. Crowfoot, and Kathleen M. Kenyon, *Samaria-Sebaste III: The Objects from Samaria* (London: Palestine Exploration Fund, 1957) 397 no. 80; 393 fig. 92:80.

11. The seal was found in Area D1 at the southern end of the mound. Its number is 55339, and it was uncovered in Locus 5620.

edly apotropaic role.[12] A typical example is a Persian Period scarab-stamp discovered in the Atlit tombs (fig. 10).[13] The third influence, *Greek* mythology, has also been discovered on stamps dating from the end of the fifth century B.C.E., and this influence reached a peak during the fourth century. On these stamps, the figure of the Greek hero Herakles replaced that of the Persian king or the Egyptian Bes, for he was identified with Melqart, the main Phoenician god. A whole group of this type was uncovered in some of the Atlit tombs.[14] Herakles is usually depicted lifting his club in one hand and holding a lion on his hind legs in the other (figs. 8–9, 11).

Type E

In the fourth century B.C.E., during the last stage preceding the final victory of Greek-Hellenistic culture over Palestinian culture, another motif appears in different variations on coins that were later known as "Philisto-Arabian" or "Palestinian."[15] Many of these coins depict either the Persian king or the god Bes.[16]

In this section I have traced the Assyrian motif from the time of its introduction into Palestine, the coming of the Assyrian administration, through its immediate use for glyptics by the local officials, its continued use during the Babylonian Period, and on to the time of the Persians, when it was mass-produced on stamps and coins.

The King Stabbing a Lion

Next let us turn our attention to the use in Palestinian glyptic of a second motif that, from the standpoint of distribution and popularity, is the best known of all. Here too the various stages illustrated above are represented,

12. See E. Stern, "Bes Vases from Palestine and Syria," *IEJ* 26 (1976) 183–87; Veronica Wilson, "The Iconography of Bes in Cyprus and the Levant," *Levant* 7 (1974) 77–103; W. Culican, "Phoenician Demons," *JNES* 35 (1976) 21–24.

13. C. N. Johns, "Excavations at ʿAtlit (1930–1931): The South-Eastern Cemetery," *QDAP* 2 (1933) 41–104; 99 fig. 85; pl. 14:935.

14. Ibid., 70–71, fig. 30, pl. 14:496; 85, fig. 59, pl. 14:687; 86, fig. 62, pl. 14:705.

15. See G. F. Hill, *Catalogue of Greek Coins of Palestine* (London: British Museum, 1914) 83–89; A. Kindler, "The Greco-Phoenician Coins Struck in Palestine in the Time of the Persian Empire," *Israel Numismatic Journal* 1 (1963) 2–6, 25–27.

16. Y. Meshorer, *American Numismatic Society SNG*, vol. 6 (1981) nos. 39–40; and cf. now Y. Meshorer and S. Qedar, *The Coinage of Samaria in the Fourth Century B.C.E.* (Jerusalem: Numismatic Fine Arts International, 1991).

Fig. 6.

Fig. 7.

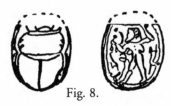

Fig. 8.

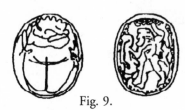

Fig. 9.

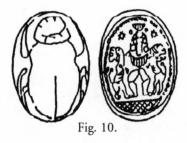

Fig. 10.

Fig. 11.

but I wish also to point out additional details. This motif depicts the Assyrian King holding an upright lion by the head or neck with his left hand and stabbing it with a dagger held in his right hand.

In its original form, this stamp (which also has very old Mesopotamian prototypes) represented the Assyrian royal house itself. A. J. Sachs and A. R. Millard have devoted special discussions to it, proving that it was the "royal Assyrian seal."[17] It has been found stamped on bullae attached to documents registering shipments to or from the royal house throughout the entire period of the Neo-Assyrian Empire (from the days of Shalmaneser III, 859–824, to the late seventh century B.C.E.). During this long period, the motif achieved an almost standard form, and it was used often as a decoration on stone orthostats in the Assyrian royal palaces. Sachs also includes among the "royal stamps" one impression on a clay bulla found at Samaria by the Harvard Expedition (fig. 12).[18] The bulla from Samaria must be an impression either from a "royal" stamp that was used to seal documents sent *to* the governor of the province or a stamp that belonged solely to the Samarian governor himself. In either case, this is the first appearance of the motif in Palestine. It is not surprising, therefore, that it served as a model for local imitation, first of all by the exiles returning from Assyria. One stamp, while slightly different in style and technique of execution, depicts a similar motif: a hero holding with his left hand the head of a winged monster standing upright.[19] This motif is one of two appearing on a stamp attributed by N. Avigad to an Ammonite official from the Assyrian Period who borrowed both his name and motifs from the Assyrian repertoire (fig. 13). The Ammonites were not the only people who adopted this motif at an early date. The first were (as usual) the Phoenicians, who made extensive use of it on their stamps, decorated metal bowls, stamped clay vessels,[20] and pottery vases, all of which were common in Phoenician contexts, especially during the seventh to sixth century B.C.E., in Palestine, Transjordan, and Cyprus.[21]

The main period during which this motif flourished in Palestine was the Persian Period, as was the case for the first motif. There is no doubt that the

17. A. J. Sachs, "The Late Assyrian Royal Seal Type," *Iraq* 15 (1953) 167–70, pls. XVIII–XIX; A. R. Millard, "Royal Seal Type Again," *Iraq* 27 (1965) 12–16.

18. G. A. Reisner, C. S. Fisher, and D. G. Lyon, *Harvard Excavations at Samaria: 1908–1910* (Cambridge: Harvard University, 1924) vol. 2, pl. 56:a; Sachs, "The Late Assyrian Royal Seal Type," pl. 19:3.

19. N. Avigad, "Seals of Exiles," *IEJ* 15 (1965) 222–32, pl. 40:B.

20. E. Stern, "New Types of Phoenician Style Decorated Pottery Vases from Palestine," *PEQ* 110 (1978) 11–21.

21. G. E. Markoe, "A Terracotta Warrior from Kazaphani, Cyprus, with Stamped Decoration in the Cypro-Phoenician Tradition," *Rivista di Studi Fenici* 16 (1988) 15–19, pls. 1–4.

Assyrian royal motif was adopted by the Persian administration also, as proved by many finds at Ur, Persepolis, and other major Achaemenian sites.[22] This motif was used by Persian officials in Palestine and is found on a number of bullae; four from Samaria—two from Samaria itself and two from the cave at Wadi ed-Daliyeh—deserve special mention here.

One variation of this stamp motif was found by the Harvard Expedition to Samaria, an impression in which the Assyrian king is replaced by a Persian king, with his typical crown and cloth. It is important to note that this impression survived on the edge of a clay tablet (it is not a bulla), perhaps sent from Persia to Palestine (fig. 15).[23] The same motif is also depicted on a bulla found at Samaria by the Joint Expedition.[24] On the other side of the bulla, traces of papyrus can be seen (fig. 14).

Two similar impressions were found on bullae in the cave in Wadi ed-Daliyeh and published by F. M. Cross (fig. 16).[25] Both were found attached to a papyrus document that had been preserved. Judging by the contents and the names of the witnesses preserved, none of the individuals was Persian. In the same cave, a coin with the same motif was also found (fig. 18).

A good example of the mass-produced stamps is the one found at the Phoenician site of Tell Keisan in the ꜥAkko Valley (fig. 17).[26]

The primary use of the motif during the Persian Period was on coins, because the motif was adopted by the city of Sidon (fig. 19).[27] A large quantity of coins from Sidon depicting the stabbing of a lion by the Persian king have been found at all of the major coastal cities of Palestine: ꜥAkko, Tell Abu-Hawam, Dor, Jaffa, and elsewhere.[28]

---

22. L. Legrain, *Ur Excavations X: Seal Cylinders* (New York: British Museum/University Museum, 1951) nos. 752–55; E. F. Schmidt, *Persepolis* (OIP 69; Chicago: University of Chicago Press, 1957) vol. 2, pls. 3:1, 11–37, 13:50–59; G. Richter, "The Late Achaemenian or 'Greco-Persian' Gems," *Hesperia Supplement 8* (Shear Volume; Athens: American School of Classical Studies, 1949) pl. 31:3. K. Ballkan, "Inscribed Bullae from Daskyleion," *Anatolia* 4 (1950) pl. 33, 9, b.

23. See Reisner, Fisher, and Lyon, *Harvard Excavations at Samaria*, 378, pl. 57h; J. Nougayrol, *Cylindres-Sceaux et Empreintes de Cylindres Trouves en Palestine* (Paris: Geuthner, 1939) 61, pl. 6.

24. Crowfoot, Crowfoot, and Kenyon, *Samaria III*, 88, pl. 15:42.

25. Cross, "Papyri and Their Historical Implications," 28, pl. 62:4, 22a.

26. Jacques Briend and Jean-Baptiste Humbert, *Tell Keisan: Une cité phénicienne en Galilée* (Paris: Gabalda, 1980) 277, pl. 89:21.

27. G. F. Hill, *Catalogue of the Greek Coins of Phoenicia* (London: British Museum, 1910) pls. XVIII:5, 7; XIX:9–11; XX:5; XXI:3.

28. C. Lambert, "Egypto-Arabian, Phoenician and Other Coins of the Fourth Century B.C. Found in Palestine," *QDAP* 2 (1932) 1–10; pl. I:21–34 (from Tell Abu-Hawam).

Fig. 12.

Fig. 13.

Fig. 14.

Fig. 15.

Fig. 16.

Fig. 17.

Fig. 18.

Fig. 19.

It should be pointed out that Sidon was not the only city to borrow the second motif for coins. Some Palestinian coins with the motif have recently turned up as well. The most interesting of these add the name of the city of Samaria.[29] I have pointed out in a previous study the strong Sidonian influence on Samaria from the Assyrian Period through the Persian era.[30]

Conclusion

The two motifs discussed above are but a few of many, and many more could have been adduced. For the purposes of this discussion, the two are sufficient to show the following:

1. The Assyrian occupation of Palestine opened a new chapter in its material culture, and the resulting changes can be observed in many of its artifacts, including relics of glyptic art. Mesopotamian glyptic appeared suddenly in Palestine, and shortly afterward local people—from all the region's different nations—started to imitate Assyrian motifs.
2. The continued occupation of the land of Palestine by the two succeeding Mesopotamian empires, Babylon and Persia, resulted in continual influx of new motifs. For this reason, we should regard the three historical periods as one cultural unit.
3. The imported seals and later imitations were absorbed into local repertoires all over the country. In addition to accurate imitations of Mesopotamian glyptic, some seals were altered according to the special tastes of the local nations. The changes took place mainly in "cultic" motifs, less often in official ones.
4. At the end of the period (fifth to fourth centuries B.C.E.), these stamps were mass-produced from cheap materials, glass or faience, and also appear on Phoenician and Palestinian coins. At this stage some Greek and Egyptian motifs were added to the old Assyrian and Persian motifs, and this combining of motifs was consistent with the mixed culture of Palestine during the period.[31]

29. Meshorer and Qedar, *The Coinage of Samaria.*

30. E. Stern, "A Phoenician Art Centre in Post-Exilic Samaria," *Atti del I Congresso Internazionale du Studi Fenici e Punici* (Rome: Herder, 1983) 1.211–12.

31. On the peculiarity of this cult, see E. Stern, *Material Culture of the Land of the Bible in the Persian Period* (Warminster, England: Aris & Phillips, 1982) 158–95; idem, "A Favissa of a Phoenician Sanctuary from Tel Dor," *JJS* 33 (Essays in Honour of Yigael Yadin; 1982) 35–54; idem, "The Beginning of the Greek Settlement in Palestine in the Light of the Excavation at Tel Dor," *AASOR* 49 (1989) 107–24.

Archaeological Indications on the Origins of Roman Mithraism

Lewis M. Hopfe †

B ETWEEN THE END OF THE FIRST century C.E. and the last part of the
fourth century a mystery religion called Mithraism was extremely popular among soldiers, merchants, and civil administrators in the Roman Empire. Today more than four hundred locations of Mithraic worship have been
identified in every area of the Roman Empire. Mithraea have been found as
far west as England and as far east as Dura Europas. Between the second and
fourth centuries C.E. Mithraism may have vied with Christianity for domination of the Roman world.[1]

Evidence for Mithraism comes from several sources. It is mentioned in
early Christian writings.[2] The Christians' view of this rival religion is extremely negative, because they regarded it as a demonic mockery of their own
faith. One also learns of Mithraism from brief statements in classical Greek
and Roman authors.[3] These rare literary sources are of little help in understanding the beliefs and practices of Mithraism. Apparently, Mithraism was
truly a "mystery" religion in that its devotees never committed its rituals or

The publisher thanks Prof. Gary Lease, who read the proofs of Dr. Hopfe's article.

1. The French historian Ernest Renan stated that if Christianity had not developed,
the world would have become Mithraic (*Marc-Aurèle et la fin du monde antique* [Paris:
Calmann-Lévy, 1923] 579).

2. See Tertullian, *De praescriptione haereticorum*, 40 and Jerome, Epist. 107 *ad Laetam.*

3. The Emperor Julian made brief reference to his devotion to Mithras (Helios) in
Oration 4, *Hymn to King Helios Dedicated to Sallust.*

theology to writing. If the tenets of Mithraism ever were written down, no evidence of such writings has so far come to light.

By far the greatest evidences for Mithraism are found in its many remaining places of worship. Throughout the Roman Empire Mithraists worshiped in underground rooms. The typical Mithraeum was built in a rectangular form, with benches installed along each wall. Along the back wall was the taurectone, the central image of the cult, which depicted Mithras slaying the sacred bull. An altar was often placed in front of the taurectone. The ceilings of the Mithraea were frequently painted blue, with stars representing the heavens. Sometimes the walls of these meeting places were decorated with frescoes that showed scenes from the story of Mithras or moments in the initiatory rites. Some Mithraea have adjoining side rooms for instruction or other rituals. A Mithraeum in Ostia has mosaic floors portraying symbols of the various grades of the Mithraic orders.[4] In addition, Mithraea often contain plaques of dedication revealing the names of the Mithraists who worshiped at these locations and, because they are dated, the periods during which the shrine was in use. From these paintings, statues, mosaics, and dedication plaques it is possible to draw only an outline of the religion of Mithraism.

The Origins of Mithraism

The question of the origin of Mithraism has intrigued scholars for many years. Franz Cumont, one of the greatest students of Mithraism, theorized that the roots of the Roman mystery religion were in ancient Iran.[5] He identified the ancient Aryan deity who appears in Persian literature as Mithra with the Hindu god Mitra of the Vedic hymns. Mithra/Mitra was a solar deity. With the coming of Zoroastrianism to Persia in the sixth century B.C.E., Mithra was demoted to a minor rank among the angels that served the supreme Zoroastrian god Ahura Mazda. The Magi, who were Zoroastrian priests, carried the message of Mithra first to Babylon and then into Asia Minor as they established religious colonies. After the collapse of the Persian Empire in the fourth century B.C.E. and the dominance of the Hellenistic rulers, the Magi continued to worship Mithra. In the religious and philo-

4. Samuel Leuchili, ed., *Mithraism in Ostia* (Evanston: Northwestern University Press, 1967).

5. F. Cumont, *Textes et Monuments Figurés Relatifs aux Mystères de Mithra* (Brussels: H. Lamertin, 1896–99).

sophical ferment of Asia Minor in the first and second centuries B.C.E., Mithraism began to take its distinctive shape. Cumont pointed to the use of the name Mithradates among the rulers of Asia Minor during that era and statuary showing them receiving power from Mithras as evidence for Mithraism's crystallization in this place and time. He admitted that the precise location and time of the development of Mithraism is uncertain. However, by the first century C.E. Cumont believed that Mithraism had developed its distinctive theology and rituals. Cumont accepted Plutarch's statement that the pirates of Cilicia were devotees of Mithras.[6] It was believed that these pirates acquainted the Romans with Mithraism. For many years Cumont's theory of the origin of Mithraism was widely accepted.[7]

In 1971 at the First International Congress of Mithraic Studies, John Hinnells, the organizer of the Congress and editor of the two-volume collection of papers presented there, challenged Cumont's position on the Iranian origin of Mithraism.[8] Hinnells attacked Cumont's interpretation of the Mithraic symbols and his identification of them with elements in Iranian religion. At the same conference R. L. Gordon also attacked the theory of Iranian origin.[9] Both scholars accused Cumont of circular thinking. According to Hinnells and Gordon, Cumont believed that Roman Mithraism developed from Iranian religion, found Iranian parallels to the symbols of Mithraism, and then used these parallels to prove the Iranian foundations for Mithraism.

Even though Hinnells and Gordon effectively destroyed Cumont's theory, neither offered an alternative hypothesis. Hinnells believed that Mithraism still had a basic Iranian origin, though his belief was not based upon Cumont's theories. Gordon frankly admitted ignorance of the true source of Mithraism and postulated that no one will never know its origins.

Recently another theory of the origin of Mithraism has been set forth by David Ulansey.[10] Ulansey theorizes that Mithraism arose in the city of Tarsus in Asia Minor. He believes it was devised and propagated by a group of Stoic philosophers who thought they had discovered astronomical evidence to

6. Plutarch, *Life of Pompey* 24:5.

7. Essentially the same theory of the origin and development of Mithraism is expressed by A. D. Nock (*Conversion* [1933; repr. Lanham, Maryland: University Press of America, 1988] 41ff.).

8. John Hinnells, "Reflections on the Bull-Slaying Scene," in *Mithraic Studies* (ed. John Hinnells; Manchester: Manchester University Press, 1975) 2.290–313.

9. R. L. Gordon, "Franz Cumont and the Doctrines of Mithraism," in *Mithraic Studies* (ed. John Hinnells; Manchester: Manchester University Press, 1975) 1.215–48.

10. David Ulansey, *The Origin of the Mithraic Mysteries: Cosmology and Salvation in the Ancient World* (New York: Oxford University Press, 1989).

prove the existence of a new and powerful god. They identified this god with Perseus, one of the hero gods of Tarsus. Since the constellation of Perseus was directly above the constellation of Tarsus the bull, the philosophers believed that Perseus dominated the bull. This new religion became popular with the Cilician pirates who had close ties to the intellectual circles of Tarsus and who were interested in astral religion. They changed the name of the hero god from Perseus to Mithra in honor of Mithridates VI Eupator, the last of the dynasty of rulers of Pontus before Roman rule. It was this group of pirate-sailors who gave Mithraism its form and spread the religion to the Roman world.

All theories of the origin of Mithraism acknowledge a connection, however vague, to the Mithra/Mitra figure of ancient Aryan religion. They all point to Persian influence in Asia Minor during the Hellenistic era and to the religious ferment of that period. All see the city of Tarsus as a starting point of Roman Mithraism. Plutarch's single statement about the Cilician pirates carries enormous weight, and as a result, all theorists accept them as the missionaries who carried the new religion to Rome.

The theories of the origin of Mithraism from Cumont to Ulansey remain only theories. Because of a dearth of literary evidence we cannot be certain that Mithraism developed in a certain place or a certain time. However, the weight of scholarly opinion has clearly moved away from the long-held theory that Mithraism began in Persia and moved westward across Babylon, Syria, Asia Minor, and into Rome.

Archaeological evidence is the strongest source of information about Mithraism. The remains of hundreds of Mithraic worship sites, the sculpting and painting of those sites, and the dedicatory plaques reveal a religion widespread across the Roman Empire from the second through the fourth centuries C.E. Current archaeological evidence may bear out the critics of Cumont's theory of the origin of Mithraism. If, as Cumont believed, Mithraism began as an Iranian cult and then moved west into Syria and on to Rome, one might expect to find well-established cult centers in Roman Syria. An examination of a map showing the locations of Mithraic centers in the Roman empire reveals that this is not so. While Mithraic materials have been found throughout the empire, the heaviest concentration is located in central Italy and northern Germany. East and west of these centers, archaeological evidence grows thinner. In Asia Minor Mithraic sites are relatively rare. They are even more scarce in Roman Syria. At the present only three Mithraea and a scattering of Mithraic artifacts have been located in Roman Syria.

The Mithraea of Roman Syria

Within the geographical dimensions of Roman Syria only three Mithraea have been discovered and excavated. They are located at Dura-Europas on the far eastern border of Roman Syria, at Sidon on the Mediterranean coast of Phoenicia, and at Caesarea Maritima on the Mediterranean coast of Roman Palestine.[11]

Dura-Europas is located on the extreme eastern border of Roman Syria on the banks of the Euphrates River. The city was established by Seleucid rulers about 300 B.C.E. to protect trade routes. Roman occupation of the city began in 164 C.E. and continued until 256, when it was conquered by the Sassanians.

During the ninety years of Roman occupation Dura-Europas was apparently inhabited by diverse religious populations. Archaeological excavations carried on in the 1920s and 1930s revealed a Christian chapel, a Jewish synagogue and a Mithraeum. The results of these excavations were thoroughly published,[12] and as a result, students of Syrian Mithraism know more about the Dura-Europas Mithraeum than any other site.

The Dura-Europas Mithraeum was apparently begun in the late second century C.E. Its first phase was probably a small room in a private home. Unlike other Mithraea, which were built underground to simulate Mithra's actions in the sacred cave, the Dura-Europas Mithraeum was above ground. Certain details were added to make it appear to be a cave. The furniture and arrangement of this Mithraeum are fairly typical of the period. It contained two carved reliefs of Mithras killing the sacred bull (*taurectone*), benches ran the length of the room, there were two altars, and the Mithraeum contained two dedicatory plaques naming Roman military leaders among its patrons.

In the early third century C.E. the Dura-Europas Mithraeum was apparently destroyed and rebuilt. The second phase was larger and more elaborate than the first. Dedications in this phase reveal that the rebuilding was done during the reign of Septimius Serverus. The revised and enlarged Mithraeum probably indicates a larger Mithraic community in this outpost city. This phase is distinguished by a series of drawings illustrating aspects of the life of

11. For a more complete description of the Mithraea and the Mithraic materials discussed here, see L. M. Hopfe, "Mithraism in Syria" (*Aufstieg und Niedergang der Römischen Welt* 2/18/4.2214–35).

12. M. I. Rostovtzeff, *Das Mithraeum von Dura* (Mitteilungen des Deutschen Archäologischen Instituts, Römische Abteilung 49; 1934) 180–207; M. I. Rostovtzeff, et al., *The Excavations at Dura-Europos: Preliminary Report of the Seventh and Eighth Seasons of Work* (New Haven: Yale University Press, 1939).

Mithras and the life of the worshiping community. Some aspects of these drawings are truly unique in Mithraism.[13]

In the middle third century the Dura-Europas Mithraeum was again enlarged. The altar area was raised, additional rooms were built, and new paintings were added. This may indicate further growth in the popularity of the religion in this region.

Dura-Europas was conquered by the Sassanians in 256 C.E., driving the Roman army and influence from this eastern frontier of the empire. The Mithraeum was destroyed, and Mithraic worship apparently came to an end. The Sassanians, who were Zoroastrian, had no use for a Roman Mithraeum.

A second center of Mithraic worship that has been excavated in Roman Syria is found in the ancient city of Sidon. Sidon was located on the Mediterranean coast of Roman Syria approximately halfway between Tyre on the south and Berytus (modern Beruit) on the north.

A Mithraeum was excavated in Sidon in the late nineteenth century. The results of the excavation of this site were reported by the journalist E. Durighello and repeated by S. Reinach.[14] Generally, students of Mithraism are dissatisfied with these reports, feeling that they are incomplete.[15] After the completion of the excavation, the site was covered and no further excavation was possible. Today all that remains of the Sidon Mithraeum are eleven pieces of sculpture now housed in the Louvre.

With only limited archaeological materials available it has been difficult to assign a date to the Sidon Mithraeum. Several dedicatory plaques from the building give the name of Fl. Gerontios and the year 500. If normal standards of Roman Syrian chronology are applied, the date of the building of the Mithraeum would have been approximately 188 C.E. Ernest Will disputes this chronology and places the dedication in the late fourth century C.E.[16] The earlier date for the building of this Mithraeum would be more in keeping with the Mithraea at Dura-Europas and Caesarea Maritima.

---

13. For a more complete discussion of these drawings, see F. Cumont, "The Dura Mithraeum" (*Mithraic Studies*, ed. John R. Hinnells; Manchester: Manchester University Press, 1975) 1.151–214.

14. E. Durighello, [no title], originally published in *Le Bosphore Egyptien*, 19 August 1887; reprinted in *Revue Archéologique* (1888) part 1, 91–93; and subsequently reprinted with a brief critical introduction in Salomon Reinach, "Sidon," *Chroniques d'Orient* 1 (Paris: Didot, 1891) 434–46.

15. M. J. Vermaseren, *Corpus Inscriptionum et Monumentorum Religionis Mithraicae* [= CIMRM] (2 vols. The Hague: Martinus Nijhoff, 1956–60) 1.73; Israel Roll, "The Mysteries of Mithras in the Roman Orient: The Problem of Origin," *Journal of Mithraic Studies* 2 (1977) n. 8.

16. Ernest Will, "La date du Mithraeum de Sidon," *Syria* 27 (1950) 261–69.

The extant pieces of sculpture from the Sidon Mithraeum include a bas-relief of the *taurectone*, including the twelve signs of the zodiac; a statue of the *taurectone*; a statue of Mithras carrying a sacred bull; a statue of a winged, lion-headed figure with a set of keys; four statues of the companions of Mithras, usually identified as Cautes and Cautopates; a statue of the triple-headed earth goddess, Hekate; and two statues of Venus.

The most recently discovered Mithraeum in Roman Syria was found during the excavation of Caesarea Maritima in 1973.[17] Caesarea Maritima is located on the Mediterranean coast of Roman Palestine.[18] The city was built on an essentially virgin location between 22 and 10 B.C.E. by Herod the Great.[19] It was named for and dedicated to his sponsor, Augustus Caesar. Among the many unique features of this city was a hugh artificial harbor. Since Palestine had so few natural ports on the Mediterranean coastline, Caesarea Maritima became the natural location for the disembarkation of Roman troops and administrators during the troubled first and second centuries C.E. Soon after its dedication Caesarea Maritima became the political capital of Palestine. It remained one of the leading cities of Syria until long after its conquest by the Muslims in 640 C.E.

Because of its location and massive remains Caesarea Maritima has long been the site of archaeological activity. During the 1973 season the Joint Expedition to Caesarea uncovered an underground vaulted room in the sand dunes just off the Mediterranean coast. Although this large room lacked the massive statuary and dramatic paintings that are frequently associated with Mithraea, and although there are no known literary references to Mithraism at Caesarea Maritima, sufficient evidence was found to identify it as a site of Mithraic worship. At the present this is the only Mithraeum known in Roman Palestine.

Excavation of the room revealed the typical participants' benches running along either side. At the east end of the vault was a small, almost square stone, which was identified as the base for an altar. Beside the altar stone was found a collection of Roman-era lamps and a small, circular, engraved marble piece. This medallion was inscribed with the *taurectone* image and three small scenes

17. See L. M. Hopfe and G. Lease, "The Caesarea Mithraeum: A Preliminary Announcement," *BA* 38/1 (1975) 2–10; R. Bull, "A Mithraic Medallion from Caesarea," *IEJ* 24 (1974) 187–90; J. A. Blakely, *The Joint Expedition to Caesarea Maritima, Excavation Reports: The Pottery and Dating of Vault 1: Horreum, Mithraeum, and Later Uses* (Lewiston, New York: Edwin Mellen, 1987).

18. This city is known as "Caesarea Maritima" to distinguish it from the other Caesareas of Roman Syria.

19. The construction and magnificent features of Caesarea Maritima are described by Josephus (see *Ant.* 15.9.6).

from the life of Mithras. On the walls of the vault were the faint remains of frescoes that may have depicted scenes from initiatory rituals. the ceiling showed slight traces of blue paint. During its days as an active Mithraeum the entire ceiling may have been painted to represent the sky and the stars.[20]

It is difficult to assign an exact date to the founding and life of the Caesarea Maritima Mithraeum. No dedicatory plaques have been discovered that might aid in the dating. The lamps found with the *taurectone* medallion are from the end of the first to the late third century C.E. Other pottery and coins from the vault are also from this era. Therefore it is speculated that this Mithraeum was developed toward the end of the first century and remained active until the late third century.[21] This matches the dates assigned to the Dura-Europas and the Sidon Mithraea.

Mithraic Articles from Roman Syria

In addition to the fully developed Mithraea of Dura-Europas, Sidon, and Caesarea Maritima, a few articles of Mithraic worship have been discovered in the area of Roman Syria.

A rectangular relief of the *taurectone* (CIMRM Mon. 71, cf. Plate V; cf. n. 15 above) was found in northeastern Syria at Arsha-wa-Qibar in 1932. Though the engraving of the relief is not clear, most of the elements of the *taurectone* can be identified. These include the bull, Mithras, the snake, the dog, the raven, Sol and Luna, and Cautes and Cautopates. The relief contains no inscription, and it is impossible to assign a date or to connect it to a Mithraeum.

Sahin, located in northern Syria, has yielded a Greek inscription that seems to be a dedicatory plaque to Mithras. Some letters on this plaque are missing, and its meaning is not absolutely clear. However, the best guess connects it to the worship of Mithra.[22] It appears to have been written in the early third century C.E.

Two Mithraic reliefs were found in the ruins of the temple of Dusares at Secia located southwest of Sidon.[23] Both of these rectangular reliefs are

---

20. For a more complete description of the furnishings of the Caesarea Maritima Mithraeum, see Hopfe and Lease, "Caesarea Mithraeuim," and Bull, "A Mithraic Medallion from Caesarea."

21. For the most detailed development of the Caesarea Maritima Mithraeum, see Blakely, *Joint Expedition*, 150.

22. The Mithraic reading of this inscription has been challenged by R. Mouterde, *Mélanges de l'Université Saint Joseph* 31 (1954) 334.

23. Ernest Will, "Nouveaux Monuments Sacres de la Syrie Romaine," *Syria* 29 (1952) 67–93.

carved from basalt and appear to be the work of the same sculptor. Both show the *taurectone* scene with all its figures. In the first (CIMRM Mon. 88) only Cautes is present, while in the second both Cautes and Cautopates are visible. Cumont suggested that at some point Mithras had become identified with Dusares, "the Arab Dionysus"[24] and speculates that the temple of Dusares contained these *taurectone* reliefs.

The Aleppo museum contains a relief showing the head of Mithras. The exact source of this relief is not known, but it was probably found on the Mediterranean coast between Lattakieh and Tartous. Though the relief is badly worn, it shows the head of Mithras with its typical curls, Phrygian cap, and nimbus. This head may have been carved in the first half of the second century C.E.[25]

A cippus found at Sidon bears an inscription in Greek that is a dedication to the god Asclepios by Theodotos, *hiereus* of Mithras.[26] The cippus may have been a gravestone. This inscription is dated 140/141 C.E. and is therefore the earliest reference to Mithras from Roman times in Syria.

A knife found at Niha in central Lebanon was apparently connected to Mithraism.[27] Its handle is elaborately carved and includes the head of a bull. It also contains the heads of a lion, a bear, a snake, a scorpion, as well as a krater, a Phrygian cap, and two busts. Because several of these items are a part of the *taurectone*, it is believed that this knife may have been connected to Mithraism in this region. The knife bears no indication of date or place of origin.

In the late nineteenth century the British Museum received a small bronze lion-headed figure from Beirut. The object is approximately three inches long and has a human body and wings. There is some indication that once there may have been a snake attached to the body. Even though the object was not found with other Mithraic materials, it is assumed to be an image of Kronos.[28] Barnett speculates that the figure may have belonged to the Sidon Mithraeum.[29]

---

24. F. Cumont, "The Dura Mithraeum," in *Mithraic Studies* (ed. John R. Hinnells; Manchester: Manchester University Press, 1975) 1:160.

25. See Will, "Nouveaux Monuments," 67.

26. M. Dunand, "Le Temple d'Echmoun à Sidon," *Bulletin du Musée de Beyrouth* 26 (1973) 27–44.

27. H. Seyrig, "Un Couteau de Sacrifice," *Iraq* 36 (1974) 229–30.

28. R. D. Barnett, "A Mithraic Figure from Beirut," *Mithraic Studies* (ed. John R. Hinnells; Manchester: Manchester University Press, 1975) 466–69.

29. Ibid., 466.

Conclusion

In the brief survey presented in this paper it is clear that the number and quality of Mithraic materials uncovered in Roman Syria is extremely limited. Only three Mithraea have been excavated in the region. The Dura-Europas Mithraeum on the eastern frontier of the empire was apparently a full temple, the equal of any. It has been fully excavated and fully reported. The Sidon Mithraeum remains something of a mystery because of the incomplete reports of its excavation. The Caesarea Maritima Mithraeum was apparently poor in its furnishings and relatively small. In addition, time and the atmosphere have deteriorated many of the frescoes that might have told a more complete story at this site. Beyond these three Mithraea, there are only a handful of objects from Syria that may be identified with Mithraism.

Archaeological evidence of Mithraism in Syria is therefore in marked contrast to the abundance of Mithraea and materials that have been located in the rest of the Roman Empire. Both the frequency and the quality of Mithraic materials is greater in the rest of the empire. Even on the western frontier in Britain, archaeology has produced rich Mithraic materials, such as those found at Walbrook.

If one accepts Cumont's theory that Mithraism began in Iran, moved west through Babylon to Asia Minor, and then to Rome, one would expect that the religion left its traces in those locations. Instead, archaeology indicates that Roman Mithraism had its epicenter in Rome. Wherever its ultimate place of origin may have been, the fully developed religion known as Mithraism seems to have begun in Rome and been carried to Syria by soldiers and merchants. None of the Mithraic materials or temples in Roman Syria except the Commagene sculpture bears any date earlier than the late first or early second century.[30] While little can be proved from silence, it seems that the relative lack of archaeological evidence from Roman Syria would argue against the traditional theories for the origins of Mithraism.

30. Mithras, identified with a Phrygian cap and the nimbus about his head, is depicted in colossal statuary erected by King Antiochus I of Commagene, 69–34 B.C.E. (see Vermaseren, CIMRM 1.53–56). However, there are no other literary or archaeological evidences to indicate that the cult of Mithras as it was known among the Romans in the second to fourth centuries C.E. was practiced in Commagene.

THE HEBREW BIBLE AND
ITS LATER USES

Laws Concerning Idolatry
in the *Temple Scroll*

Lawrence H. Schiffman

THE SECTION OF THE TEMPLE SCROLL that extends from column 53 to 66 has been described elsewhere as the "Deuteronomic Paraphrase."[1] This section was included by the author/redactor of the complete scroll in order to give it the character of a complete Torah, covering much of the legal material appearing in the Pentateuch. In this section, the author worked through large parts of Deuteronomy 12–23, the legal section of Deuteronomy. In constructing the complete scroll, he used this material, as well as various other sections he composed, along with a number of sources at his disposal. These sources, I maintain, were to some extent Sadducean in character.[2] The author/redactor's general intent was to bring this material together in order to express his own unique vision of Israel's Temple, its ritual, the Land of Israel, its government, and the laws by which the Jewish people were to live. It was through this medium that the author sought to propose

---

Author's Note: This paper was written during my tenure as a Fellow of the Institute for Advanced Studies of the Hebrew University at Jerusalem, Israel. I thank the Institute and its staff for their support of my research. This paper is offered in memory of Professor H. Neil Richardson, with whom I shared an interest in Qumran studies and with whom I had the privilege of working for three seasons at the excavations at Dor, Israel.

1. L. H. Schiffman, "The Deuteronomic Paraphrase of the *Temple Scroll*," *RQ* 15 (1992) 543–67.

2. L. H. Schiffman, "The New Halakhic Letter (4QMMT) and the Origins of the Dead Sea Sect," *BA* 53 (1990) 64–73.

---

an ideal society and ritual, which he hoped would become reality in the present, premessianic age.

That the topic of idolatry was a central concern of the scroll is apparent from the opening column of the preserved portion of the scroll. In column 2 the author adapts Exod 34:10–17 with additions from Deut 7:5, 25–26. He states there the obligation to destroy idolatrous cult objects and to avoid idolatrous worship. He emphasizes that covenants with the inhabitants of the land will result in idolatry and intermarriage. This passage is probably to be read in the historical context of early Hasmonean times in which the author/ redactor sought to strengthen the separation of Jews from pagan worship and intermarriage. At the same time, we will see that actual pagan worship did not constitute a *major* issue in the legislative context of the scroll.

In the context of the deuteronomic paraphrase with which he concluded his scroll, the author dealt with the various laws regarding idolatry that are included in Deuteronomy.[3] Specifically, the scroll treats these matters in five passages: (1) 11QTemple li 19–lii 3 prohibits various idolatrous practices. (2) 11QTemple liv 8–18 deals with a prophet who incites idolatrous worship. I call him, for the sake of convenience, the idolatrous prophet. (3) 11QTemple liv 19–lv 1 deals with an individual who entices others to idolatrous worship. He is designated here the enticer (rabbinic *mesit umediah*). (4) 11QTemple lv 2–14 deals with an idolatrous city (rabbinic *ʿir hanidaḥat*). (5) Finally, lv 15– lvi 4 discusses the idolatrous individual.

Essentially, the scroll presents us with five laws dealing with idolatry in one form or another. While the first is located independently, the last four constitute a collection, only three of which appear together in Deuteronomy.[4] The first section, prohibiting idolatrous practices, is clearly placed where it is (li 19–lii 3) because the source of parts of this law (Deut 16:21– 17:5) appears immediately after the command to establish judges (Deut 16:18–20, 11QTemple li 11–18). The second, third, and fourth sections proceed from the text of Deuteronomy 13 and appear in the same order as in

---

3. Num 15:22–31 was taken by the tannaim to refer to idolatry (*Sipre Numbers* 111–12, ed. H. S. Horovitz [Jerusalem: Wahrmann, 1966] 116–22; *m. Hor.* 1:5). This passage from Numbers is not represented in the *Temple Scroll* but is utilized in 4Q375. See J. Strugnell, "Moses-Pseudepigrapha at Qumran: 4Q375, 4Q376 and Similar Works," *Archaeology and History in the Dead Sea Scrolls: The New York University Conference in Memory of Yigael Yadin* (ed. L. H. Schiffman; Sheffield: Sheffield Academic Press, 1990) 224–34. Omitted from consideration here is 11QTemple lix 2–4, the rebuke for the king, which mentions idolatry, and 11QTemple lx 16–lxi 1, which prohibits magical and superstitious practices.

4. The Deuteronomic laws pertaining to idolatry are seen as a corpus by A. Rofé, *Mavoʾ Le-Sefer Devarim* (Jerusalem: Akademon, 1988) 60–65.

Deuteronomy. The final law, from Deuteronomy 17, is placed here because the author wanted to group this law with the others pertaining to idolatry.[5]

The study that follows undertakes the detailed analysis of each of these laws, placing emphasis on its relationship to the deuteronomic texts on which it is based. In addition, where appropriate, I compare these laws with the interpretations in rabbinic literature.[6]

The Prohibition of Idolatrous Practices

In the context of the scroll's brief treatment of Deuteronomy 16,[7] 11QTemple li 19–lii 3 deals with the outlawing of idolatrous practices and is basically an expansion and reshaping of Deut 16:21–22.

> Do not do in your land as the nations do: Everywhere[8] they sacrifice and plant for themselves Asherot[9] and erect for themselves pillars and set up for themselves figured stones to bow down to (or: on) them. And they build for themselves [. . . .][10] You may not plant [for yourself any tree as an Asherah next to my altar which you shall (or: must) make for] yourself. Nor may you erect for yourself a pillar [which I despise], n[or] shall you make for yourself (anywhere) in your entire land a [fi]gured [st]one to bo[w] down to (or: on) it.

5. This decision led the author to continue in col. lvi with other laws from Deuteronomy 17, culminating in the substantial original composition, the Law of the King (11QTemple lvi–lix). On this section of the scroll, see L. H. Schiffman, "The King, his Guard and the Royal Council in the *Temple Scroll*," *PAAJR* 54 (1987) 237–59.

6. For rabbinic attitudes toward idolatry, cf. E. E. Urbach, "Hilkhot ʿAvodah Zarah We-Ha-Meṣiʾut Ha-ʾArkheʾologit We-Ha-Historit Ba-Meʾah Ha-Sheniyah U-Va-Meʾah Ha-Shelishit," *Me-ʿOlamam shel Ḥakhamim* (Jerusalem: Magnes, 1988) 125–78, and S. Lieberman, *Hellenism in Jewish Palestine* (New York: Jewish Theological Seminary of America, 1950) 115–38. In the course of this study, no relevant material was found in Philo or Josephus.

7. The bulk of chap. 16 (dealing with festivals) was not included in the scroll, which drew its festival calendar (11QTemple xiii 10–xxix 10) primarily from Numbers 28–29.

8. The words *bekol maqom* were omitted in the translation by Yigael Yadin (*The Temple Scroll* [3 vols.; Jerusalem: Israel Exploration Society, 1977/1983] 2.230, 393). The English translations used in this paper are my own.

9. Cf. 11QTemple ii 7, where the destruction of ʾašerîm is commanded, in accord with Exod 34:13.

10. The lacuna consists of some seven lines (01–07), and in the first readable line (1), there is a lacuna sufficient for approximately nineteen letters. The initial section should probably be restored with the word *bamot*, as suggested by Yadin (*Temple Scroll*, 2.231), who compares 2 Kgs 17:8–11.

The text begins with an opening formula, which although having biblical parallels, is essentially a composition of the author or his source. This material (*lo?.... hemmah*) has a parallel in 11QTemple xlviii 11, in which almost identical phraseology applies to laws of burial. The passage in xlviii 11ff. appears to be based on Lev 22:24, 18:3, and Ezek 8:13.[11] Nonetheless, the correspondence is not close enough to classify this clause as anything but the author's own.[12] The opening words, *lo? ta?asu be?arṣekemah*, are dependent on Lev 22:24, *ube?arṣekem lo? ta?asu*, words dealing in their original context with the offering of animals whose genitals have been mutilated. The connection of *lo? ta?asu* with *haggoyim ?osim* is based on Deut 12:2–4 and 30–31, which do in fact deal with idolatrous worship.

Verse 8 warns that sacrifice is to be prohibited throughout the Land of Israel. The discussion in the corresponding chapter of Deuteronomy of the centralization of sacrificial worship indicates that the words *bekol maqom* (11QTemple li 19) are to be understood with the following, rather than the previous, words. These words are taken from Deut 12:2, where the Israelites are commanded to destroy *kōl hammĕqōmôt ?ăšer ?ābĕdû šām haggoyim*, and v. 3, where they are to extirpate the names of the pagan gods *min-hammāqôm hahû?* Note that in Ezek 8:13 the subject is the elders of Israel, whose abominations (*tô?ēbôt gĕdōlôt*) are described as *?ăšer hēmmāh ?ōśîm*. Lev 18:3 supplied the notion of not following the ways of the Gentiles and the formulation: *kĕma?ăśēh ?ereṣ-miṣrayîm . . . lō? ta?ăśû ûkĕma?ăśēh ?ereṣ-kĕna?an . . . lō? ta?ăśû.* The author of this section of the scroll composed freely in a biblical style that seems to have as its base Deuteronomy 12 and other materials, which the author reworked extensively.

After this, the text turns back to its basic source, Deuteronomy 16. Whereas there vv. 21 and 22 are prohibitions, the *Temple Scroll* author first borrows them to create a description of the pagan worship of "the nations": they plant Asherot and erect pillars. In creating this list of idolatrous practices, he moves to create a harmonization of his base text in Deut 16:21–22 with Lev 26:1,[13] which also mentions figured stones or pavements.[14] Despite the fact that both of these verses list the pagan cult objects in the singular, the

11. Yadin, *Temple Scroll*, 2.209.

12. For this reason Yadin seems to find here historical reference to the Hellenistic Period (*Temple Scroll*, 2.130). See below, p. 174.

13. Cf. G. Brin, "Ha-Miqra? Bi-Megillat Ha-Miqdash," *Shnaton* 4 (1979/80) 207; E. Tov, " 'Megillat Ha-Miqdash' U-Viqoret Nusaḥ Ha-Miqra?," *Eretz-Israel* 16 (Orlinsky Volume; Jerusalem: Israel Exploration Society, 1981/82), 103.

14. Cf. Yadin, *Temple Scroll*, 2.230, and J. Blidstein, "Prostration and Mosaics in Talmudic Law," *Bulletin of the Institute of Jewish Studies* 2 (1974) 19–39.

scroll author switched to the plural, since his point was that they do this throughout the land (*bekol maqom*).[15]

Somewhere at the top of column lii, which is not preserved, the scroll turns to the prescriptive laws relating to idolatry and again takes up Deut 16:21–22. These verses now repeat the MT verbatim (although partly restored), except that the first person is introduced for God (*mizbeḥi*, and as restored, *sane²ti*). It is readily apparent that the changes and abridgements used in this same text above (li 20) were exegetical and do not constitute actual textual variants.[16] Once again the scroll turns to harmonizing with Lev 26:1. Here 11QTemple copies Leviticus only in the second half of the verse, using the singular *maskit*, agreeing with the singular usage in Deuteronomy, which it has copied as well. The author avoids the plural in constructing his negative commandment, since the plural would be misleading, creating the impression that only more than one pagan cult object is forbidden.

A few minor variations are also introduced. 11QTemple has *ta²aseh lekah* in lii 3 for Lev 26:1 *tittĕnû* and *be-kol ²arṣekah* for the MT plural *bĕkol ²arṣĕkem*. 11QTemple *ta²aseh* may be the result of the occurrence of this word in Deut 16:21.[17] While these variants are not attested otherwise, we cannot be certain that they are not textual variants of the synonymous variety. The end of Lev 26:1, "for I am the Lord your God," is omitted here since it is unnecessary in light of the first-person, divine-discourse prohibition wording.

It is impossible to claim that there is a textual tradition lying behind the divergences from the MT in this law. These changes are exegetical and harmonistic, with the exception of two possible minor examples for which we cannot be certain. No proof has been found that there was a source for this law other than the canonical Pentateuch itself. The text does not introduce a single exegetical or halakhic detail not found in the Torah. The activity of the author/redactor is entirely literary in that he has created a new text.

The Idolatrous Prophet

In 11QTemple liv 8–18 the *Temple Scroll* paraphrases the law of the prophet who advocates idolatrous worship[18] found in Deut 13:2–6.

---

15. For the plural, cf. Num 33:52 (Yadin, *Temple Scroll*, 2.231).

16. This text is preserved partly in 4QDeut^c Frgs. 30 and 32, with no sign of variation (S. White, *A Critical Edition of Seven Manuscripts of Deuteronomy: 4QDt^a, 4QDt^c, 4QDt^f, 4QDt^g, 4QDtⁱ, and 4QDtⁿ* [Ph.D. dissertation, Harvard University, 1988] 80–83).

17. Tov, "Megillat Ha-Miqdash," 103.

18. This "prophet" is not to be confused with the false prophet of Deut 18:20–22 (cf. Rofé, *Mavo² Le-Sefer Devarim*, 62). *Tg.Ps.-J.* Deut 13:2 conflates these two types of "prophets" incorrectly.

If there shall arise among you a prophet or a dreamer (or: seer) who had (previously) given you a sign or wonder, and this sign or wonder had come to pass for you, saying: "Let us go and worship other gods" which you had not known, do not listen[19] to the word of that prophet or to that dreamer. For I am testing you to determine whether you love the Lord, the God of your fathers, with all your heart and with all your soul. You should follow (lit.: walk after) the Lord your God and worship (only) Him, and revere (only) Him, obey His voice and cleave to Him.[20] And that prophet or dreamer must be put to death[21] because he spoke rebelliously against the Lord your God Who took you out of the land of Egypt—and I have redeemed you from the house of bondage—to lead you astray from the way in which I commanded you to go. In this way shall you purge the evil from among you.

For MT *kî* 11QTemple has *ʾim*, a modernizing linguistic variation known from elsewhere in the scroll.[22] In line 9 the scroll adds *ʾelekah*.[23] It is difficult to understand any reason for this plus. In light of the occurrence of this word further on in the verse, this seems not to be a genuine textual variant but an expansion on the part of the scroll or a *Vorlage*.

The substitution in 11QTemple of *haʾot ʾo hamopet* (the *ʾalep* of *ʾo* is a correction suspended above the line) for MT *hāʾôt wĕhammôpēt* is both harmonizing (with v. 2) and exegetical, since it clarifies that the Torah intends either a sign or a miracle, not both together. The identical reading is found in the LXX.[24] In the latter part of v. 3, the scroll has moved *wenaᶜobdem* from the end of the verse to the direct discourse of the idolatrous prophet. This is to remove the ambiguity of the prophet's statement in the MT. The wording of the MT gives the impression that he stated all of verse 3b (from *nēlĕkâh*). The 11QTemple version makes clear that the words *ʾăšer lōʾ yĕdaᶜtem* are not

19. So MT and Samaritan. 1QDeut[a] (D. Barthélemy and J. T. Milik, eds., *Qumran Cave I* [Discoveries in the Judaean Desert 1; Oxford: Clarendon, 1955] 55), the LXX, and *Targum Pseudo-Jonathan* have the plural.

20. Cf. 4QDeut[c] Frg. 20, in which parts of Deut 13:5–6 appear (White, *Seven Manuscripts of Deuteronomy*, 60–61). Note that this MS has *tlkwn*, which agrees with 11QTemple as opposed to MT *tlkw*. The same reading is found in 1QDeut[a]. Where the MT and 11QTemple have *tdbkwn*, 1QDeut[a] has a word ending in what appears to be a *reš*, leading the editors to restore [*tšm*] *r*. It is not clear why they restored a defective form.

21. According to *Sipre Deuteronomy* 86 (ed. L. Finkelstein; New York: Jewish Theological Seminary of America, 1969), 151, execution was to be by strangulation.

22. Brin ("Ha-Miqraʾ Bi-Megillat Ha-Miqdash," 214–17; followed by Tov, "Megillat Ha-Miqdash," 101) argues that this is a linguistic modernization on the part of the author, but Yadin rejects this view (*Temple Scroll*, 2.247).

23. Omitted in the translation by Yadin (*Temple Scroll*, 2.244, 399). 1QDeut[a] does not have this addition.

24. Tov notes that the Samaritan here agrees with the MT ("Megillat Ha-Miqdash," 106).

to be included in the direct discourse of the false prophet. Accordingly, it is possible to conclude that this is an exegetical change made intentionally by the author or his *Vorlage*. Further, this change effected a harmonization with Deut 13:14, a similar verse.[25]

11QTemple *debar*, used for MT *dibrê* in v. 4, may be a genuine variant, as may be 11QTemple *la-ḥolem* for MT *ʾel ḥôlēm*, although this difference may also be the result of sloppiness. Spelling *menaśeh* with *śin* rather than *samek* is simply a linguistic variation.[26]

In line 12 11QTemple switches from the third to the first person, as is usual, but in line 13 it preserves the third-person usage of the biblical text with the substitution of *ʾelohe ʾabotekemah* for MT *ʾĕlōhêkem*. This may be a variant but may also be influenced by Exod 3:16.[27] In v. 5 the scroll switches the order of some of the clauses and deletes, perhaps by mistake, the reference to observing the commandments.[28] The change in word order may have been present already in the author's *Vorlage*, since this reading is also in evidence in 1QDeut^a.[29] The omission by the scroll of the second *hahûʾ* in v. 6 must be an error, since it is required in order to make sense.[30] In line 16 *ʾelohekah* appears in the scroll for the MT's plural *ʾĕlōhêkem* (v. 6). The reading in the scroll of *ʾašer hoṣiʾakah* for MT *hammôṣîʾ ʾetĕkem* is designed to avoid the ambiguity caused by the usage of a participle. The scroll author has replaced the MT participle with the past tense: another example of an exegetical variation.

Note also the shift from a plural object in the MT to a singular object in 11QTemple. In cases of shifting from plural to singular, the scroll agrees with the LXX and the Samaritan Pentateuch. In the case of the scroll, it is probable that the variations were in the author's text of Deuteronomy. These changes seem to be intended to eliminate the awkward shift in the MT from plural "you" (*ʾetĕkem*) to singular "you" (*happōdĕkā*).[31] It is true that the scroll, like the LXX and the Samaritan, is more consistent grammatically here, but the language then proceeds to shift to the first person, creating a more glaring awkwardness. Furthermore, at the end of v. 10 there is another shift from the third person to the first.[32]

25. The appearance of Deut 13:14 in 11QTemple lv 4 will be taken up below.
26. For other examples see Yadin (1.32; 2.244 [liv 12]).
27. Yadin, 2:244.
28. Tov sees this as omission resulting from intentional shortening ("Megillat Ha-Miqdash," 103).
29. Ibid., 109.
30. Cf. Tov, "Megillat Ha-Miqdash," 103.
31. So also 1QDeut^a, *wh[pwdkh]*.
32. Cf. Brin, "Ha-Miqraʾ Bi-Megillat Ha-Miqdash," 211–12.

In this passage, then, there seems to be evidence of genuine textual variants, which, however, are of minor contextual significance. At the same time, several harmonizations and exegetical variations, or changes to eliminate ambiguity, have been introduced into the text by the author of the *Temple Scroll* or his source. In some of these cases, the LXX and Samaritan Pentateuch share the same traditions. Yet absolutely no halakhic details have been included. Again, the text of the scroll follows the biblical legislation exactly.

The Enticer to Idolatry

11QTemple liv 19–lv 1 includes the law of Deut 13:7–12 regarding one who attempts to entice others to idolatrous worship (*mesit umediaḥ*) The text and restoration proposed here make use of the recently published fragment from Cave 11.[33]

> And if your brother, the son of your father or the son of your mother, or your son or your daughter, or the wife of your bosom,[34] or your neighbor who is like you,[35] shall entice you secretly saying, "Let us go and worship other gods,"[36] which you have not (previously) known, you [and your father, from among the gods of the nations which are around you, whether near you or far away from you, from one end of the earth to the other end of the earth, you shall not agree with him nor shall you listen to him. You (lit.: your eye) shall not have pity on him nor be merciful to him, nor cover up for him. Rather, you must put him to death. Your hand[37] shall be first to execute him, and the hand of the entire people shall be last. You shall stone him to death with rocks. For he attempted to lead you astray from the Lord your God, Who took you out of the land of Egypt, from the house of bondage.

33. A. S. van der Woude, "Ein Bisher unveroffentlichtes Fragment der Tempelrolle," *RQ* 13 (Memorial Carmignac; 1988) 89–92. This fragment was published earlier by J. P. M. van der Ploeg ("Les manuscrites de la grotte XI de Qumrân," *RQ* 12 [1985] 10). There it was incorrectly identified as a fragment of Deuteronomy. This fragment is described by van der Ploeg (p. 90) as being in the same hand as 11QTemple[b], but somehow he failed to identify it properly. Apparently the fragment of Lev 13:58–59 on p. 10 should also be ascribed to 11QTemple[b].

34. Rashi notes that this means the wife with whom you sleep.

35. *Targum Pseudo-Jonathan* translates: *deḥabib ꜥalak kenapšak* 'who is as dear to you as yourself'.

36. From the parallel in 11QTemple liv 10 it is certain that the author understood the statement of the enticer to end here. Cf. above, pp. 164–65.

37. Here and below in this verse, the LXX (13:10) has the plural, *hai cheires*. This reading is most probably the result of an exegetical tendency on the part of the LXX, which saw Hebrew *yād* here as a collective noun.

And all Israel shall listen; and see and not continue to do (anything) like this evil thing in your midst.]

This text essentially follows Deut 13:7–12 verbatim. *We³im* has replaced MT *kî* as part of the process of linguistic updating.[38] The conjunction *and* is used here by the scroll because this law, both in Deuteronomy and in the *Temple Scroll*, connects directly to the one that precedes it in context.

The spelling of *yeśitkah* with *śin* for MT *samek* is a linguistic variant (orthographic),[39] as is the pausal (lengthened) *wenaᶜabodah* for MT *wĕnaᶜobdâh*. The presence in 11QTemple of *ben ³abikah ³o*, not found in the MT, is in agreement with 4QDeutᶜ,[40] the LXX, and the Samaritan Pentateuch,[41] demonstrating that possibly in Hellenistic times the fuller reading was most widespread. The spelling *ryᶜyk* in 11QTemple reflects a singular (as in MT *rēᶜăkā*), since a plural would make no sense.[42] MT singular *yādaᶜtā* is here replaced by *yedaᶜtemah*, the plural. This shows an attempt to correct the deuteronomic text in order to bring about agreement with the plural that follows, *³attâh wa³abōtêkā*.[43]

Column lv 01–1 (eight lines) was restored by Yadin according to Deut 13:7–12 (starting with the last word in v. 7). That restoration can now be re-evaluated in light of the recently published fragment from 11QTempleᵇ (11QTemple xx).[44] The fragment reads as follows:

> your] father or the son of [45] [your mother
> w]ho is like you secretly
> your fa]thers, from among the gods[
> from y]ou, from the ends[46] of the earth and to[

38. See above, n. 22.

39. See above, n. 26.

40. Frgs. 21 and 22 (White, *Seven Manuscripts of Deuteronomy*, 62–63).

41. Tov, "Megillat Ha-Miqdash," 106; van der Woude, "Unveröffentlichtes Fragment," 91. Philo has simply *adelphos* 'brother', with mention of neither parent (*Special Laws* 1.316).

42. Cf. Yadin, *Temple Scroll*, 1.31.

43. Yadin, *Temple Scroll*, 2.245.

44. For a full restoration of the fragment, see below, appendix.

45. Van der Woude ("Unveröffentlichtes Fragment," 91) is certainly correct that this line is not to be restored *ysyt]kh ³ḥ[ykh.* . . . Yet he does not note that such a restoration is impossible since the partial letter at the end of the first line cannot be a *ḥet* since it slants too far to the right as it descends. This can only be a *waw*. His restoration in line 1 of *³immekah* must be corrected to *ben ³immekah*.

46. Van der Woude ("Unveröffentlichtes Fragment," 91) notes that *mqṣy*, plural, appears here, while the MT has *mqṣh*, singular.

> your] eye upon him nor be merciful t[o him
> f]irst to execute him and the hand[
> to lead]you astray[

This fragment indicates several things about the text and restoration proposed by Yadin. First, it confirms the reading of 11QTemple, which includes mention of the father in line 19, in agreement with other ancient witnesses, as opposed to the MT, which contains only a reference to the mother. Second, the clear *ᶜayin* in line 5 indicates that the text added *ᶜalayw* after *taḥmol*, as found in the LXX but not in the MT or Samaritan.[47] Yadin's restoration of lv 3–4 should most probably be revised in this light. In this connection, one must at least consider the possibility that in Yadin's line 6, the divine reference should not be restored in the third person, as in the MT, but rather in the first, as is characteristic of this scroll. However, such a restoration would result in difficult syntax and the need for extensive change. The text would then have had to read: *meᶜalai ᵓašer ᵓanoki hoṣeti ᵓotkah.* Since in such cases the author of the deuteronomic paraphrase usually leaves the third person intact,[48] Yadin's restoration of line 6 is most probably correct.

Here again the *Temple Scroll* follows the deuteronomic text, diverging only in minor textual variations. No significant halakhic or exegetical activity can be ascribed to the scroll in this passage.

The Idolatrous City

11QTemple lv 2–14, dealing with the city that becomes idolatrous (*ᶜir hanidaḥat*), generally follows Deut 13:13–19.

> If you hear regarding on[e of your cities which] I give you [in which] to dwe[ll], the following:[49] "Some worth[less] peo[p]le among you have gone out and have led astray all the [in]habitants of their city, saying,[50] 'Let us go and worship gods' which you have not known,"[51] then you must ask, inquire and investigate carefully.[52] If the accusation turns out to be true (and) correct, (that) this abomination has been per-

47. Ibid.
48. Brin, "Ha-Miqraᵓ Bi-Megillat Ha-Miqdash," 210–12.
49. This is the meaning of *leᵓmor* in this context.
50. 1QDeutᵃ preserves Deut 13:13–14 in fragmentary form (Barthélemy and Milik, *Qumran Cave I,* 55). No variants from the MT, except those occasioned by Qumran orthography, can be found there.
51. See above, pp. 164–65.
52. *Heṭev* here modifies all three verbs, not only the first, as in Yadin's translation (*Temple Scroll,* 2.247, 401).

formed (or: abominable transgression has been committed) among (the people of) Israel, you must kill all the inhabitants of that city by the sword, destroying[53] it and all (the people) that are in it. And all its domesticated animals[54] you must kill by the sword.[55] Then you must gather all the spoil (taken) from it into its town square and burn the city and the spoil (taken) from it with fire as a whole burnt offering to the Lord your God. It shall be an eternal mound never to be rebuilt. None of the property to be destroyed should remain in your possession. (You shall do all this)[56] in order that I shall be appeased from My anger and show you mercy, and have compassion on you and increase you as I promised to your forefathers, provided that you obey My voice to observe all My commandments which I command you this day so as to do what is right and good before the Lord your God.

The scroll substitutes *ʾim* for MT *kî* twice (lines 2, 13), as part of its "modernizing" tendency.[57] Further, the text switches to the first person, as usual, but preserves the third person in lines 9–10 and 14.[58] Note the interesting shift in the referent of the first person (*ʾānōkî*) from Moses in Deut 13:19 to God in the scroll. This shift in meaning results from the change in context occasioned by the move to first person, direct divine discourse.[59]

11QTemple adds *kol* indicating that all the inhabitants must worship idols for this law to apply (line 3) and again that all the inhabitants be killed (line 6). This is clearly a halakhic modification and in both cases agrees with the LXX.[60] In line 8 the scroll even adds *kol* again to say that all animals must be destroyed. But the parallel with the LXX proves that these changes may have taken place in the *Vorlage* of the author and may not be original to him.

In the case of the requirement that all the inhabitants be led astray to idolatrous worship for this law to apply, the view of the scroll contrasts with

53. Taking *haḥarem* as an infinitive absolute used in the gerundive sense, rather than as an imperative.

54. I.e., permissible, edible animals.

55. 4QDeut[c] Frg. 24 (White, *Seven Manuscripts of Deuteronomy*, 66–67) preserves the words *weʾet behemtah*. As noted by White, the phrase is missing in some Greek manuscripts as a result of homoioarchton. Based on this reading, Rofé would omit the entire phrase (up to the end of the verse) from the text of Deuteronomy (*Mavoʾ Le-Sefer Devarim*, 64 n. 14).

56. The clause that follows (vv. 18b–19) applies not simply to the avoidance of the *ḥerem*, as in Yadin's translation (*Temple Scroll*, 2.248, 401), but rather to the entire procedure outlined in Deut 13:13–19.

57. See above, n. 22.

58. Cf. Brin, "Ha-Miqraʾ Bi-Megillat Ha-Miqdash," 210–11; J. Maier, *The Temple Scroll: An Introduction, Translation, and Commentary* (Sheffield: JSOT Press, 1985) 122.

59. Brin, "Ha-Miqraʾ Bi-Megillat Ha-Miqdash," 210–11.

60. Tov refers only to the addition in line 3, where he notes that the Samaritan text is in agreement with the MT ("Megillat Ha-Miqdash," 106).

that of the tannaim, who require only that the majority of the inhabitants worship idolatrously (*m. Sanh.* 4:1). The scroll may have been influenced here by Gen 18:24–25, in which Abraham asks God how he can take the lives of the righteous along with the sinners.[61] Ezek 18:1–20, which likewise expects that only those who violate the law will suffer divine punishment, may also have been an influence here. In any case, according to the *Temple Scroll*, collective responsibility was not possible. Only those who actually worshiped idols could be included in the idolatrous city.

The statement that all the inhabitants are to be killed, also emphasized by the scroll, contrasts with the view of some tannaim that the children of the idolatrous city are to be spared (*t. Sanh.* 14:3). The notion that all the animals are to be killed disagrees with the tannaitic view that certain animals designated as offerings are to be saved (*t. Sanh.* 14:5).[62] It seems that these three additions of *kol* in the scroll or its *Vorlage* were intended to be polemics against specific views that we know from later tannaitic sources.

The omission of *ʾăḥērîm* from v. 14 in 11QTemple is no doubt an error in our text.[63] In 11QTemple the order of verbs is *šʾl, drš, ḥqr*, whereas in MT it is *drš, ḥqr, šʾl*. This is most likely an editorial change designed to place the steps of investigation in order of intensity, "asking" being an earlier stage than detailed investigation. The occurrence of *beyisraʾel* in 11QTemple for MT *bĕqirbekā* may be simply a contamination or harmonization based on Deut 17:4.[64] The same reading is found in some manuscripts of the LXX.[65] It is certainly not a midrashic variation, because the scroll makes no analogy between the idolatrous city and the idolatrous individual of Deut 17:2–7, the laws of which follow immediately in the *Temple Scroll*.

The addition of *takkeh* in line 8[66] seems intended to increase clarity, but this variation may be a textual variant. The addition of the preposition *le-* to *tel* seems to be explanatory. Substitution of the root *dbr* for MT *šbᶜ* in the *Niphal* may be a case of synonymous variance[67] or may have been a textual variant in

---

61. Yadin, *Temple Scroll*, 2.247.

62. Cf. *Sipre Deuteronomy* 94 (ed. Finkelstein, p. 156). The Tosepta records disagreement about the kinds of offerings to be exempted, whereas the *Sipre* includes all offerings.

63. *Contra* Tov, "Megillat Ha-Miqdash," 103.

64. Yadin, *Temple Scroll*, 2.248; see also below, p. 173.

65. Tov ("Megillat Ha-Miqdash," 106 [cf. 104]) notes that the Samaritan agrees with the MT.

66. Not noted by Yadin, *Temple Scroll*, 2.248.

67. Maier suggests that it may be an attempt to avoid anthropomorphism (*Temple Scroll*, 122). J. Milgrom notes, however, that these usages are synonymous in Deuteronomy itself ("Further Studies in the Temple Scroll," *JQR* 71 [1980–81] 100).

the author's *Vorlage.* 11QTemple *wehaṭob,* which is not in the MT but which is found in the LXX and Samaritan,[68] seems to be a harmonizing variation influenced by Deut 6:18 and 12:25. It may have appeared already in the author's *Vorlage.* The 11QTemple use of *lipne* for MT *bĕʿênê* has been explained as a move away from anthropomorphism,[69] but this does not seem likely in light of other passages where *lipne* remains. The very same variation exists in 11QTemple liii 8. In any case, this does seem to be an exegetical variation.

While this passage shows the types of variations we have observed above, it also contains changes introduced by the author or readings adopted by him to indicate specific Jewish legal rulings that he proposed or accepted. This is what we mean when we refer to halakhic variations. Apparently the case of the idolatrous city interested the author/redactor of the paraphrase, who sought to express his own views on its laws in the scroll.

The Idolatrous Individual

The final passage in the scroll dealing with idolatry is the law of the idolatrous individual from Deut 17:2–7, which is found in 11QTemple lv 15–lvi 4.

> If there be found in your midst, in one of your gates (i.e., cities) which I give to you, a man or a woman who does what is evil in My sight, (namely) to trespass my covenant, and he (or she) goes and serves other gods and bows down to them, either to the sun, or to the moon, or to any of the host of heaven, and they inform you regarding him (or her), then you shall listen to this charge, and you shall seek out and investigate well. If the accusation turns out to be true (and) correct, (that) this abomination has been performed among (the people of) Israel, then you shall take out that man or that woman and stone them with rocks[70] [to death. According to (the testimony of) two witnesses or according to (?)[71] three witnesses[72] shall the executed be put to death; he may not be put to death according to (the testimony

68. Tov, "Megillat Ha-Miqdash," 109.
69. So Brin ("Ha-Miqraʾ Bi-Megillat Ha-Miqdash," 218–20), followed by Tov ("Megillat Ha-Miqdash," 110). Contrast Yadin (*Temple Scroll,* 2.238), who suggests that this change was effected to introduce *lipne ʾadonai* because it is more common in a sacrificial context.
70. The remainder of this law is restored in Yadin (*Temple Scroll,* 2.250) based on Deut 17:5–7.
71. Yadin places the second *ʿal pi* in parentheses in his restoration of line 1, since these words are not found in the MT but help to supply a line of sufficient length (*Temple Scroll,* 2.250).
72. On the problem of the number of witnesses in Qumran legal texts, see L. H. Schiffman, *Sectarian Law in the Dead Sea Scrolls, Courts Testimony and the Penal Code* (Chico, California: Scholars Press, 1983) 73–88.

of) one witness. The hand of the witnesses shall be against him first to execute him, and the hand of the rest of the people afterwards. In this way shall you purge the evil from among you.]

This passage is largely a quotation of Deut 17:2–7.[73] It has been placed here by the author/redactor of the *Temple Scroll* because of its similarity to Deut 13:13–19 in both subject matter and actual literary form.

As part of the tendency toward linguistic updating observed above, the scroll replaces MT *kî* with *ʾim*.[74] The reference to *ʾadonai ʾĕlōhêkâ* in Deut 17:2 is replaced by the first person pronoun *ʾanoki*, as is usual in the scroll's adaptation of deuteronomic material. In the same way Deuteronomy's *bĕʿênê ʾadonai ʾĕlōhêkâ laʿăbōr bĕrîtô* is changed to *beʿenay laʿabor beriti*. 11QTemple *wehalak weʿabad* replaces MT *wayēlek wayaʿăbōd* as part of the process of linguistic updating, as does *wehištaḥaweh* for MT *wayîšttaḥû*.

The scroll has *ʾo lašemeš* where Deuteronomy has *wĕlašemeš*. This seems to be a genuine textual variant, since it is in evidence also in some manuscripts of the LXX.[75] This variant, however, has exegetical and halakhic significance, and it may be reflected in the *Temple Scroll* for this reason. One could gather from the MT that to violate the law of Deut 17:2–7, one had to worship both other gods and the astral entities. By substituting *ʾo* for the conjunctive *we-*, the scroll and the other witnesses to this reading clarified the law and indicated that it referred to one who worshipped *either* other gods or astral objects.

MT *ʾăšer lōʾ ṣiwwîtî* does not appear in 11QTemple. The omission of these apparently unnecessary words may either have been a genuine variant in the scroll's deuteronomic *Vorlage*, or an omission designed to remove ambiguity.[76] MT *wĕhuggad lĕkā* has been updated to *wehiggidu leka alayw*. The same reading is found in the Samaritan.[77] 11QTemple has added *ʾet hadabar hazeh* after *wešamata(h)*. While this change is no doubt influenced by v. 5, *ʾet haddābār*

---

73. Deut 17:2–7 is partially preserved in 4QDeut^c frgs. 30 and 32 (White, *Seven Manuscripts of Deuteronomy*, 80–85). In its preserved sections it is equivalent to the MT.

74. See above, n. 22.

75. Yadin (*Temple Scroll*, 2.249); Tov notes that the Samaritan is in agreement with the MT ("Megillat Ha-Miqdash," 106).

76. Yadin suggests that these words "weaken the command and lend themselves to divergent interpretations" (*Temple Scroll*, 2.249). Yet his reference to *Sipre Deuteronomy* 148 (ed. Finkelstein, p. 203) does not seem relevant. Rashi and Ibn Ezra understand this phrase to refer to worship that God had not commanded. Apparently they also saw the need to stress that it was not the astral entities that God had not commanded, since it was he who had created them; it was the worship of them as gods.

77. Tov, "Megillat Ha-Miqdash," 106.

hārāᶜ hazzeh. it seems to be an exegetical change as well, not just a textual harmonization. The text of 11QTemple wants to clarify that after hearing this charge, then you shall conduct the investigation, so that the hearing is to be separate and is to precede the investigation. This seems to be an attempt to eliminate ambiguity.

The addition of *wehaqaretta,* clearly based on Deut 13:15,[78] represents harmonization with the law of the idolatrous city (Deut 13:13–19, in 11QTemple lv 2–14, treated above), which is of similar literary character and content.[79] Most of the remainder of this sentence (*wĕhinnēh . . . hazzōt*) is common to Deut 17:4 and 13:15. While 11QTemple lv 20 follows Deut 17:4 in concluding with *bĕyîśrāʾēl,* 11QTemple lv 6, based on the idolatrous city, instead of concluding with *bĕqirbekā* as in MT Deut 13:15, reads *beyîśrāʾēl,* clearly under the influence of our passage in Deuteronomy and in the *Temple Scroll.*[80] In the parallel to Deut 17:5, the scroll does not have the text *ʾăšer ᶜāśû . . . hāʾiššāh,* probably the result of homoioteleuton in the scroll's deuteronomic *Vorlage* or an error in the scroll itself. Indeed, various LXX manuscripts omit either all or part of this section.[81]

Here again, we have only minor modifications of the deuteronomic material. The scroll makes no original contribution at all.

Conclusion

In approaching the prohibition of idolatrous practices, the first passage studied here, Yadin suggested that the scroll's formulation constituted "a rebuke of Hellenizers in the Hasmonean Period and of Temple practices."[82] Yet the formulation of this entire law is based on Scripture. When we investigate the laws pertaining to idolatry in the *Temple Scroll* in detail, curiously, the only area in which the author/redactor made specific contributions of halakhic character is in regard to the idolatrous city. Here his rulings tended to minimize the possibility of the enforcement of this law, since the requirement as he saw it

---

78. Yadin, *Temple Scroll,* 2.249; Tov, "Megillat Ha-Miqdash," 104.

79. This addition is not found in 4QDeutᶜ frgs. 30 and 32 to Deut 17:4 (White, *Seven Manuscripts of Deuteronomy,* 80).

80. See above, p. 170.

81. See Yadin, *Temple Scroll,* 2.249, where, however, the reference to "several manuscripts of the Vatican Codex" is confused, and Tov ("Megillat Ha-Miqdash," 109), who notes that *ʾăšer . . . šĕᶜārêkā* is omitted in the LXX and Samaritan. Some LXX manuscripts omit only *ʾet-hāʾîš ʾô ʾet-hāʾiššāh.*

82. Yadin, *Temple Scroll,* 2.230.

was for every last citizen to turn to idolatry. This approach should be compared with the view of some tannaim that this law was never intended to be enforced (*t. Sanh.* 14:1).[83] It may be that here the author was polemicizing against the destruction of cities by the Hasmoneans in their effort to extirpate paganism from the Land of Israel. However, it has been shown that the author of the *Temple Scroll* adopted a stricter view because he required the execution of even children and sacrificial animals.

With this exception, the author seems to have had little need to add to the Torah's legislation regarding idolatry. We must conclude that this entire topic is treated in the *Temple Scroll* in a context in which idolatrous practice by Jews was not a substantial problem of the times. Such an analysis fits the Hasmonean Period better than Yadin's conclusion, because the Hasmoneans had extirpated idolatry, both Jewish and non-Jewish, from the Land of Israel. Contrary to Yadin's analysis, emphasis on idolatry in the scroll would have argued against the Hasmonean dating he proposed, and which we accept, and would have supported an earlier dating during the years leading up to the Hasmonean revolt, a view which we cannot accept. It was during this period that idolatrous practices were beginning to make inroads among extremely hellenized Jews, who after the hellenistic reform attempted to bring such practices into the Jerusalem Temple.

From a literary point of view, the examination of these passages (like others in the deuteronomic paraphrase) shows that the author/redactor of the *Temple Scroll* worked from pentateuchal texts quite similar to the Masoretic Text, but exhibiting variants like those known to us from the Qumran manuscripts of the Bible. He based his work on what we may call the canonical Torah, which he rewrote and reredacted so that it would carry his message of sanctity and holiness for the Hasmonean Period in which he lived.

---

83. Although this view is presented anonymously in the Tosepta, from the continuation it is apparent that other tannaim did not agree. The Tosepta states that the purpose of this law was "*deroš weqabbel sakar*, study (it) and receive a reward (for the study of the Torah)." This must mean that the law was intended as a deterrent.

Appendix
11QTemple^b = 11QTemple liv 19–lv 6

48 (55)	(מקרבכה)]] VACAT [[ואם ישיתכה אחיכה בן אבי]כה און] בן אמכה או בנכה או	1
63	בתכה או אשת חיקכה או ריעיכה א]שר כנפשכה בסת]ר לאמור נלכה ונעבודה	2
56	אלהים אחרים אשר לוא ידעתמה אתה ואב]ותיכה מאלוהי]ן העמים אשר	3
64	סביבותיכמה הקרובים והרחוקים ממ]כה מקצי הארץ ועד] קצי הארץ לוא תואבה	4
63	לו ולוא תשמע אליו ולוא תחוס עינ]כה עליו ולוא תחמל ע]ליו ולוא תכסה	5
60 (67)	עליו כי הרוג תהרגנו ידכה תהיה בו ברא]ישונה להמיתו ויד] כול העם (תהיה בו)	6
66	באחרונה וסקלתו באבנים ומת כי בקש לה]דיחכה]מעל יהוה אלוהיכה המוציאכה	7

Notes to Restoration

This restoration is based on average line lengths similar to those proposed in the instances in which Yadin was able to restore the width of the columns of fragments of this manuscript, 11QTemple^b.[84] For translation and textual notes, see above, pp. 166–67. The numbers to the left are the number of letters and spaces in each line, with numbers in parentheses indicating additions.

Line 1. It was necessary to assume a closed paragraph (*parašah sětumah*) before the start of the law of the enticer to idolatry, since otherwise the lines would not line up evenly. From comparison with the length of such spaces elsewhere in the manuscript we opted to restore only the last word of the previous law. Less likely, but indeed possible, is an indentation at the beginning of the line, a practice followed occasionally by the scribe of 11QTemple.

Line 2. Our restoration assumes the odd spelling of *ry*^{c}*ykh* as in 11QTemple. Perhaps substitute *r*^{c}*k*. The *dalet* at the end of the preserved portion of the line in van der Woude's edition is probably a typographical error.

Line 6. The reading *khmytw* in van der Woude must be corrected to *lhmytw*. At the end of the line, considerations of space indicate that the words *thyh bw* may have been repeated.

84. See Yadin, *Temple Scroll*, 2.80, 91.

Method in Septuagint Lexicography

Gary Alan Chamberlain

C ONSIDER THE OPENING SENTENCE IN the LXX: Ἐν ἀρχῇ ἐποίησεν ὁ θεὸς τὸν οὐρανὸν καὶ τὴν γῆν. It is simple Greek: every word is common not only in the New Testament, but also in Xenophon, Herodotus, and Homer.[1] For most of the words on every page of the LXX, the same is true. Of the 120 most common words, which together would account for perhaps 80% of the words on a typical LXX page, only three (ἐνώπιος, κύριος, λαλέω) are not found in either Homer or Herodotus—though the first is found in Alcaeus (ca. 600 B.C.E.), the second is used in Aeschylus, and the third (with the meaning 'chatter') occurs in Sophocles (all three are, of course, exceedingly common in the New Testament).

I have surveyed these 120 most common words throughout Rahlfs'[2] text and find only a few instances where the meaning is unclear in relation to normal Greek usage.[3] This does not mean that LXX Greek is always typical or refined,[4] but it is generally comprehensible. Even when there are distinctly

---

1. Of course, in Homer there is no definite article, and ὁ, ἡ, τό remains a demonstrative.

2. A. Rahlfs, ed., *Septuaginta* (Stuttgart: Deutsche Bibelgesellschaft, 1935).

3. E.g., the use of σύν to translate the *nota accusativa*, אֶת (as though it were the same as the preposition "with") in Ecclesiastes. This (with other hyperliteralisms) is a regular feature of the translator Aquila.

4. Native Greek speakers certainly would not have recognized the various stratagems for dealing with the common Hebrew construction of infinitive absolute paired with finite verb (participle and finite verb, Gen 43:7; cognate dative with finite verb, Gen 43:3; cognate accusative with finite verb, Isa 42:17), nor would the frequent καὶ ἐγένετο have seemed "natural."

odd expressions clearly reflecting Semitic usage, the meaning often seems to come through. For instance, the use of πρόσωπον in phrases relating to favor or favoritism reflects the Hebrew idiom נשא פנים ('lift up the face, show favor'), leading to the LXX expression λαμβάνειν τὸ πρόσωπον, from which arise the New Testament words προσωπολημψία ('favoritism, partiality') and cognates. In this case the meaning of the LXX words in context has been sufficiently comprehensible to shape New Testament idiom, as well as the idiom of the Greek Church.[5]

Of the approximately 1,300 words that occur more than 30 times in the LXX, all but 61 (over 95%) are to be found in Bauer's New Testament lexicon.[6] Though there are exceptions (some of which are discussed below), Bauer's treatment of these words generally is sufficiently clear and comprehensive to enable New Testament students to interpret the LXX usages accurately. And the bulk of the rest of the New Testament vocabulary is also used in the LXX,[7] so that the reader familiar with Koiné Greek will find Bauer adequate for perhaps 98% of all the words encountered on a typical page. For ancient Hellenistic readers, the same would have been true: they would have experienced no difficulty with the vast majority of LXX words.

In addition, most now would agree with the conclusions of such scholars as Bauer, Friedrich, Lee, and Horsley,[8] that the vocabulary of "Biblical" Greek is for the most part that of the common popular language of the Hellenistic Age. When it fails to conform to the norms of "classical" usage, this is only occasionally due to Semitic influence or to the formative power of religious

5. The word group also appears in Barnabus, Polycarp, and the Didache, as well as various ecclesiastical authors through at least the eighth century C.E.

6. W. Bauer, *A Greek-English Lexicon of the New Testament and Other Early Christian Literature* (2d ed.; trans. and augmented by F. W. Gingrich and F. W. Danker; Chicago: University of Chicago Press, 1979). A new German edition (the sixth) has appeared: W. Bauer, *Griechisch-deutsches Wörterbuch* (ed. K. and B. Aland; Berlin: de Gruyter, 1988).

7. A. Schmoller's *Handkonkordanz zum griechischen Neuen Testament* (adapted by B. Köster to the Nestle-Aland 26th Edition; Stuttgart: Deutsche Bibelgesellschaft, 1989) indicates words not found in the LXX; excluding proper names, the non-Septuagint words apparently constitute only about 15% of the total. Despite his emphasis on the widest possible search for parallels, Bauer himself notes that the LXX is still the most important force in shaping New Testament language (*Lexicon*, xxi).

8. Bauer, *Lexicon*, xi–xxi; G. Friedrich, "Pre-History of the *TDNT*," *Theological Dictionary of the New Testament* (ed. G. Kittel and G. Friedrich; Grand Rapids: Eerdmans, 1976) 10.613–61; J. A. L. Lee, *A Lexical Study of the Septuagint Version of the Pentateuch* (Atlanta: Scholars Press, 1983); G. R. H. Horsley, "The Fiction of Jewish Greek," *New Documents Illustrating Early Christianity* 5 (New South Wales: Ancient History Documentary Research Centre, 1989) 5–40.

experience and ideas. We should not overstress the "popular" level of Biblical Greek, as though its style were equivalent to that of the most vulgar papyri; even the New Testament aims at describing a new realm of reality and experience with some literary elevation, and the LXX authors and translators are consciously presenting a "foreign" way of life and generally striving for an even higher cultural level.[9] But the point is that time after time, examination of LXX usage does not reveal anything other than what is found in the standard classical[10] and New Testament lexicons.

For examples of standard usage, Lee cites the completely idiomatic use of many terms, such as the words for 'washing'.[11] Other examples are easy to find. The Hebrew idiom שלח יד ('put forth the hand'), meaning 'to raise a hand against' or 'to attack', is generally rendered ἐπιφέρω χεῖρα (e.g., 1 Regn 24:7), a well-chosen corresponding Greek idiom common since Homer. Or consider the use of the verb συγγίνομαι, which in Classical or Hellenistic Greek can mean either "to make someone's acquaintance" or "to have sex" (like the English phrase "have intercourse with"). In the LXX it is always used to mean "have sex"[12] but in contexts where the sex is improper or illicit—hence the deliberate and precise use of an ambiguous term, not unlike the use of Hebrew ידע meaning 'to know, to have sex with', which συγγίνομαι renders in Gen 19:5. This deliberate and idiomatic usage is also employed to good effect in Jdt 12:16, where Holophernes is trembling with the desire to "get to know Judith better." One wonders if the underlying Semitic root was ידע, though Jerome's rendering (*concupiscentia*) is straightforward, to say the least. As a last example, there are the two instances of ἀβλαβής, a noun that can mean either 'harmless' (Sap 18:3) or 'unharmed' (Sap 19:6); it is intriguing that both meanings can also be found in a single classical text—Plato's *Republic* 357b and 342b.

---

9. Cf. the oral remark by F. Danker that the inscriptions, not the papyri, most closely correspond to the public and proclamatory intent of the LXX translators. We should not forget that the whole LXX is intended to render a sacred tradition; nothing in it is as "occasional" as the letters of Paul or as "vulgar" as Revelation.

10. Liddell, Scott, Jones, *Greek-English Lexicon* (Oxford: Clarendon, 1940; supplement 1968). It should be noted that LXX usage often does differ from Homeric and Attic usage, but good parallels to LXX idiom are found not only in LSJ's treatment of inscriptions and papyri, but also in such late classical authors as Aristotle or Xenophon and Hellenistic authors such as Polybius.

11. Lee, *Lexical Study*, 36–40.

12. *Contra* C. A. Moore, *Daniel, Esther, and Jeremiah: The Additions* (Anchor Bible; Garden City, N.Y.: Doubleday, 1977) 97, who confuses the verb with its cognate noun συγγενής.

Gary Alan Chamberlain

For these reasons I believe that LXX lexicography needs to begin with the assumption that, for most words, most of the time, the common Greek meanings are what the translators or authors intended and are even more probably what the ancient readers would have understood. One implication, if this thesis is correct, is that thorough study of most LXX words will not add anything to meanings already found in the standard lexicons; one wonders how great the advance in knowledge would be from doing a full-scale (probably multivolume) LXX lexicon.

I turn now to categorizing the few remaining LXX words, meanings that are not paralleled in other Greek sources, and begin with the LXX text of Gen 1:2: ἡ δὲ γῆ ἦν ἀόρατος καὶ ἀκατασκεύαστος, καὶ σκότος ἐπάνω τῆς ἀβύσσου, καὶ πνεῦμα θεοῦ ἐπεφέρετο ἐπάνω τοῦ ὕδατος. The word ἀκατασκεύαστος does not appear in Bauer. It occurs only here in the LXX but can also be found in Theophrastus, with the meaning 'unformed'. The verb κατασκευάζω, though generally meaning 'prepare, make ready', can also mean 'organize' or 'administer'.[13] On the model of Bauer, then, but drawing the information from LSJ (sometimes checked against the cited texts) and the standard LXX Concordance,[14] I propose the following lexical article:

ἀκατασκεύαστος,-ον (Theophr) *unformed, disorganized*, Gen 1:2.*

A person wanting to study the word ἐπιφέρω would find no suitable meaning (nor any reference to the middle voice) in Bauer. It would be helpful in this case, then, from LSJ to supplement Bauer's treatment as follows:

ἐπιφέρω 2.c. (mid) *rush upon, bear down upon* Gen 1:2.

These are the only additions to Bauer that any New Testament student would need in order to produce an adequate translation of the verse.

So far, then, the words of the LXX may be divided into two categories. The first consists of the common classical and Koiné words that Bauer or notes based on LSJ can make clear to anyone familiar with the New Testament or with any classical author. The second category is usage based on Hebrew idiom but sufficiently expressive or comprehensible to have shaped the language of the early Church and therefore to have been included in Bauer.[15]

13. E.g., Xenophon, *Anabasis* 1.9.19.
14. E. Hatch and H. A. Redpath, *A Concordance to the Septuagint* (Oxford: Clarendon, 1897; reprinted Graz, Austria: Akademische, 1975).
15. As discussed in relation to προσωπολημψία above. Another example is στόμα μαχαίρης ('mouth—or edge—of a sword') Luke 21:24; Heb 11:34.

To this second category may be added transliterations such as χερούβ and loanwords such as σάββατον and ἀρραβών.[16] LXX words not found in Bauer, such as σεραφιν 'seraphim' (Isa 6:2, 6) and κινύρα 'lyre',[17] are also easily glossed for lexical purposes and present no problems of method.[18] I presume that some of the transliterations were generally understood in Greek, as they are in English, where *cherubim, seraphim,* and *Sabbath* are common within the worshiping community. But for LXX lexical purposes, whether the terms were comprehensible or not, the notation "translit.," with the definition of the Semitic word, will suffice, e.g.:

αιλ, αιλαμ, αιλαμμειν, αλαμμω(θ), αιλαμμω(ν), αιλευ (57) all translit. of אֵיל *door-post,* אֵילָם *vestibule,* alw. concerning Jer. temple, 3 Regn 6:3, 2 Par 3:4; 49x in Ezek 40, 41.

Continuing to read the LXX, noting instances where Bauer does not provide sufficient guidance for understanding,[19] one quickly encounters instances in which LSJ also gives no satisfactory definition. Sometimes the context compels the adoption of new, unattested meaning. One needs read no further than Gen 1:10, where the word σύστημα, not treated in Bauer, occurs. In LSJ the definition 'accumulation' is suggested for this text, with a Hippocratic parallel. This meaning does not precisely fit the Genesis text, nor does it describe the use of the word in the LXX as a whole. In military contexts, 'corps, army' (a usage found in Polybius) fits the context of 1 Par 11:16, or the more general term 'assembly' for 3 Macc 3:9. For Genesis, I suggest 'collection, body (of water)'; though this meaning is unparalleled outside the Bible, it is also appropriate for Ezek 31:4, and Jer 28:32 contains a related mistranslation. The proposed lexical entry therefore would be:

σύστημα,-ατος τό (8, Pla+) 1. *army* 1 Par 11:16, 2 Macc 8:5; *assembly (of people)* 3 Macc 3:9. 2. *collection, body (of water,* no ||) Gen 1:10, Ezek 31:4. Jer 28:32 mistrans. of אגם 'bulwark' as though אגם 'pool'.

Another good example of unparalleled meaning is the common noun τραυματίας. In Classical Greek (since Herodotus) and secular Koiné, it means

---

16. Ἀρραβών was, of course, a Semitic loanword that had been used in Greek from the time of Aristotle and Menander and is common in nonbiblical Hellenistic texts.

17. Κινύρα occurs in Josephus as well as the LXX; cf. Hebrew כִּנּוֹר.

18. The loanwords are generally found in LSJ, and Rahlfs accents them; true transliterations are unaccented in Rahlfs and generally not treated in LSJ.

19. The suggestion for undertaking a preliminary LXX lexicon in this way came from a conversation with Dr. Robert Kraft.

Gary Alan Chamberlain

'wounded man', a meaning also found in the LXX.[20] But in several passages (such as Gen 34:27), one is driven by the context to the unparalleled meaning 'corpse'. A lexical article, then, might look like this:

τραυματίας,-ου ὁ (85, Hdt.+) 1. *wounded man* 2 Macc 4:42 etc.   2. *corpse* (no ‖) Gen 34:27, 2 Regn 1:19, 1 Macc 1:18, Ps 87:6, Ezek 6:7.

Note that I am not postulating new meanings based on the meaning of the Semitic source. Rather, I speak only of meanings indicated *by the Greek context*.[21] LSJ, however, has a disconcerting habit of proposing novel definitions for LXX words, apparently solely on the basis of the (presumed) underlying Hebrew. For instance, the Hebrew word רְאֵם ('wild ox')[22] is often rendered μονόκερως ('unicorn'); only for LXX texts does LSJ suggest 'wild ox' as a meaning for the Greek word. That the Greek translators misunderstood the Hebrew and never intended any unusual meaning for μονόκερως, is demonstrated by the fact that Jerome also misunderstood the Hebrew and translated both רְאֵם and μονόκερως with the Latin *unicornus* in his two versions of Ps 21:22.[23]

A general rule, then, is that any LXX word means precisely what it would be taken to mean in Classical or Hellenistic Greek, unless this is clearly impossible. Any other assumption implies that the translators expected the readers either already to know the Hebrew text (in which case there would be no need for a translation) or to read the Greek through the lens of some specifically "Jewish-Greek" dialect, for which there is no real evidence.[24] Nor is this error

20. The clearest instance is 2 Macc 4:42, a text composed in Greek rather than translated. In many translated passages, this same meaning would probably be presumed by most ancient readers, regardless of the underlying Hebrew.

21. Stereotypical translation is the major way that the semantic range of a Greek word is extended to include aspects of the underlying Hebrew term; cf. κρίσις (usually 'judgment', etc.) in 4 Regn 1:7, which translates מִשְׁפָּט and which, again from context, must mean something like 'customary manner, usual appearance'. On the other hand, ψυχή in Ps 68:2 does *not* mean 'throat'; that is the meaning of the Hebrew, but no Greek reader would infer that meaning from the context.

22. This example is drawn from G. B. Caird, "Toward a Lexicon of the Septuagint," *JTS* 19 (1968) 453–75; 20 (1969) 21–40, reprinted in R. Kraft, ed., *Septuagintal Lexicography* (Missoula: Scholars Press, 1975) 110–52. But Caird, as we shall see, does not consistently apply the principle used here of presuming that the common Greek meaning is the one intended by the translator and perceived by the reader.

23. The "Gallican" psalter is Jerome's revision of an Old Latin rendering of the LXX, while his "Psalterium iuxta Hebraeos" was done from the Hebrew.

24. We would also be assuming that the translators were working with our received Masoretic Text and that they correctly understood it—both of which assumptions can be demonstrated to be false in hundreds of instances.

in method confined to LSJ. Caird also tries to define on the basis of the underlying Hebrew, as exemplified in his translation of the word γομφιάζω as 'set on edge' in Ezek 18:2.[25] I contend that it must mean 'grind one's teeth', just as Caird rightly translates it in Sir 30:10. Bauer also makes this error in his discussion of the terms διατίθημι and διαθήκη. He himself, under διατίθημι, cites Aristophanes' *Birds* 439f., where the phrase διατίθημι διαθήκην means 'conclude an agreement'. But, misled by the extensive discussions concerning the meaning of בְּרִית,[26] Bauer postulates a "biblical" meaning 'issue a decree'.[27] The LXX texts he cites, Ps 104[105]:9 and 2 Par 7:18, do not support his meaning 'decree, ordain' for διατίθημι (for which secular parallels do not exist). The Psalm text refers precisely to the phrase in question, "establish a covenant." The Chronicler, on the other hand, is speaking of David's dominion, so that for this text 'confer, assign' (Bauer's second meaning; cf. Luke 22:29) is preferable. Nor is the argument advanced by the additions of Barn 10:2, PsSal 9:10, and T. Naphth 1:1 as supporting evidence in the latest German edition. The use of διατίθημι in T. Naphth. is no different from that in T. Zeb., T. Levi, or T. Benj. and is better translated with the usual meaning of διατίθημι 'make one's last will and testament'. PsSal 9:10, despite the fact that διαθήκη is the object of a preposition, is related to the phrase in question and should be rendered 'you offered yourself in a covenant to our fathers concerning us'. And finally, Barn. 10:2 alludes to Deuteronomy, using διατίθημι nearly elliptically to mean 'make a covenant, confer a relationship', as Lake rightly translates.[28]

I repeat, it is usually best simply to assume that the likely meaning for a normal Greek reader is the way the LXX should be construed. Such instances as τραυματίας are not modifications of this principle: the indication ⟨no ||⟩ in a lexical article simply means that the ancient reader would have had to infer that meaning from the context, regardless of any familiarity with the Semitic original, or with any presumed special Jewish usage or custom. If the context does not compel the reader to see that the 'wounded' are also 'dead', then the normal meaning is to be preferred. In a similar way, in English military usage, the word *casualties* refers to both 'wounded' and 'killed', and the reader is

25. As reprinted in Kraft, *Septuagintal Lexicography*, 122.

26. Continental scholars have resisted equating this term with German "Bund" or French "alliánce." The discussion has been enormously complicated by attempts to derive the covenant forms of the Hebrew Bible from the Hittite vassal treaties; the issues are surveyed, with negative conclusions for the Hittite origins, in my own dissertation, *Exodus 21–24 and Deuteronomy 12:26: A Form-Critical Study* (Boston University, 1976).

27. The German phrase *Verfügung erlassen* is still retained in Alands' 6th edition.

28. K. Lake (trans.), *The Apostolic Fathers I* (LCL; Cambridge, Mass.: Harvard University Press, 1912).

forced to seek from context any clarification about how many soldiers actually died. As for διατίθημι and διαθήκη, one should assume that a normal Greek reader of the LXX would not construe them legalistically (the same would be true of νόμος, which in the LXX generally means 'custom' or 'traditional practice'), at least not until the Roman Period made written decrees and "law" the "customary" way of ordering society.

Having said all of this, I come now to the handful of exceptions, the words and phrases for which neither customary Greek usage nor literary context suggests a suitable meaning. Inevitably, these exceptions are crucial words in a sentence, the opaque and frustrating enigmas that turn most students of the Bible away from all efforts to consult the LXX, the words that are the lexical and textual riddles, sometimes subverting even the most competent commentators. These words demand treatment that is particular *in method* if they are to be apprehended.

It is at this point that it becomes impossible to proceed with an LXX lexicon as one would with any nontranslated corpus, purely on the basis of the Greek context. It is necessary always to be attentive to the textual and linguistic problems in the Semitic sources, as well as the Greek witnesses.[29] Yet it is precisely in those cases where the Semitic source has not been preserved— where the LXX is an expansion of the Hebrew Bible or reflects a *Vorlage* different from the Masoretic Text—that the LXX has received the most attention. Whether one is translating the deuterocanonicals for which Semitic *Vorlagen* have been lost or seeking to emend the Masoretic Text,[30] the textual and linguistic interactions of both the Hebrew and Greek witnesses must be sorted out before the LXX can be honestly and reliably used.

A great weakness in biblical and historical studies is the failure first to read the LXX itself as a literary collection. Failure ever to engage the LXX except in relation to a textual problem in the Hebrew Bible results in failure to understand the LXX itself the way it would have appeared to an ancient reader. This lack of understanding leads to postulating false textual or lexical possibilities. That is why it is imperative first to ask what the ancient reader would have understood in order to form a proper judgment about what the translator *meant* in any particular instance. This is true for four fundamental reasons.

29. Cf. above all P. Walters, *The Text of the Septuagint* (Cambridge: Cambridge University Press, 1973) esp. p. 279, Iud 5:16, where the B text (without variant in Rahlfs) reads ἀγγέλων, but the true reading must be ἀγέλων 'flocks'; the difficult metonymy of 'the piping of the flocks' invited the copyist's substitution of 'angels'.

30. The problems here are well discussed in E. Tov, *The Text-Critical Use of the Septuagint in Biblical Research* (Jerusalem Biblical Studies 3; Jerusalem: Simor, 1981).

(1) The translator may have aimed at something other than the rendering of the Semitic meaning. I refer here to the well-known instances of homophony. While these instances are not common, the renderings of בָּמָה by βωμός (only in the Prophets; in the Torah and Joshua βωμός always translates מִזְבֵּחַ), of מוּם or מְאוּם by μῶμος (in all instances), and of תֹּךְ by τόκος (Ps 71:14 [72:14]), all show more concern for sound than for meaning. Once again, then, the *Greek* context is the guide; τόκος means 'interest' (on loans) rather than 'oppression' in a more general sense, and μῶμος means 'blame' unless the context forces the meaning 'blemish'.

(2) The reader may find a meaning not intended by the translator or the original[31] that becomes the operative meaning of the text in the later history of the tradition. This principle is illustrated in the use of Ps 8:6 by the writer of Heb 2:5–9. The phrase βραχύ τι can mean either 'by a little bit' (the un-ambiguous meaning of the underlying Hebrew) or 'for a little while'—the meaning that makes possible a christological use of the text. The modern translator might assert that the author of Hebrews was "wrong" to use the text in this way, but the fact is that the Greek does permit this construal. Hence LXX lexicography must respect the interpretation of the Greek text that the *reader* might have perceived or risk missing the actual operation of the LXX in the history of Jewish and Christian tradition. There are implications for textual criticism and the history of doctrine in recalling that every copyist was a *reader*, not a translator.[32] This can be seen in the confusion between πόλις and πυλή. In 4 Regn 10:8, where B and others read "the door of the gate of the city," Lucian simplifies to "the gate of the city," and the remaining wit-nesses read "the door of the city." Lucian's rendering is the most natural but is clearly secondary, resulting (as does the B reading) from the conflation of the variants πυλή 'gate' and πόλις 'city'. Rahlfs' emendation, τὴν θύραν τῆς πύλης 'the door of the gate', is unsupported—were it not for the fact that it is the equivalent of the Masoretic Text *and* has the virtue of being the *lectio difficilior* in that the phrase would seem redundant to the reader unfamiliar with Hebrew idiom. The easy transition to "the door of the city," from which arose the doublets and the Lucianic rationalization, is the best explanation for the origins of all the readings and confirms the correctness of Rahlfs' emenda-tion. This instance should lead to questioning the twenty or so other in-stances where the LXX apparently has rendered Hebrew שַׁעַר with πόλις. Is it

31. Cf. the discussion of ἐκδέχομαι in Lee, *Lexical Study,* 59–60.
32. The great exception is the hexaplaric tradition that so confuses our efforts to re-construct the text of the "Old Greek," because Origen had consulted the Hebrew in a form virtually identical to the Masoretic Text.

not highly probable that copyist's error has produced all of these instances
(Gen 22:17, 24:60; Deut 12:15ff., Iud 5:8B,11, etc.), even though only a few
(such as 2 Regn 10:8; 1 Par 16:42; Ier 52:7, and perhaps 1 Macc 5:22) retain
traces of confusion in the manuscript tradition?[33]

(3) The translator may have found the text incomprehensible and intended to leave the question of meaning to the reader. A striking instance is
Ps 89:5, where it says: τὰ ἐξουδενώματα αὐτῶν ἔτη ἔσονται 'their contemptible things will be years'. This is instructive first of all in that ἐξουδένωμα is,
according to LSJ, a *hapax legomenon*. Yet the meaning can be derived from
normal principles of word formation alone.[34] Comparison with the Hebrew
shows that the translator misread the word זְרַמְתָּם 'you sweep them away', as
though it were pointed זִרְמָתָם as it is in Ezek 23:20, where it means 'phal-
luses'! He also mistook שֵׁנָה for the word 'year' rather than its correct meaning 'sleep'. The fact that the resultant sentence neither bears any relation to
the Hebrew ('you sweep them away as they sleep') nor makes any sense at all
was no deterrent to the translator, nor need it be to the modern reader. It is
possible to see what the translator *intended* as soon as one interprets the Greek
words with the meanings an ordinary Hellenistic reader would give them.

(4) The translator may have misunderstood the text, and by determining
the reader's probable comprehension of the text, one is able to deduce the
translator's error. Sir 25:15 is a good example. Here the word κεφαλή makes
no sense ("there is no head like the head of a serpent") until one recognizes
that behind the difficulty is the Hebrew word ראש, meaning 'poison', a rare
homonym of the common word 'head'. Once again the lexicographer should
not postulate new meanings for the Greek word, since the context would never
lead a Greek reader to think 'poison'. It is obvious that the translator had no
aim apart from the ordinary use of the Greek word and rendered the Hebrew

---

33. Note also the confusion in Deut 12:5, 14, where πόλις appears as a variant for
φυλή 'tribe'.

34. Hence LSJ is wrong in offering the definition 'contempt'; both from its use in the
plural and from its structure, 'contemptible thing' is the necessary definition. Cf. M. Stehle,
Greek Word Building (rev. H. Zimmermann; trans. F. F. Church and J. S. Hanson; Missoula:
Scholars Press, 1976) 3–4. 'Contempt' would be ἐξουδένωσις, which actually occurs in
Ps 30:19. Similarly, the word μακροημερεύω, though it occurs seven times (Deut 5:33, 6:2,
etc., Iud 2:7, Sir 3:6) is not even listed in LSJ (including the Supplement). It (and its cognates, which are found in LSJ) derive from the Hebrew ארך ימים ('length of days', 'long
life') and related phrases. But one need not postulate any special "Jewish-Greek dialect,"
since the normal principles of word formation, along with the literary context, made the
word comprehensible to Greek speakers even if it was an *ad hoc* coinage by the translator.
Nor can one discern any cultural or theological "freight" borne by these terms.

as he (mis)understood it. When modern translators render the sentence using the word 'poison', I conclude that they are right to point out what was clearly the intent of the Hebrew original but that an LXX lexicon should not do anything other than explain the confusion of roots that led to the meaningless Greek sentence. The lexical article, as a supplement to Bauer, might read:

κεφαλή 3. Sir 25:15 mistrans. of Heb. ראש *poison* as if *head.*

The above examples are readily understood and are chosen simply to illustrate the principles: first, look at the Greek text *as a text*, not in relation to any actual or supposed Semitic original. Then check Bauer first, followed by LSJ, for the ordinary senses of the words. At that point Bauer may be supplemented with brief lexical notes that make the LXX understandable to anyone familiar with the New Testament or other ancient Greek works. Presupposing that the reader (or copyist) would have construed any words (except transliterations and loan words) in a normal Greek sense (unless compelled to do otherwise by the *Greek* context) should produce insight into the textual and linguistic history of the LXX. One foreseeable offshoot of this method (if in fact it proves to have heuristic power) would be further to discredit the supposition that there was a special "Jewish-Greek" dialect that was shared by the translators and readers.

Next I turn my attention to three additional, more complex problems of interpretation that may be clarified by applying the above method, thereby lending their support to it. First let us examine two instances involving the word περιλαμβάνω 'encompass, surround'. Let us begin with Lam 4:5, for which both Rahlfs and the Göttingen text read περιεβάλοντο κοπρίας 'they clothed themselves with dung'. The Greek phrase as it stands seems clear (but see below on κοπρία) and even makes sense in context. Whence then comes the variant περιέλαβον in A or περιελάβοντο in other witnesses? The usual meaning of περιλαμβάνω is evidenced in the LXX (Ps 47:13, Isa 31:9), but it sometimes renders the Hebrew word חבק 'embrace'[35] and some contexts compel that meaning for the Greek (Gen 29:13, 4 Regn 4:16, Sir 30:20). It is used stereotypically (again rendering חבק) in Eccl 4:5, where it must mean 'fold or clasp' (one's hands). Now חבק is also the word in the Hebrew of Lam 4:5, so the original LXX text must have been περιέλαβον, intended to mean 'embrace' or 'cling to' (trash heaps). I am not postulating here a new "meaning" for περιλαμβάνω; on the contrary, it was a copyist's inability to make

---

35. Outside the Bible, LSJ cites only one instance—Xenophon's *Anabasis* (7.4.10)—for this meaning.

sense of the text—which to him him meant 'surround the trash-heap'—that
led to his "emendation": -βαλ- for -λαβ-.[36] The lexical article, then, would
read like this:

περιλαμβάνω (13, Hdt.+) 1. *encompass, surround* Ps 47:13, Isa 31:9   2. *embrace*
(X. *Anab.* 7.4.10) Gen 29:13, 4 Regn 4:16, Sir 30:20; *put one's arms around* Iud
16:29. Eccl 4:5 stereot trans of חבק 'fold clasp' (hands) as if 'embrace'. Lam 4:5
(*recte*; Ra, Gött. περιβάλλω but cf. Heb.) stereot trans of חבק 'cling to' (trash-
heap) as if 'embrace' (scribe read 'surround', hence emendation -βαλ- (for -λαβ-) is
if 'put on, wear'.

It is interesting to note that this construal establishes 'dunghill, trash-
heap', and not simply 'trash, refuse', as the meaning of κοπρία. In fact, LSJ
only lists two instances of κοπρία meaning simply 'refuse' (rather than the
place trash is dumped); one is Luke 14:35, where Bauer correctly gives the
more usual meaning. The other is Sir 27:4, where I believe (*pace* both Rahlfs
and Ziegler) that the correct form should be κόπρια (neut. pl. of κόπριον, a
change of accent only; of course the singular verb with a neuter plural subject
is typical Greek), whose usual meaning is 'dirt, refuse', as the context requires. In other words, there are no instances of κοπρία meaning simply
'dung, trash'; thus the meaning of περιεβάλοντο κοπρίας is more problematic
than it first appeared.

Turning to Gen 19:17, we find the word συμπαραλαμβάνω, again in both the
Rahlfs and Göttingen texts. P 961 clearly reads συμπεριλαμβάνω. LSJ offers no
instance of either word meaning what this context requires: (pass.) 'be also over-
taken'. Which should be preferred? For the single compound παραλαμβάνω LSJ
offers but one instance of the passive meaning 'be captured' (Polyb. 3.69.2), and
even this is not quite what the Genesis passage requires. But for περιλαμβάνω
the meanings 'intercept, overtake, catch', (pass.) 'be caught, trapped' are frequent from the times of Herodotus and Aristophanes. By principles of normal word formation, συμπεριλαμβάνω is the superior reading. Proper lexical
method, then, can also assist LXX scholars in textual criticism.

The second example shows that proper method can also lead to insights
that are strictly lexical. In Obad v. 1 the word περιοχή occurs, which one
commentator[37] asserts means 'passage' (of scripture), as it may in its only
New Testament occurrence (Acts 8:32). The secular equivalent is 'section' (of
a book, in Plato). But one doubts that this meaning would seem natural to
the Greek reader of Obadiah, when there is nothing about books in the con-

36. Note the similar textual confusion of -λαβ- and -βαλ- in Job 22:22.
37. H. W. Wolff, *Obadiah and Jonah* (Minneapolis: Augsburg/Fortress, 1986) 33.

text. Other occurrences of the word περιοχή in the LXX do not suggest this meaning; generally, it is used in the sense of 'siege' or 'enclosure'. But it also shows up in mistranslations of words taken to derive from the roots צור/צרר 'constrict, harrass' (4 Regn 19:24, Ezek 12:13, etc.). I believe that in Obadiah the Greek translator mistook the noun ציר 'messenger' for the homonym 'pang, convulsion'. Note that according to LSJ περιοχή is defined by one lexicographer (Photius, ninth century C.E.) as equivalent to περιπετεία 'overturning' or θλῖψις 'constriction, harassment' (the latter word not infrequently used to render words derived from the Hebrew צור/צרר). The latter meaning for περιοχή is attested in the meaning 'siege'; the former, 'upheaval', 'sudden reversal', suits the context in Obadiah and conforms to the postulated misunderstanding of the Hebrew. The lexical article:

περιοχή,-ῆς, ἡ (23; Theophr., Polyb.+; B: *passage of Scripture*) 1. *fortified enclosure* (no ‖) 1 Regn 22:4–5, 2 Par 32:10, Ps 30:22, Ier 28:20.   2. *siege* 4 Regn 24:10, Nah 3:14, Ier 19:9. 4 Regn 19:24 mistrans. of מצור 'Egypt' as if from צור 'constrict, harrass'; Ezek 12:13, 17:20 mistrans. of מְצוּדָה 'net' as if מְצוּרָה 'fortified enclosure'.   3. *sudden reversal, overturning* (= περιπετεία, cf. LSJ). Obad 1 mistrans. of ציר (2) 'messenger' as if ציר (3) 'upheaval, convulsion'.

This example shows that the LXX, by its relation to the Hebrew original, sometimes provides direct evidence for the correctness of some of the Byzantine lexicographers' equivalencies, in the absence of other classical or Hellenistic evidence.

Third, I take up the strange case of στήριγμα in 4 Regn 25:11.[38] One usual classical meaning of the word is 'foundation' or 'support', the meaning found in the LXX in such passages as 2 Esdr 9:8, Tob 8:6, Ps 104:16, and Sir 3:31. The underlying Hebrew terms vary; the most common is מַטֶּה 'staff' or 'prop'. In 2 Regn 20:19, however, the translator was baffled by the word אֱמוּנִים 'faithful', which he translated etymologically with στήριγμα, based on the root אמן 'be firm'. It is not surprising, therefore, that in 4 Regn 25:11, faced with the unusual word אָמוֹן 'artisan', he did the same. Unfortunately, after the translation was done, the Hebrew itself was corrupted, and the word אָמוֹן became הָמוֹן 'crowd', or in other contexts, 'army'. Perhaps the Hebrew copyist was influenced by the sense that all Judah went into exile, or perhaps he himself did not know the less common word. But אָמוֹן is the word preserved in the parallel text Ier 52:15, and is doubtless correct, as is confirmed by the etymological rendering of the LXX.

---

38. Some of the material in this section was presented to the Old Testament Textual Criticism section of the 1984 meeting of the Society of Biblical Literature in Chicago.

In the footnotes of *Biblia Hebraica Stuttgartensia*, however, the LXX evidence is unmentioned, and what should have been a *textual* problem is addressed *lexically*. That is, the editor proposes a new and otherwise unattested Hebrew word, אָמוֹן, based on a supposed Akkadian etymology (*ummanu*) and defined by the Latin word *exercitus*, apparently (from the appended Syriac notice) intended to mean 'army'. There are compounded levels of confusion here. First, the proposed Akkadian word is actually one of two words, one of which corresponds to אָמוֹן 'artisan', and the other to הָמוֹן 'army'; they are homographs because Akkadian does not distinguish the two initial sounds (as Greek did not, until breathing marks were added). Second, the Latin definition is itself ambiguous because, remarkably enough, Latin has a pair of homographs *exercitus*, the fourth-declension noun 'army' and the first-second declension adjective that can mean 'skilled person'! So the two Akkadian words correspond precisely to the two Hebrew words already known, and there is no Akkadian evidence for Hebrew 'army' with initial ʾalep. The proposed new Hebrew word, along with its etymology, is spurious and is in fact unmentioned in the Baumgartner lexicon.[39] Consequently, since the use of στήριγμα is etymological and apparently results from the translator's inability to understand the Hebrew, it is time to return to the rule of thumb that the word means what a Greek reader would take it to mean—'support' or 'foundation'. As before, taking this rule into account helps to clarify the translator's aim (and limitations). I dismiss out of hand Caird's suggestion[40] to translate στήριγμα as 'solid citizens'; not only is the meaning unparalleled (and the Greek word singular in number), but the suggested meaning could never occur to anyone unfamiliar with the *emended* Hebrew text!

But there is a further harvest to be reaped. As noted above, in 2 Regn 20:19 the translation στήριγμα is etymological, based on אמן, with the meaning 'foundations', rather than on אֱמוּנִים 'faithful ones'. Similarly, στήριγμα appears in Ezek 7:11 because the translator has assumed that מַטֶּה means 'support' or 'prop'[41] just as it does in 4:16 and Ps 104:16. There is another book in which στήριγμα makes its appearance, the book of 1 Maccabees (2:43, 6:18, and 10:23). In 1 Maccabees, of course, there is no surviving Semitic original, and my suggestions are inevitably speculative. Goldstein, in the Anchor Bible,[42] translates this word 'help' or 'aid', and the NRSV uses

39. Ludwig Koehler and W. Baumgartner, *Hebräisches und aramäisches Lexicon zum Alten Testament*, fasc. 1 (Leiden: Brill, 1967).

40. As reprinted in Kraft, *Septuagintal Lexicography*, 147.

41. Admittedly, the text of Ezek 7:11 is confused. But it is possible to see that Greek στήριγμα corresponds to MT מַטֶּה, which here probably means 'rod' (for punishment).

42. J. A. Goldstein, *I Maccabees* (AB 41; Garden City, N.Y.: Doubleday, 1981).

'strengthening' and 'reinforcing'. Perhaps the latter translations are justifiable if the underlying root is assumed to be אמן and the translation stereotyped and etymological. Note once again that I am not saying that στήριγμα *means* something like 'reinforcement', but that, as with κεφαλή in Sir 25:15, it is justifiable to aim for the sense of the underlying Hebrew when the Greek witnesses to the translator's incapacities.

The Anchor Bible, on the other hand, seems to be inferring an extended meaning from the Greek context, and an argument can be made for this meaning. There is a word more commonly used, however, to translate 'aid' or 'help', and that word is βοήθεια, which is in fact the word used in 10:24 (just following στήριγμα in 10:23). In terms of lexical method, I still prefer holding to the meaning 'support' as the only "meaning" that στήριγμα demonstrably carries in the LXX.

There is one more possibility. I believe that at least in 1 Macc 2:24 (and perhaps the other two passages as well) the Hebrew word did not stem from אמן, but was הָמוֹן, meaning 'army'. If the Hebrew text of 2 Kings had already been corrupted, the translator of 1 Maccabees would have been misled by the false equivalence of στήριγμα in the LXX with הָמוֹן in the Hebrew. The sentence in the original Hebrew of 1 Macc would therefore have been: וַיִּהְיוּ לָהֶם לְהָמוֹן 'and they became for them an army'. This makes excellent sense in context, but without the textual corruption and mistranslation of 2 Kgs/4 Regn 25:11, no one ever would have known how such a Hebrew text came to be rendered as it is in 1 Macc 2:43.

My thesis has been that one should always presume the common meanings of Greek words in the LXX unless the Greek context forces an expansion of their semantic range. Even when a translational or textual error can be identified, the Greek reader's point of view is the best clue to discerning the translator's aim. In negative terms, this thesis opposes the theory that Jews in Alexandria (or Antioch, Ephesus, or Rome) were speaking or writing a special dialect of Greek. For the study of the New Testament and the Christian fathers, as well as early Judaism, this thesis is beneficial to an appropriate comprehension of the texts.

The Semantic Field
of the Term 'Idolatry'

Charles A. Kennedy

I DOLATRY IS A TERM WITH POTENTIAL reference to a wide range of activities, a term defined variously according to individual speakers'—or translators'—theological biases. In all likelihood most translators in the past have
never seen the actual artifacts referred to in the Scriptures as "idols," yet they
felt free to characterize them as "dead idols" or "filthy idols" or collectively as
"abominations." The reason for this is not hard to discover: dogma tri-
umphed over the text. The word *idol* is defined as an illicit image, prohibited
in the cult. For some this prohibition can be carried a step further to include
all images. A major problem arises for these extremists, however, when the
text describes licit images allowed in the cult. The cherubim on the ark and
in the temple of Jerusalem are the most notable examples. Because of these
allowable images, a distinction has sometimes been made between "idolatry"
and "iconolatry," the former being condemned, the latter permitted, indeed
enjoined. Idols are bad, but icons are good.

The interplay between the words *idol* and *image* (or *icon*) in the western
tradition is epitomized in the dialogue between William Tyndale and Thomas More. Tyndale preferred to translate *eidōlon* as 'image'. In so doing he
broke with the tradition perpetuated in the Vulgate of transliterating, not

Author's Note: The material in this paper was first presented at the International Meeting
of the Society of Biblical Literature, Heidelberg, Germany, August, 1987.

translating, *eidōlon* ('idol'). For his intellectual honesty he was vilified by Thomas More. Images, said More, were pictures of Christ, the Virgin Mary and the saints; idols were of the Devil. If Tyndale could not tell the difference between them, Tyndale would be guilty of loving both God and the Devil and thus liable to drastic punishments in this world and the next.[1]

The debate between Tyndale and More is but one example of the ongoing debate about words and meaning among translators. Tyndale was anxious to translate the Greek text of the New Testament in such a way as to remove the contaminating accretions of the medieval church and thus restore the pristine purity of the gospel. In the end, More's dogma prevailed over Tyndale's innovative translation and the word *idol* was enshrined in the text of the Authorized Version.

The advances made in philology, lexicography, and linguistic analysis in this century raise questions about the ways in which ancient texts are to be translated and understood. I propose here to examine the concept of *idol* as it appears in the MT and to compare that usage with the way in which the translators of the LXX understood it. I will discuss briefly the transition of the term into Latin, showing the pivotal role of Tertullian and Jerome in the process of fixing the meaning of the word for Christian tradition.

The oldest catalog of idol terminology is found in the rabbinic commentary *Sifre Lev.* 19:4:

> *ᵓlylym*: This is one of the ten derogatory names by which idols are called: *ᵓlylym* because idols are pierced (*ḥlwlym*); *psl* because they are carved; *mskh* because they are melted; *mṣbh* because they stand; *ʿṣbym* because they are made limb by limb (*nᶜsym prqym prqym*); *trpym* because they decay (*mrqybym*); *glwlym* because they are abominable (*mglᶜym*); *šqwṣym* because they are detestable; *ḥmnym* because they stand in the sun (*ᶜwmdym bḥmh*); *ᵓšrym* because they receive beatitude from others (*mtᵓšrym mtᵓḥrym*).

This exercise in philology, Pfeiffer noted, enlisted etymology in the holy war against heathenism.[2]

When the Hebrew text was translated into Greek, some changes in vocabulary occurred. To the rabbinic list of ten words the LXX added seven more words, all of which it translated as *eidōlon*: *ᵓl, ᵓlh, ᵓlwh, bᶜl, hbl, mplṣt,* and *ṣlm* At the same time the LXX deleted three words from the list (*mskh,*

1. Louis A. Schuster et al., *The Complete Works of St. Thomas More* (New Haven: Yale University Press, 1973) 8/1.4–5, 174–75.

2. R. H. Pfeiffer, "The Polemic against Idolatry in the Old Testament," *JBL* 43 (1924) 238.

mṣbh, and *ʾšrym*). *Mskh* and *mṣbh* are translated by their Greek equivalents, 'molten image' and 'stele', respectively. The Asherim were more problematic, since presumably no one in living memory had seen them. The result was the translation 'grove' which was carried over into the AV.[3] Taken together, these words provide a working vocabulary for studying the concept of idolatry in early and late Israel.

In his study, "The Polemic Against Idolatry in the Old Testament," Pfeiffer analyzed the attitude toward images in the documentary sources of the Pentateuch. He distinguished three stages in the history of idolatry. The first was designated the period before 621 B.C.E. and the Deuteronomic Reform. At that point images, pillars, and memorials were mentioned, but not idolatry. Although J demonstrated no knowledge of sacred images, there were household shrines with images (Judges 17 and 18), which appear to have been acceptable to the narrator. The second phase, that of the Deuteronomic Reform and the time of Ezekiel, evidenced a polemic against images and idols in the name of and for the sake of the cultic reform in the Jerusalem temple. Pfeiffer placed all the pentateuchal laws prohibiting images in the period after 621 B.C.E. The third phase began with the rededication of the temple after the Exile. By this time, according to Pfeiffer, information about the ancient cults of Canaan had to be derived solely from the text of the emerging scriptures, not from firsthand knowledge of the shrines themselves. With the development of the concept of Israel as the Chosen People, all other nations were deemed accursed and their gods literally "unspeakable." Even in reading the text of the Bible, substitute names were to be read in place of Molech, Baal, Astarte, and others.[4] It was this third phase that provided the context for the interpretation of these words in the Jewish and Christian traditions.

It is difficult not to agree with this schematization as far as the textual evidence goes. But by confining himself to the literary evidence, Pfeiffer ignored the archeological evidence that was beginning to accumulate even at the time he wrote. Pfeiffer did not adequately consider the probability that the family shrines, so acceptable in the first phase, survived much longer than the literary evidence indicates. The historical narratives of the Bible do not reveal much about the Persian and Greek periods, but the archeological record certainly does with regard to tombs and burial customs. Rock-cut tombs and hypogeia continued to flourish down to the Roman period. The religious life of

---

3. The AV added three more words to idol vocabulary: *ʿwn, ʿymh, ṣʿyr*, none of which were idols in the MT or the LXX.

4. See Exod 23:13: "Make no mention of the names of the other gods, nor let such be heard out of your mouth."

the people included rites at these tombs, however much the priesthood in Jerusalem wished otherwise.[5]

A second study of idolatry often cited is that of C. R. North.[6] North explored the principles underlying the manufacture and worship of idols, hoping thereby to discover the "ethos of idolatry." He classified a group of words pertaining to idols in two categories: terms describing the process by which they were made ('carved', 'molten') and terms of opprobrium ('weaklings', 'onerous things', 'revolting things'). In both categories, nothing positive or favorable is ever implied about images or the gods/goddesses they represent. North thereby confirms the sense of the AV that idols are by nature evil things.

North explained the prohibition of images by citing the Decalogue and concluded, "One God, therefore, it would seem, no idol; no idol because only one God."[7] This somewhat enigmatic conclusion seems to mean that no idols of the One God were permitted on the basis of a rather straightforward logic: there could not be a replication (a second) to the One and still have the One remain one. Clement of Alexandria quotes Antisthenes in much the same vein: "God is like none else, wherefore none can know him thoroughly from a likeness" (*ex eikōnos*).[8] But why should this prohibition be extended to include other images as well (see Deut 4:12ff.)? Pfeiffer solves this by including all the legal prohibitions in his second phase, as part of the Deuteronomic Reform.[9] The fact is, however, that Israel never did totally reject images in the temple or the synagogue. From the decoration on the Ark of the Covenant, to both the First and Second Temples, to the synagogues of Galilee and Dura-Europos, images of animals, plants, imaginary beings, and even people continued to be used with enthusiasm. This pictorial plethora leads Faur and others to posit a licit iconolatry, by which he means acceptable decorative motifs, as opposed to illicit idolatry involving worship of images.[10]

5. Ephraim Stern, *Material Culture of the Land of the Bible in the Persian Period 538–332 B.C.* (Warminster: Aris & Phillips, 1982), esp. chap. 3, "Burials," and chap. 6, "Cult Objects"; E. R. Goodenough, *Jewish Symbols in Greco-Roman Period* (New York: Pantheon, 1953) 1.61ff. If *t. ʿAbod. Zar.* 6:8 is to be believed, there were still three places in Israel where Asherah was worshiped in the Common Era.

6. C. R. North, "The Essence of Idolatry," in *Von Ugarit Nach Qumran* (ed. J. Hempel; Berlin: Alfred Töpelmann, 1958) 151–60.

7. Ibid., 156.

8. Clement of Alexandria, *Exhortation to the Greeks* (LCL; trans. G. W. Butterworth; Cambridge, Mass.: Harvard University Press, 1968) 159.

9. Pfeiffer, "Polemic against Idolatry," 235.

10. J. Faur, "The Biblical Idea of Idolatry," *JQR* 69 (1978) 1–15.

The second essential feature of idolatry posited by North is that it exalts the worship of the *élan vital* instead of the worship of the Transcendent Creator. He sees the basis of paganism as being the nurturing of the life-force, from which fertility cults, agricultural festivals, and seasonal rituals also stemmed. By contrast, Israel's covenant was with the God in history, the God who brings his people out of the house of bondage in Egypt. On the conceptual level there is a difference between a pagan cyclical notion of life and the biblical linear progression from creation to consummation. North, however, overlooked another operative factor on the practical level, which became especially important for the later generations who knew of the Exodus only as story, not experience. Nature and the *élan vital* are not moral. The uniqueness of Israel's revelation, which it shares with the other monotheistic faiths, is that God is not simply Power, but Righteousness, Justice, and Grace. These are attributes that do not readily translate into the symbolism of thunderbolts or balance scales. To this extent one can agree with North's contention that the one God must of necessity be aniconic.

Nevertheless, North's study stopped short in that it took into account only a small part of the vocabulary relating to idols. If the semantic field of a word is to be plotted, it is essential to include as many meanings as possible in order to capture the various nuances of the word. To do less is to run the risk of skewing the evidence in favor of some predetermined interpretation or theological position. It is also essential to consider the contributions of modern linguistics to the translation of ancient texts.

In the biblical field the study of languages has been dominated by the science of philology and its seemingly endless search for Akkadian, Arabic, Aramaic, Ugaritic, and even on occasion hypothetical Sumerian roots. For example, ʿ*ṣb* is usually associated with a root meaning 'grieve'; therefore idols are "grievous things that cause grief to the worshiper or to God." On the face of it this appears to me to be comparable to the Hellenistic etymology in which puns played a more important role than scientific philology.[11]

Today the ongoing work of translating the Bible into living languages provides insights into the process of the translation of ancient languages. Eugene Nida makes an important distinction between the specific linguistic context of a word, which gives a form linguistic meaning, and the practical-world (non-linguistic) context, which provides what is more generally understood by the meaning of a word. He goes on to say:

---

11. Cf. the tradition that identifies the fruit that brought evil (Lat. *malum*) into the world as an apple because of the phonetic similarity of the Greek word (*mēlon*).

The cultural distribution must, however, reckon not only with objective events but with evaluations of the events and the corresponding symbols. The emotion which a patriot feels when he uses the phrase "Old Glory" is utterly unintelligible to a Nuer of the Sudan, who neither has nor understands banners. But when he dances before a favorite bull and calls out its name, he experiences a similar "thrill" in having uttered an emotionally charged expression.[12]

The difficulty with etymologies is that, however interesting they may be from a historical perspective, "they are no guarantee whatsoever that the historical influence is a factor in the people's actual use of such linguistic units."[13] The translator must understand that actual use, and not some historically accurate (or even plausible) explanation, determines what a word means at a given moment.

The word *idol* raises all of these problems. At the outset it is important to remember that the English word *idol* derives from a *transliteration*, not a translation, of the Greek word *eidōlon*, which had a history of its own before it became a Christian technical term. The Greeks did not use the word *idol* to designate a class of religiously abhorrent images.

To penetrate behind the layers of interpretation that influence the core meaning of a word, Nida proposes plotting its semantic field, analyzing the word in its cultural setting. To do so in the case at hand, it is necessary to assemble the various Hebrew terms and their referents and compare them with the Greek vocabulary of the LXX. This will generate two charts: a componential chart listing the various forms and functions of the word *idol* and a chart showing the cultural acceptability or rejection of the words used.

The componential chart (chart 1) lists the Hebrew words that were translated *eidōlon* in the LXX.[14] The frequency is listed under each of the terms plotted. The vertical column lists the forms and kinds of activities associated with the words as they are described in the passages in which they occur.

At this point it is appropriate to list some observations that are useful in interpreting these charts.

1. Note that *mskh* and *mṣbh* are never *eidōla*. They are translated directly into Greek ('molten image' and 'stele'), with no further explanation

---

12. Eugene A. Nida, "Analysis of Meaning and Dictionary Making," *International Journal of American Linguistics* 24 (1958) 283.

13. Eugene A. Nida, "Implications of Contemporary Linguistics for Biblical Scholarship," *JBL* 91 (1972) 85.

14. Four cases of *hapax legomena* have been omitted (*ʾl, ṣʿir, bmh,* and *mplṣt*), along with the three instances of *hbl,* which occurs sixty times with no less than sixteen meanings in the AV.

Chart 1. Componential Plot of Images

Word	Hebrew words translated as eidōlon										not eidōlon	
	גלולים	עצב	אליל	פסל	אדה	אליל	בעל	חמנים	צלם	שקוץ	מצבה	מסכה
Frequency	17	12	7	5	4	4	3	3	2	2	33	18
Associations												
carved	?	X	X	X	X		?	X	X	X	X	
molten	?	X		X	X	X	X	X				X
anthropomorphic	X	X		?			?	X	X			X
zoomorphic	X											X
private display		?	X					X			X	
public display	X	X	X						X	X	X	X
high places	X	X								X	X	
memorial	?										X	X(child)
sacrifices	X(child)	X	X			X					X	
incense	X	X	X				X					?
priest	X											
divination		X						X				X
sexual acts		X										X

needed or given in accordance with the translator's rule of the non-specification of shared information: the source text does not draw attention to that information which is shared by the source and the receptor languages.

2. 'God' and 'god' (*ʾlh*) appear to be as interchangeable in Hebrew as in other languages. The four occurrences of *ʾlh* are all in Daniel and refer to the *ṣlm / eikōn* of gold, but whether the image is that of a god or of the king is never specified.

3. *Psl* usually (47 times) is translated on the analogy of *mskh*, using the Greek for 'carved imaged.' Only 5 times does it become an 'idol.'

4. *Trpym* are 'idols' in only 3 of 15 occurrences, all in Gen 31:19ff.—the story of Rachel's theft of the household gods. Elsewhere the LXX simply transliterates the Hebrew, perhaps because there was no equivalent term in Greek, or, what is more likely, because the later translators did not know how to explain *trpym* any more than they could draw a picture of cherubim.

5. The word *glwlym* occurs most frequently, apparently confirming this strange word as a special term of opprobrium. The dictionaries offer the choice of deriving the word from *gll* I, 'large idols rolled about on wheels' (so Young's *Concordance*) or from *gll* II, 'dungy things'. The high frequency also indicates the widest range of circumstances from which to plot the term. It is obviously the most inclusive term for the cult image, and therefore plotting its cultural context is necessary for determining its function.

Chart 2 classifies the various Hebrew terms according to their cultural acceptability or lack of it. Brackets have been added to image or idol words that are not translated as *eidōla* in the LXX. The numbers indicate how many times a word is translated 'idol' and the total number of its occurrences in the MT. Some interesting patterns of interpretation emerge.

1. I begin with culturally disfavored words. The most frequently used negative word for pagan images is never translated *eidōla*. *Mskh* and *mṣbh*, as we have already noted, are translated directly into Greek. The word *ʾšrym* is an example of the translators' missing the forest for the trees! *Mṣbh* is found almost as many times on the positive side of the chart because of its association with the pillars erected by the patriarchs. The Greek word *stēlē* suits the sense very well, being appropriately "neutral" in its connotations, much like the term *monument* in English.

2. *ʾlylym* and *šqwsym* are euphemisms meaning 'weaklings' and 'loathsome/revolting things'. The LXX translators opted for the nonpejora-

Chart 2. *Semantic Distinctions of Eidōla*[a]

Culturally Favored		Culturally Neutral				Culturally Disfavored	
[כרובים]	(0/92)	צלם	(2/16)			[אשרים]	(0/40)
[מצבה]	(0/12)	[תמונה]	(0/10)	[סמל]	(0/2)	[מצבה]	(0/19)
תרפים	(3/15)	[דמות]	(0/19)	עצב	(12/17)	[מסכה]	(0/18)
				גלולים	(17/47)	פסל	(5/52)
						אלה	(4/16)
						אלוה	(7/57)
						אלילים	(4/18)
						שקוץ	(2/27)

[a] Numbers indicate frequency of translation as 'idol' / total occurrences in MT. Words in brackets are not *eidōla*.

tive 'image' as a more readily understood meaning for the somewhat obscure sense of the Hebrew.

3. On the positive side, the only 'idol' word is *trpym*, which, as Pfeiffer noted, carries no sense of condemnation in the biblical narrative, either in Genesis or later when Michal uses one as a ruse to cover David's escape (1 Sam 19:13ff.). The *trpym* may also be interpreted as being the *ʾlhym* referred to in Exod 21:6. In this passage a slave may become a lifetime member of the family by being brought before his master's god(s) for the ritual boring of the ear.[15] This ceremony is comprehensible if the master's gods were in fact the images of the family ancestors.

4. Cherubim are never *eidōla*, although they are images that are carved (*mqlʿwt*, not *pslym*; 1 Kgs 6:32). Since there is no unanimity among Jewish commentators as to the form or design of the cherubim and it is clear that the cherubim were a prominent part of the temple furnishings, the safest route for the translator was to treat the word as a technical term and transliterate it.

5. In the middle of the chart there are two sets of words. *Ṣlm* (usually *eikōn* in the LXX) can be negative (Num 33:5 and 2 Chr 23:17, with reference to a Canaanite shrine and the house of Baal). Yet in 1 Samuel 6 the word *ṣlm* refers to a likeness (*homoiōma*) of the mice and tumors

---

15. Paul Walters (Katz), *The Text of the Septuagint* (Cambridge: Cambridge University Press, 1973) 251.

that were votive offerings intended for the God of Israel and so perhaps deemed acceptable. *Tmwnh* and *dmwt* are never *eidōla*.

6. One would expect to find *ʿṣb* on the negative side of the chart, but Wolff calls *ʿṣb* a "neutral" word derived from a root meaning 'to form'. He notes, however, that the word has acquired "an undertone of contempt" from its homophone *ʿṣb* II 'to hurt, pain, grieve'.[16] To insure that this negative resonance comes through, Wolff translates *ʿṣbym* as 'dead idols', and he includes in this category not only the Calf of Samaria, the Ashtaroth, and *trpym*, but also the pagan plaques and statuettes in private use. On the basis of our study, Wolff is wrong to include the *trpym* in this catalog, for as we have seen above (no. 3), *trpym* are positive, not negative, images.

The derivation of *ʿṣb* from a meaning 'to form' is confirmed by the LXX, where *eidōlon* is the preferred translation. Linguistically, it is not difficult to see why. For those speaking Greek, *eidōlon*, 'a form, shape or appearance', is the same sort of "neutral" word that Wolff finds in *ʿṣb*. The shift to the negative sense for *eidōlon* can be traced to Tertullian, who on linguistic grounds accurately reproduces the sense of the Greek but who on theological grounds then proceeds to denounce idolatry. In *De idolatria* 3–4 Tertullian explains the origin of the word to his Latin audience: "*Eidos* is the Greek term for *forma*: from *eidos* a diminutive was formed, viz., *formula*. Thus every *forma* or *formula* must be called *idolum*." When Tertullian takes *latreia* 'service (to a god)' and joins it with *eidōlon*, the result is 'service to an image (of a god)' and *eidōlon/ idolum* by itself becomes no longer 'image', but 'image of a god', which comes to mean 'image of a (false) god'.

The shift to the negative for *ʿṣb* is also influenced by the way the word is used in the Prophets. Wherever it occurs it is in parallel with a negative term: *carved image, molten image* (two classes prohibited by the Law) and *abominations* and *weaklings* (euphemisms).[17] The Vulgate completes the shift to the negative by transliterating these *eidōla* as

---

16. H. W. Wolff, *Hosea* (Hermeneia; Philadelphia: Fortress, 1974) 139. In Wis 14:15ff. another connection between image and grief is given. A father bereft of his young son has an image (*eikōn*) of the boy made as a memorial. Fulgentius (*Myth.* 1:1) derives 'idol' from *idos dolu*, "which in Latin we call appearance of grief." As in the Wisdom of Solomon, Fulgentius cites the story of a grieving father, commissioning a picture of his dead child as the origin of the word. In both cases the etymology is determined by analyzing the segments of the word, then combining them. This can be a risky procedure; witness the common erroneous derivation of 'sincere' from the Latin *sine cera* 'without wax'.

17. Mic 1:7, Hos 13:2, Jer 50:2, Isa 10:11, and Isa 48:5.

idola. The process can be followed in Jerome's retranslation of the Psalms. Where the LXX of Psalms have *simulacra*, Jerome substitutes *idola* (97:7 [96:7], 115:4 [113:12], 135:15 [134:15]). In two places Jerome "corrects" the LXX of Psalms. At 127:2 [126:2] the *lḥm ᶜṣbym* = *panem doloris* (RSV: "bread of anxious toil") becomes *panem idolorum*.[18] At 139:24 [138:24] the *drk ᶜṣbym* = *via iniquitatis* becomes *via idoli*. With this consistent equating of *ᶜṣb* with *idolum* by Jerome, the western tradition was fixed.

The use of *simulacrum* to translate *ᶜṣb* in Psalms LXX was rejected after Tertullian suggested that the Itala version preserved a sense of ambivalence about images. *Simulacrum* covers a wide range of meanings. The *Thesaurus Lingua Graeca* 10, 322 lists such meanings as *xoana*, *agalmata*, *eidōlon*, *aphidruma*, etc. Tertullian, with a lawyer's desire for precision, was in search of a more accurate description for the unsuitable images. Since the Latin words were too general, he introduced a Greek loanword, *idolum*, which he then had to explain to his Latin audience. As a result *idolum* became a technical term in Latin and a negative one at that. A similar history can be recounted for the term *daimōn*, which in Greek was used both positively and negatively. When it was employed in Christian Latin, however, it came to denote specifically an evil spirit.

7. *Glwlym* affords the biggest surprise. To the translators of the LXX this term was not considered negative but neutral. Only in 1 Kgs 20:26 [21:26] is it translated 'abomination'. In the other cases it is most frequently rendered 'image' or 'thought', 'invention, device' (*enthymēma* fifteen times). In Ezek 14:2, 3 the word is taken to mean not a physical image, but a mental one (*dianoēma*), a concept that Tertullian eagerly endorsed: it is possible to practice idolatry without any physical images. "The doctrines of heretics have the same effect as the idols of the nations."[19] Their words are *idola*.

The variety of terms used in the LXX for *glwlym* suggests that in addition to the Hebrew etymologies of the term, the Greek derivation was not from *gll*, but *glh* 'to appear, to reveal, to discover'. In Ps 98:2 the Lord reveals (*gllh*) his vindication in the sight (lit., 'before the

---

18. Jerome's "bread of idols" may be related to the "food offered to idols" (*eidōlothuton*) in 1 Cor 8:1ff. In Psalm 127 a family heritage with many offspring is the work of the Lord, not the family ancestor. Offerings should therefore be made to God, not the deceased fathers.

19. *Adv. Prax.* 18.

eyes') of the nations. In the Book of Consolation Jeremiah applies a similar blessing to Israel: "See . . . I will reveal to them abundance of prosperity and security" (33:6). In both cases the emphasis is on seeing the manifestation of God's activity. A noun derived from this verb would thus be an 'appearance', something seen with the eye, which is the definition of *eidōlon* in Epicurus and the classical authors. The LXX is quite consistent in using the general term for image to cover a wide range of meanings in Hebrew. The probable explanation for selection of a generic term for *image* in Greek is that the nuances of various Hebrew words were no longer relevant or meaningful to the Greek audience, as the case of the Asherim demonstrates.

This study has examined the LXX translators' understanding of the concept of idolatry in the MT. In cases in which a Hebrew term conveyed a clear sense to them, for example "carved or molten images," the translators preferred to use a comparable Greek equivalent such as *glupta* or *chōneuma*. A word like *mṣbh*, on the other hand, could have positive associations when it occurred in connection with the patriarchs, but negative connotations in references to the Canaanite cults. Here the translators preferred a neutral term in Greek, *stēlē*, which conveyed the general sense of an upright pillar. In the case of words that were already euphemisms in Hebrew (e.g., *glwlym*), the translators preferred to drop the original meaning and substitute the generic term 'image' for the sake of clarity.

The pejorative sense of *eidōlon* as 'idol' did not emerge until Tertullian transliterated the Greek term into Latin as *idolum*. He coined a technical term for the western church that quickly lost the meaning 'image' and assumed the negative sense of 'representation of a false god'.

The Use of Hebrew Scripture in Stephen's Speech

Robert T. Anderson

❦

The Use of the Temple in Stephen's Speech

S TEPHEN'S SPEECH AS REPORTED IN the Book of Acts has provoked considerable discussion concerning the traditions he (or Luke) reflects.[1] The central subjects in the climactic part of the speech are David, Solomon, and the temple/tabernacle. They are the focus of Acts 7:45b–50, from the latter part of the speech, which reads (in the RSV):

> So it was [a tabernacle rather than a temple] until the days of David, who found favor in the sight of God and asked leave to find a habitation for the God of Jacob. But it was Solomon who built a house for him. Yet the Most High does not dwell in houses made with hands; as the prophet says, "Heaven is my throne, and earth my footstool. What house will you build for me, says the Lord, or what is the place of my rest? Did not my hand make all these things?"

Issues related to genre and motive of speeches in the ancient Mediterranean world, or of Acts in particular,[2] need not long detain us. Like Thucydides (and unlike Herodotus), Luke was a contemporary of the speakers he reports

---

1. J. Bowman, *The Samaritan Problem* (trans. Alfred M. Johnson Jr.; Pittsburgh: Pickwick, 1975) 83–86; S. Lowy, *The Principles of Samaritan Bible Exegesis* (Leiden: Brill, 1977) 50–57; J. Purvis, "The Fourth Gospel and the Samaritans," *NovT* 17 (1975) 174–77; A. Spiro, summarized in J. Munck, *The Acts of the Apostles* (AB; Garden City, N.Y.: Doubleday, 1967) 285–300.
2. M. Dibelius, *Studies in the Acts of the Apostles* (London: SCM, 1956) 139–85; H. Cadbury, *The Making of Luke–Acts* (London: SPCK, 1958) 185–89.

and would be familiar with the context, if not the exact words, of his orators. While he undoubtedly used the speeches for his own purposes, both his integrity as an accomplished *literati* and the shared knowledge of much of his audience would require that the speeches be appropriate to the time and character of his speakers. Luke's companionship with Paul could have enriched his knowledge of Stephen and the speech, since Paul was likely present at its delivery: indeed it may have been a catalyst for Paul's conversion experience.

The complex sources within the speech militate against the supposition that Luke made up the speech of whole cloth. Divergent scriptural recensions are used[3] and appeal is made to traditions of varied sectarian sources. Although this variety may support some theories about the purpose of Luke's use of the speech, it more likely indicates that Stephen represented a heterodox position within Judaism. It is recorded that he was a Hellenist, and some scholars feel, as indicated below, that there is strong evidence that he was a Samaritan. Regardless of which voice is represented, Stephen's or Luke's, Christian, Hebrew, or Samaritan, the Jerusalem Temple was challenged in this speech and, at least implicitly, the city, the monarchy and priesthood associated with it.

Negative attitudes toward the temple are reflected elsewhere in the New Testament: Heb 9:11 (no temple, but a tent of Christ's priesthood); Rev 21:22 (no temple in the heavenly Jerusalem and possible questioning of the significance of the city of Jerusalem itself);[4] and Jesus' comments about the temple in Mark 13:1–2 and 14:58, which are echoed by the statement in Stephen's speech (and Heb 9:11) about a temple "built with hands."

Much of the Christian concern about the temple could have eschatological overtones. The synoptic gospels link the death of Jesus with the destruction of the temple and expect the church to replace all that the temple had represented.[5] Even Paul, despite his focus on the Jerusalem Temple and the likelihood that his contributions to the temple were somehow related to eschatological hopes for it, explicitly states that the church is the temple of the living God (2 Cor 6:16).

Criticism of the Jerusalem Temple is found in the literature of other Jewish sects as well. The Qumran community rejected the temple because of its un-

---

3. A. Spiro summarized in Munck, *Acts*, 285.

4. A. Beagley, *The "Sitz im Leben" of the Apocalypse with Particular Reference to the Role of the Church's Enemies* (BZNW 50; Berlin: de Gruyter, 1987), as reviewed by C. DuRousseau in *JBL* 108 (1989) 169–71.

5. J. Chance, *Jerusalem, the Temple, and the New Age in Luke–Acts* (Macon, Georgia: Mercer University Press, 1988) 19.

worthy priests and inaccurate calendar; the Samaritans disowned it because it was located at the wrong site. Evidence in Isaiah (66:1–2) and elsewhere in the Hebrew Scripture indicates that the temple and its associated institutions and concepts did not receive universal Jewish sanction. The Samaritan attitude is the classic expression of sentiment against the Jerusalem Temple. On this basis Abraham Spiro, John Bowman, and others have assumed that Stephen was a Samaritan. But there are other options to account for Stephen's position. S. Lowy is one who has explicitly argued against Spiro and Bowman's thesis.[6] Haenchen believes that the Acts 7 speech was put into the mouth of Stephen by Luke on the basis of an argument ultimately derived from Hellenistic rationalism,[7] and Klijn understands the allusion to the tabernacle to mean serving God in a purely spiritual sense.[8]

At this point some observations from a diachronic reading of the sources in the Hebrew Scripture relating to Jerusalem, monarchy, temple, and priesthood, illuminate Luke's use of sources and the motives for the content of Stephen's speech. This is particularly true in the light of recent literary studies.

Cult Traditions in Hebrew Scripture

The two earliest cult documents, J and E, represent opposing sides in the basic Moses/Sinai–David/Zion tensions, but an anti-temple sentiment is expressed in both. E's position, an essentially northern, post-Solomonic tradition, is not surprising, but J also seems to question the temple implicitly by emphasizing the altars of Abraham and Noah and declining to make any mention of the temple. There may be other subtle indications. Consider with Coote the status given to the smith in J. In Canaanite myth the smith was instrumental in the building of the temple, but in J the smith is a murderer, perhaps an early indication by J of the contrast between a proper earthen altar cult and an improper temple cult, an implication not likely to be missed by the bedouin sheiks who were essential in David's bid for power.[9]

J and E part company in their attitudes toward the monarchy. Each stage of the J story—the preflood narratives, the ancestral accounts, and the focus on Moses—plays a significant role in supporting the United Monarchy. The bedouin ancestors of Genesis 12–50 are not unlike the tenth-century bedouin sheiks for whom J was writing, because they also sought to survive in

6. Lowy, *Samaritan Bible Exegesis*, 50–57.
7. E. Haenchen, *The Acts of the Apostles* (Philadelphia: Westminster, 1971) 290.
8. Cited in Haenchen, *Acts*, 285.
9. R. Coote, and D. Ord, *The Bible's First History* (Philadelphia: Fortress, 1989) 39, 67.

the shadow of continuous Egyptian threat.[10] The Moses stories, where Coote suggests reading "David" for "Moses," could subtly reassure bedouin living along the Palestinian-Egyptian border that they had a protector in David.[11] The monarchy is envisioned in J's scenario as akin to the Garden of Eden, where all would enjoy prosperity and peace.[12] The E document, informed by the experience of the United Monarchy, has no such delusions. Solomon is the new tyrannical pharaoh who enslaves Israel, and Jeroboam is the deliverer.[13] The covenant tradition takes precedence over any monarchical tradition, and the document, rather than reflecting alignment with courtly circles, seems better associated with a prophetic school.[14] E has no interest in monarchy, either southern or northern.

Furthermore, E does not join in J's implicit interest in the city of Jerusalem. "El Elyon," a divine name assigned by J for use by Abraham and the priests Abiathar and Zadok, may have had Canaanite/Jebusite origins sanctioned by J,[15] and use of this name may have reflected J's origins and support of Jerusalem. E, on the other hand, is neither geographically nor ideologically in support of Jerusalem. E's priestly ritual interests are more geographically diverse than J's. Abraham is prepared to offer the sacrifice of Isaac at an unspecified place (Genesis 22). Jacob sets up a sacred pillar at Luz that he names "Bethel" (Gen 28:17–18, 35:14); he also builds an altar at Shechem (Gen 33:20). Likewise, Moses, who is completely dissociated from Jerusalem, is involved with many ritual practices (particular in the Sinai experience described in Exodus 19–24). The various altars and open-air sanctuaries cited by E exist for ritual practice and are not only incidental memorials. Incidental memorials seem to exist in J, however, where they are downplayed in deference to the temple at Jerusalem.[16]

These two early cult documents, J and E, express a basic multidimensional tension. One focused on the prophet Moses and the holy place in the wilderness of Sinai or Gerizim; its religious edifice was the tabernacle, and its theoc-

10. G. Mendenhall, "The Nature and Purpose of the Abraham Narratives," *Ancient Israelite Religion: Essays in Honor of Frank Moore Cross* (ed. P. Miller, P. Hanson, and S. McBride; Philadelphia: Fortress, 1987) 339ff.

11. Coote and Ord, *Bible's First History*, 33–34.

12. Ibid., 54; J. Rosenberg, *King and Kin: Political Allegory in the Hebrew Bible* (Bloomington: Indiana University Press, 1986) 193, 195, 203.

13. Coote and Ord, *Bible's First History*, 215.

14. N. Gottwald, *The Hebrew Bible: A Social-Literary Introduction* (Philadelphia: Fortress, 1985) 138.

15. W. Humphreys, *Crisis and Story* (Mountain View, Cal.: Mayfield, 1990) 61–62.

16. Gottwald, *Hebrew Bible*, 349.

racy took the form of a priesthood. The other focuses on King David and the Holy City of Jerusalem. Its religious edifice was the temple, and its theocracy takes the form of a monarchy.

For a time the prophetic voice seemed to speak on behalf of one side or the other of this tension. Amos and Hosea emphasized the Mosaic covenant.[17] Then Isaiah, a product of Jerusalem and its Canaanite roots,[18] raised Jerusalem from political and ritual ultimacy to theological ultimacy with his "polis" theology.[19]

Micah and Jeremiah represent a contrary prophetic position willing to challenge city (Micah 1:5) and temple (Jeremiah 7). Fishbane does suggest that Micah and Jeremiah reflected the prophecy in 1 Kings 9 that says temple and city would be destroyed if the people were not responsible,[20] but one must not forget the more significant factors of Jeremiah's concern that the deuteronomistic reform had made an idol of both Jerusalem and the temple and that Micah saw Jerusalem as more the source of Judah's ruin than her hope.

For these reasons, then, it is possible to postulate a cult document primarily supportive of the Moses-Sinai-Tabernacle tradition (E) and a cult document primarily supportive of the David-Zion-Temple tradition (J). Each of these draws prophetic support (Isaiah vs. Jeremiah and Micah). Each vibrates with ambiguities that subsequent documents try to ameliorate.

Deuteronomy (D) and the Deuteronomic Historian (DH) present another cult tradition that over the centuries of its creation tried to blend the two polar foci of Moses and David into an acceptable reconciliation. By the time of DH, the northern kingdom with its prediliction for the Moses-Sinai-Tabernacle tradition was gone, but some of the traditions were carried south and speak in D. DH became necessary as a new basis for a temple-cult narrative.[21] It is not surprising then that the legitimacy of a northern monarchy and northern shrines was undercut by DH. He stigmatized the important tribes of Benjamin (Judges 19–21), particularly Saul's hometown of Gibeah, Jabesh Gilead (Judg 21:8–14), and the shrines at Dan and Bethel in the editing of Judges. In contrast, a positive affirmation of the Davidic Judean monarchy was underscored

17. Consider the references to the Mosaic Period: Amos 2:10, 3:1, 4:10; Hos 2:15, 11:1, 13:4, and the attacks on kings and priests who have led Israel astray.

18. J. Roberts, "Yahweh's Foundation in Zion (Isa 28:16)," *JBL* 106 (1987) 27–45.

19. G. von Rad (*Old Testament Theology* [2 vols.; New York: Harper, 1965] 1.150) is in agreement, despite minor modifications by subsequent scholars.

20. M. Fishbane, *Biblical Interpretation in Ancient Israel* (Oxford: Clarendon, 1985) 459.

21. Coote and Ord, *Bible's First History*, 41.

by D. This affirmation is borne by the chiastic interpretation of Rosenberg, who demonstrates an allegorical relationship between the DH account of David and the Adam and Eve story, underscoring again the relationship of garden, paradise, temple, and sacred enclave.[22]

On the other hand there is also rather specific DH criticism of one or another of the triad of city, temple, and monarchy. For instance the DH history makes David's threshing floor a place of theophany and oracle, though it falls far short of giving it an exact location or permanent shrine and has nothing to do with Solomon's Temple.[23] Hannah's song portrays a god who cannot be limited to a house.[24] In another instance, widespread resistance to David's sacral kingship is reflected in Nathan's response to David's desire to build a temple.[25] Rosenberg senses a subtle condemnation of the royal court in Barzillai's rejection of David's invitation to live in the royal palace (2 Sam 19:35–36).[26]

Despite these criticisms, DH paradoxically gives an impression of affirming both Jerusalem (though not explicitly mentioned) and the temple, but as demonstrated above, it does not particularly support the monarchy, since the covenant traditions that it affirms create tension and even outright conflict with the monarchy, as Gottwald has observed.[27]

These conflicting presentations of monarchy and temple reflect a reconciliatory spirit at work in DH, which is expressed elsewhere in the tradition as well. Rosenberg judges that DH makes David out to be a "Faustian technician" who intentionally plays to both sides of the Moses/David tension.[28] He suggests, for example, that the sons of David, Amon and Absalom, represent prince and shepherd in tension.[29] Whether the stories reflect the dual nature of David or the views of DH, the play to both sides served the purposes of DH. DH implies that the reason David did not build a temple did not stem from principle, but from the fact that he did not have sufficient control over the territorial arable land, which was essential for monarchy.[30] Thus neither the "Moses" voice nor the "David" voice (or better, both voices) could comfortably represent the davidic heritage.

22. Rosenberg, *King and Kin*, 202–10.
23. Ibid., 123.
24. Ibid., 114.
25. Ibid., 119–23.
26. Ibid., 186.
27. Gottwald, *Hebrew Bible*, 138.
28. Rosenberg, *King and Kin*, 173.
29. Ibid., 157.
30. Coote and Ord, *Bible's First History*, 38.

Writings from the exilic and postexilic periods required of the traditions a new focus. Isaiah 40–66 (whether representing one or two authors) is a vision that draws from and in a sense spiritualizes both the Mosaic and Davidic traditions. Sacrifice becomes a matter of inward motives in passages like 57:15, 58:1–14, and 66:3. Monarchy is hardly mentioned, nor is the temple, except in a basically critical way (Isa 66:1–3). Jerusalem is significant, but more as a contrast to Babylon than to other shrine locations in Palestine. Jerusalem is the only geographical place left for the fulfillment of Israel.

Haggai, Zecharaiah, and Ezekiel, on the other hand, make not only Jerusalem, but the temple, an important part of the vision of the restored community and are in this sense more heavily weighted toward the David/Zion tradition than the Moses/Sinai tradition or any compromise position. Likewise the Chronicler-Ezra-Nehemiah tradition strongly supports city, monarchy, and temple, providing a rationale for David not building a temple.[31] The Chronicler reconciles priestly and deuteronomic traditions, the Aaronide priesthood and the Levites, and Davidic and Mosaic authority,[32] but is very slanted toward Judah, Jerusalem, and the temple. The Chronicler portrays Solomon as carrying out rules laid down by David (including the building of the temple), which would more clearly put David into the David/Zion scheme without the ambiguity found in DH and Samaritan literature.

The Psalms express a variety of assumptions (temple-vs.-individual worship, priesthood vs. individual worship, Jerusalem psalms vs. prophetic psalms), making them suitable, as probably intended, to anyone's needs. To cite a psalm is not necessarily to support a tradition, although it is sometimes significant in analyzing a speech such as Stephen's to note which categories of psalms were used or not used. I shall return to this theme below. The most likely psalms to suggest a bias are the hymns related to Jerusalem, the temple, or kingship. In regard to kingship, Gottwald points out that rituals implicitly associated in the psalms with divine and human kingship in Israel are, on the other hand, not inconsistent with the Mosaic, covenantal tradition.[33] This may indicate a general tendency in the Psalms to reconcile the Mosaic and Davidic traditions.

This survey of the Hebrew Scripture has been selective. I have identified those traditions demonstrating a pronounced affinity with either the Moses/Sinai or David/Zion bias. I have also selected those traditions that Luke tended to cite most frequently. In general terms, Stephen's speech represented

31. Fishbane, *Biblical Interpretation*, 394ff.
32. S. DeVries, "Moses and David as Cult Founders in Chronicles," *JBL* 107 (1988) 619–39.
33. Gottwald, *Hebrew Bible*, 534.

two quite different bodies of literature, and I turn now to demonstrating this fact more specifically.

The Cult Traditions and Stephen's Speech

It is instructive to mark the topics and sources from the Hebrew Scriptures that were selected in Stephen's speech. Abraham, Moses, Solomon, David, and the temple dominate the speech. Of course Abraham and Moses are almost *pro forma* citations in the argumentation of any Jewish sectarian, from the Samaritans to Paul, and are not necessarily evidence of tension in Stephen's speech. David, as alluded to brie)y, is hardly more controversial. Even the Samaritan tradition, the Israelite sectarian tradition most likely to have trouble with a southern king, does not disapprove of David completely. In fact, according to their tradition, David actually worshiped at Mt. Gerizim: "David was (for all that) accustomed to go on pilgrimmage to Mount Gerizim, and upon it to offer tithes and sacrifices and ex-voto offerings and alms."[34] The most conservative of sectarians, then, would not find fault with the content of Stephen's speech up to this point.

It is only with the mention of Solomon and the temple that tension begins to mount. Interestingly, it provokes not the fringe sectarian movements, but the conservative Jewish element. The mention of Solomon in itself may not have engendered strong feelings, since there was a long history of conflicting opinions about him. The Samuel source, perhaps written from hindsight, may well have been describing Solomon in terms of the tyranny of 1 Sam 8:7–18. If Coote and Ord are right,[35] E wanted the reader to see Solomon as the Pharaoh who oppressed Israel. DH provides the ultimate condemnation of Solomon in order to explain the adversaries that he meets during his reign (1 Kings 11). Jews would not be shocked to hear an indictment of Solomon from Stephen's lips.

The temple, on the other hand, had become an issue in the first century, and several sectarian groups were questioning its legitimacy for one reason or another. These groups found they could draw on prophetic traditions in Hebrew Scripture that had been glossed over by the strong Jerusalem-Temple bias of most postexilic thinkers. By the introduction of this single issue, Luke drew the diverse heterodox sectarians together and isolated them from traditional Jews.

34. P. Stenhouse, *The Kitab Al-Tarikh of Abu'l-Fath* (Sidney, Australia: Mendelbaum Trust, 1985) 59.
35. Coote and Ord, *Bible's First History*, 215.

Today, the down-playing of Jerusalem is sometimes considered to be part of Luke's alleged antisemitic stance, but that view seems to be advanced by a particular segment of the Jewish population who are hostile to the Christian movement. Admittedly, Luke has moved a long way from Judaism, and the episode with Stephen is a major hinge in the swing of Christianity to the Gentile world, but in his description of that swing, Luke uses devices that are thoroughly Jewish.[36] Haenchen may consider the Jews to be the "mighty and irreconcilable enemies of Christianity,"[37] but he balances Luke's supposed anti-Jewish statements with an awareness of Luke's appreciation for the contribution of Jewry.

I believe that Luke distinguishes between the chief priest and Sadducees, whom he sees as the real foes of Christianity on the one hand, and the ordinary priests and Jews, who are at worst indifferent to Christianity on the other hand.[38] Luke is an apologist for Paul's decision to focus his mission on the gentiles. His irenic temperament dictates that he make that defense while preserving a general affirmation of the Jews.

Luke demonstrates a genuine love for Jewish Scripture, which he cites often, if somewhat selectively. His favorite sources are the deuteronomic corpus, the Book of Isaiah, and Psalms,[39] which share in common rather eclectic and conciliatory postures at important junctures in Hebrew history. In Isaiah he focuses primarily on the latter part of the book (after chap. 40), and there is no echo of the *polis* theology. None of the "Zion" psalms are used, nor are the characteristic enthronement psalms. The material on Moses reflects neither the bias of E nor J and at certain points seems to reflect the Samaritan recension of the Pentateuch.[40]

By contrast Luke practically ignores sources steeped only in the David/Zion/Temple tradition; for example he is virtually uninfluenced by a book like Ezekiel.[41] This selectivity and its implications indicate that Luke is using Hebrew tradition to clarify the distinction between Christianity and more conservative Jewish traditions while at the same time striving for reconciliation among all forms of sectarianism.

One need not go outside the Hebrew Scriptures to find the diverse attitudes toward Jerusalem, monarchy and temple reflected in Stephen's speech,

36. Dibelius, *Studies*, 169.

37. Haenchen, *Acts*, 290.

38. R. Brawley, *Luke–Acts and the Jews: Conflict, Apology, and Conciliation* (Atlanta: Scholars Press, 1987) 132.

39. Noted also by Chance, *Jerusalem*, 43.

40. Spiro as summarized by Mann in Munck, *Acts*, 285.

41. Chance, *Jerusalem*, 43.

including the widely held assumption of his repudiation of all three.[42] Yet I believe both Hebrew Scripture and Stephen's speech reflect a complex melding of different traditions. Thus it is possible that Luke/Stephen both consciously and unconsciously utilized more than one tradition. The rather unorthodox insertion of a quote from Deuteronomy into the middle of a citation from Exodus (Acts 7:37) is good evidence that Luke heard Stephen use, or assumed that he would use, such an atypical tradition, although the quotation need not be understood as an exclusively sectarian/Samaritan reading.[43]

Whether or not Stephen was a Samaritan cannot be determined simply on the basis of the differences of attitude toward Jerusalem, monarchy and temple in his speech, since the same diversity is found within the Jewish tradition, as reflected in the Hebrew Scripture. Nevertheless the purpose for the Book of Acts, as stated in 1:4, 7, was to prepare for the gospel to move outward from Jerusalem to Judea, Samaria, and the uttermost parts of the world. This goal presupposes that the Samaritans are not irrelevant. In fact, it might imply that the speech was given primarily for the benefit of the Samaritans.[44] Furthermore, although Luke's story is frequently set in Jerusalem and all the action leading up to Stephen's speech in Acts is confined to Jerusalem, the story then moves out from Jerusalem, first to Samaria, then to other parts of Judaea, and finally to distant parts of the Mediterranean world. After that, Jerusalem no longer plays a significant role.

Stephen's speech helps Luke marshal the contemporary sectarian groups: Hellenists, Samaritans, Essenes, and Christians vis-à-vis orthodox Judaism. In this way Luke prepares the reader for the spread of Christianity through those groups already alienated from Judaism. Ultimately "there exists a bond between Jew and Christian which, while it has been severed by jewish rejection of God's Messiah, will be restored after the 'times of the Gentiles' are completed."[45] Brawley focuses more sharply still: "rather than setting gentile Christianity free, Luke ties it to Judaism. And rather than rejecting the Jews, Luke appeals to them."[46]

Luke takes his cue, consciously or unconsciously, from the conciliatory posture of those works from Hebrew Scripture that he most admires. Luke, as

42. For example, H. Conzelmann, *Acts of the Apostles* (Hermeneia; Philadelphia: Fortress, 1987) 56; and Munck, *Acts*, 66.
43. Purvis, "The Fourth Gospel," 188–89.
44. For support see R. Scroggs, "The Earliest Hellenistic Christianity," *Religions in Antiquity: Essays in Memory of Erwin Ramsdell Goodenough* (ed. J. Neusner; Leiden: Brill, 1968).
45. From the last paragraph of Chance, *Jerusalem*, 151.
46. The last two sentences of Brawley, *Luke–Acts*, 159.

well as the writers of the Hebrew Scriptures, is writing at an important juncture in the history of the church, a time when extensive reconciliation is needed. Some traditions from Israel's past were more helpful in resolving the conflicts that Luke faced than others and for that his favorite triad D/Isaiah/ Psalms gave him a model, both in content and style. Luke envisions reconciliation on a much larger scale than simply a reconciliation between Jew and Samaritan and may have intentionally referred to more than one source of anti-temple sentiment in his attempt to reconcile several factions.

The Role of Isaiah in the Development of the Christian Canon

William R. Farmer

YOU MAY ASK WHY A NEW TESTAMENT specialist would volunteer to write a paper on the role of Isaiah in the development of the Christian canon. The idea for this paper first entered my mind when I started reading Tertullian's magnum opus, his monumental refutation of Marcion.[1] Marcion had advocated that Christians should reject the Old Testament on the grounds that the God of the Old Testament was not the God of the Christians. The God of the Christians, according to Marcion, had remained unknown to the human race until the time Christ appeared on earth and revealed him in the fifteenth year of the emperor Tiberius as recorded in the Gospel according to Luke. This God revealed by Christ was a God of love and compassion. The God of the Jews, among whom Christ first appeared, was a lesser god who had created the world and established justice through the Law of Moses, which he had given to the Jews for the Jews—not for the rest of the world.

In his *Antitheses* Marcion spelled out in great detail the exegetical basis for his thesis that the God of the Old Testament could not be the same God who had revealed himself in Christ. Christ could only be known through the gospel that Paul preached, which gospel could be authenticated by Paul's apostolic

Author's Note: This paper was first read to a session of the Southwest Biblical Seminar meeting at Perkins School of Theology, Southern Methodist University, Spring 1983.

1. Tertullian, *Adversus Marcionem* (ed. and trans. Ernest Evans; Oxford: Clarendon, 1972) xxiii, 658.

letters and a written gospel that Marcion used. Marcion was charged by his enemies with having created his written gospel out of one of the church's Gospels, that is, Luke. By removing the later accretions that Marcion believed had been added to Luke's original Pauline gospel, he believed he had reconstructed an apostolic gospel of canonical authority. This apostolic gospel, alongside Paul's letters and supported by Marcion's *Antitheses*, constituted the stringent Christian canon Marcion wanted the church to adopt in place of the more inclusive and diverse canon that included the scriptures of the Jews—including such Old Testament books as Isaiah. So, the immediate context in which I want to take up the question of the role of Isaiah in the development of the Christian canon is that of considering Isaiah as a book that Marcion wanted the church to reject as part of its doctrinal norm.

What has impressed me in reading Tertullian's attack on Marcion is how well Marcion knew the scriptures—both Old Testament and New Testament—and how well Tertullian knew them. Tertullian had Marcion's *Antitheses* lying before him. In the text of Marcion's *Antitheses*, Tertullian could see exactly how Marcion argued. Tertullian's point-by-point refutation of Marcion's argumentation is all that we have to go by as we attempt to reconstruct Marcion's *Antitheses*. The essentials of the controversy, in my view, are as follows.

(1) Marcion's theological program depended on the validity of the fundamental argument that the God who spoke through the Law and the Prophets was a different God from the God who spoke through Jesus Christ. In order to establish this thesis, Marcion juxtaposed sayings from the Law and the Prophets with words of Jesus from the written *Evangellion*. Marcion was successful in focusing attention on the antithetical character of statements in the Law and the Prophets compared with teachings in the Gospels.

(2) Tertullian's rebuttal was two-fold. As the first step, he set out to prove that careful examination of the texts would show that the God who spoke through the Prophets was the same God who spoke through Jesus. As the second step in his rebuttal, to rectify differences remaining between what this one God had said in the earlier and later periods, Tertullian appealed to the concept of development. What God said in the earlier period was appropriate for that time and place in the history of the human race; what he said through Jesus was appropriate for the condition of God's people at the time when God's promise to save the nations was being fulfilled.

Well-trained in legal matters, Tertullian knew that weak arguments could be easily overturned. It is characteristic of Tertullian, therefore, to illustrate his points by telling examples. Tertullian would take some saying of Jesus that appeared to belong distinctly to his teaching when compared to popular piety, including Jewish piety, and would demonstrate that what God was saying in Marcion's *Evangellion* (our Luke) could also be found being said by God through one or more of the Prophets, though often in quite different words, to be sure.

It is precisely at this point that one is able to begin to answer the question with which I began: "What role did the *Book of Isaiah* play in the development of the Christian canon?" In beginning an answer to the question, I want to emphasize that in demonstrating that the same God who spoke through Jesus also spoke through the Prophets, a demonstration crucial for the church's case for retaining the Old Testament within the Christian canon, Tertullian relied heavily on the text of Isaiah. In fact, it would not be too much to say that without Isaiah Tertullian may not have been able to refute Marcion convincingly. This may be putting the matter too strongly. This may be making claims for the importance of Isaiah too great for the evidence to bear. But I do not think so. I believe that without the *Book of Isaiah* Tertullian may not have succeeded in his goal to destroy the foundation on which Marcion rested his case for two different gods.

This is a very important point that will, no doubt, be resisted, because it seems to suggest the disputed concept of a canon-within-the-canon. Whatever one's position on this question, it is important to resist any tendency to exaggerate the canonical authority of a particular book in the canon at the expense of the authority of the whole canon.

So, at the outset, let it be understood that this paper does not concern itself with searching out this kind of canon-within-the-canon. In fact, my thesis, if valid, will demonstrate that it was chiefly Tertullian's use of Isaiah that made it possible for the church to ward off Marcion's skillful attempt to define and justify within the existing canon of Christian scriptures a canon-within-the-canon: Marcion's *Evangellion-Apostolicon*. If it should turn out that the *Book of Isaiah* has functioned in any way as a canon-within-the-canon, then, ironically, this will be a canon-within-the-canon that calls for a canon larger than itself.

Isaiah in the hands of Christian theologians calls for a canon that unites the Law and the Prophets *with* the Gospels, the Old Testament *with* the New, the promise of God that He will save the nations *with* their salvation in Christ.

This leads me to the second main point to be made about the role of Isaiah in the development of the Christian Bible. This second point is no less important than the first, though it is of a somewhat different nature, involving the theological importance of faith in God as a God who will keep his promise to save the nations.

Catholics argued that the Church needed to retain the scriptures of the Jews because, without them, an important proof that the Christian religion was of divine origin would be lost. The argument ran something like this: God, in days long past raised up certain men who spoke for him concerning the future. The fact that certain promises made by God had been fulfilled proved not only the power and faithfulness of God, but the divine origin of the religion of those who believed in this almighty God who was sovereign over the nations and exercised control over the future.

To this argument for retaining the Law and the Prophets, which told of these long-standing promises of God, the Marcionites, according to Tertullian, argued as follows: Christians do not need these promises to prove the divine origin of the Christian religion, for in the miracles of Christ, Christians have all the evidence needed to prove the divine origin of the Christian religion. To this Tertullian countered: Nonsense, the Lord himself warned against such a reliance upon miracles (Matt 7:21–23).

The church, therefore, argued Tertullian, does need the evidence of its divine origin that is afforded by certain promises made by God in the past that have been fulfilled before the very eyes of men and women in the recent past. Chief among these promises are those that entail God's promise to save the nations. The undeniable fact that a new community, a new nation, a new race had been created, made up of people from all the nations, was proof to Christians of the second century of the divine origin of the Christian religion. People who spoke different languages and practiced different customs were being saved and learning to live in harmony with one another. This had been promised by God, above all in Isaiah. The fulfillment of this promise offered proof of the divine origin of the Christian religion that was compelling, especially to Christians living in a pagan society that paid lip service to the ideals of racial and cultural harmony, but which found it so elusive and virtually impossible to achieve in any enduring way.

Moreover, said Tertullian, God has a purpose in making these promises. Instead of instantly bringing about the salvation of the nations, God made a promise to do this at some time in the future so that his chosen people's faith in his promises could be tested. I think this is a crucial point of distinction between the faith of Marcionite Christians and the faith of those of Catholic persuasion. If I understand the distinction, it is this. For Marcion, saving faith in the Christian God was faith in a God who did not require faith in the absence of evidence. For Marcionites, the experience of divine love, compassion, and forgiveness was directly appropriated through faith in Christ. One reasoned, presumably, from the fact of salvation to the existence of a God of compassion. One could be certain of the miraculous reality of this God by virtue of his miraculous love that was directly, immediately, and fully available to the believer. The stories of Christ's miracles in the Gospels only confirmed the validity of faith in such an intimate, compassionate, and loving God.

But with Tertullian it was different. Authentic faith includes faith in promises yet to be fulfilled. It is faith that may appear foolish or foolhardy, because it rests on confidence in the trustworthiness of God alone, without benefit of full and immediate confirmation. The experience of having one's faith tested is essential to God's purposes. This meant that God wanted a people who had been disciplined, who, in the words of the hymnist of the black church, knew what it meant to "hang on in there."

I think that a great deal is at stake here. At stake is the question of whether I am saved by my faith in what God has done, or whether I am saved by my faith in God's power and trustworthiness to do what he has promised he will do. I have come to the conclusion that this latter faith is essential to salvation. This is especially important to me with reference to the acute and abiding evidence of sin, distortion, hypocrisy, and destructiveness in the hatred of whites for blacks in society and above all within the Christian community. If I place my faith in the evidence provided by the Church of Christ's miraculous power to create a new humanity within the present broken North American society, I falter. I appear to myself as hopelessly utopian and am unable to function as a joyous Christian surrounded by so much that contradicts the view that it is God's intention to save the nations. The nations resolutely resist being saved. It is only when I hold on to God's promise that he will save the nations, when I experience the power of his redeeming love working in cross-racial relationships that are alive and well, and when I join with others who testify to the same—it is only then that I have a joyous consciousness that I will be saved by placing my faith in a God who has made such a great, all-encompassing, and noble promise. The negative evidence remains. But it has no power to refute God nor to deter those who believe in and hold on to his sure promises.

Now, the import of Isaiah for all of this is that, while God's promise to save the nations may not be restricted to this book, this is the book that provides Tertullian his more convincing texts. As with Marcion's doctrine of two Gods, it would be much more difficult for Tertullian to refute convincingly the arguments of the Marcionites concerning the dispensability of God's promises if he did not have Isaiah.

In any case, to the extent that Tertullian's use of Isaiah was decisive in this regard, we can see a second example of the way in which this book has played an important role in the development of the Christian canon. On another occasion I shall go on to argue that what Tertullian did was but a theological continuation of what Jesus, Paul, Matthew, Luke, and the majority of Christian theologians up until Tertullian, had done before him—namely, to appeal to the text of the book of Isaiah as a central controlling norm in the doctrinal development of Christian faith.

The Tabernacle in Samaritan Iconography and Thought

James D. Purvis

I AM PLEASED TO DEDICATE THIS ESSAY to the memory of my friend and colleague H. Neil Richardson. Professor Richardson's distinguished career included archaeological field work at Tell Balâta, the site of biblical Shechem, the original home of the Samaritan community. He maintained a long interest in the history of the Samaritans, about which we were often in conversation. It is fitting also that the two Samaritan documents that receive special attention here are presently housed in collections of the libraries of Boston University, where Professor Richardson served so meritoriously as Professor (1957–1981), and, subsequently, Professor Emeritus (1981–1988).

Although Samaritan history, literature, and theology (especially eschatology) have long been of interest to scholars, scant attention has been paid to the iconography of the community. This situation was recently redressed in the publication by Reinhard Pummer of *The Samaritans*, in the Iconography of Religions series of the Institute of Religious Iconography of the University of Groningen.[1] The term iconography is used here (as also by Pummer) in the broadest sense—that is, of representations of subjects or other "artistic" expressions, whether graphic or architectural—and not in the limited sense of representations of divine beings in human or animal form. It is the latter, and restrictive, use of the word icon (and its derivatives) that is

---

1. Reinhard Pummer, *The Samaritans* (Iconography of Religions, sec. 23, fasc. 5; Leiden: Brill, 1987) 46 pp. + 48 pls.

---

indicated in the oft-repeated cliché that Judaism is an aniconic religion. The same is true of the Samaritan religion. But although Jewish art (and hence iconography) may be said to be quite developed, the same may not be said of Samaritan art. The illustrations given by Pummer consist of calligraphy, architecture, dress, and ritual paraphernalia. The only illustration of a drawing is a chart depicting the tabernacle and its implements. In commenting on Samaritan manuscripts, Pummer notes, "None of the Samaritan MSS known so far are illuminated. The only drawings produced by them in the past seem to be depictions of the temple [sic: read tabernacle] implements on the cases of Torah scrolls or on parchment and paper leaves."[2] Elsewhere Pummer adds Torah mantles, and I would add that I have seen depictions of tabernacle vessels also on Samaritan lamps of the Byzantine Period.

It would appear then (as far as we know) that representations of the tabernacle and its vessels constitute the only avenue through which the Samaritans have found artistic expression in drawing. It is the purpose of this essay to consider this phenomenon, with reference to two such drawings and to note what has been emphasized by the Samaritans in their illustrations, as well as the ways in which their depictions agree or disagree with Jewish and Christian traditions.

The Drawings

The oldest known Samaritan drawings of the tabernacle are on parchment. One, presently housed in the Lenin State Library in Moscow, is alleged to date to the mid-seventh century.[3] A sixteenth-century parchment is also known. But most extant copies are on paper and date from the early twentieth century. The two drawings reproduced here were the subject of a study by the writer, that appeared in the twentieth-anniversary edition of *Aleph-Beth: The Samaritan News*.[4] The reader is referred to that publication for a more detailed and descriptive analysis of the charts. For purposes of this study these depictions may be considered representative. It should be noted that there are slight

2. Ibid., p. 8. See also Pummer, "Samaritan Material Remains and Archaeology," *The Samaritans* (ed. Alan D. Crown; Tübingen: Mohr, 1989) 156.

3. See Pummer, *Samaritans*, 31, for bibliography on publication in Russian. A Hebrew translation and photograph appear in *Aleph-Beth: The Samaritan News* 248 (15 November 1979) 1–7.

4. James D. Purvis, "Two Samaritan Drawings of the Tabernacle in the Boston University Library," *Aleph-Beth: The Samaritan News* 500 (15 December 1989) 105–20.

Fig. 1. Tabernacle Drawing by Jacob ben Uzzi. Photo: Boston University Photo Services.

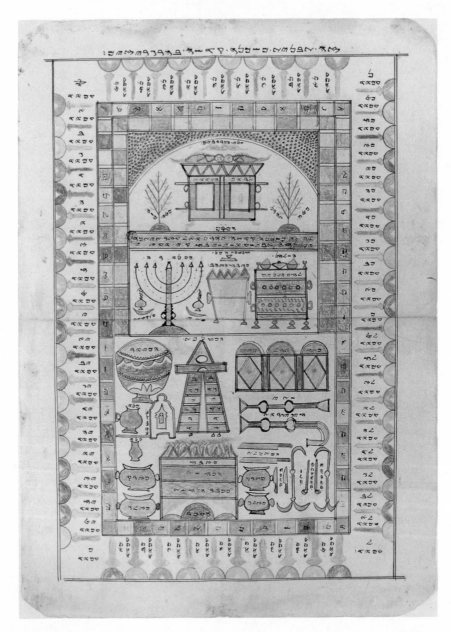

Fig. 2. Tabernacle Drawing by Jacob ben Aaron. Photo: Boston University Photo Services.

differences between the drawings, as well as between them and another known drawing by one of the artists. Thus "representative" does not connote uniformity. I am of two minds on the significance of these variations. They may reflect alternative traditions (or opinions) within the Samaritan community on the appearance and placement of certain cultic objects within the shrine or, what is more likely, simply liberties taken by the artists.

The older of these two charts was drawn (although not signed) by Jacob ben Aaron (fig. 2), the high priest of the Samaritan community at the beginning of this century; the younger was drawn (and signed) by Jacob ben Uzzi (fig. 1), most likely the grandson of Jacob ben Aaron.[5] Of the two, the latter is more artistically pleasing, not only in the appearance of the furnishings and cultic articles, but also in the medium used in its execution (ink made of metallic compound, as compared with the colored pencils used by Jacob ben Aaron).

Jacob ben Aaron was a prolific writer, being not only a copyist of manuscripts but also the author of articles and books on various aspects of Samaritan culture. Some of these were polemical tracts setting forth the claims of the Samaritans against the Jews, but many were informative essays for the benefit of those who wished to know more about the sect. A number of Jacob's writings were translated and published by William E. Barton, a Christian clergyman from Oak Park, Illinois. The two were friends and correspondents from 1903 to the time of Jacob's death in 1916.[6] A photograph of the drawing included in this paper first appeared in 1907 in a treatise of Jacob's published by Barton.[7] The only comment on the chart (other than that it was by the high

5. The chart drawn by Jacob ben Aaron is in the William E. Barton Collection of the Special Collections Division of the Mugar Memorial Library of Boston University. The one drawn by Jacob ben Uzzi is in the Percy E. Woodward Collection of Art and Archaeology of the Jefferson and Brown Museum of the Boston University School of Theology. I wish to express my thanks to Dr. Howard B. Gotlieb, Director of the Special Collections Division, and Mr. Stephen P. Pentek of the School of Theology Library, for permission to photograph and publish these documents. Thanks are also due to Ms. Margaret R. Goostray, Assistant Director of Special Collections, for her assistance, and to the Office of Photo Services.

6. See James D. Purvis, "Studies on Samaritan Materials in the W. E. Barton Collection in the Boston University Library," *Proceedings of the Fifth World Congress of Jewish Studies, 3–11 August 1969* (ed. Pinchas Peli; Jerusalem: World Union of Jewish Studies, 1972) 1.134–43 [Hebrew abstract, 1968]); "The W. E. Barton Collection in the Boston University Library, Special Collections Division," *BASOR* 248 (1982) 76.

7. Jacob ben Aaron, "The Messianic Hope of the Samaritans" (trans. from Arabic by Abdullah ben Kori; ed. with intro. by William Eleazar Barton), *The Open Court* (1907) 272–96.

priest) was that it depicted "symbols of the temple [sic] furniture to be restored by the Messiah, as illustrated on the case of the holy scroll." This article
was reprinted in booklet form, and copies were sent to Jacob for sale to tour-
ists. In his correspondence with Barton, Jacob reported that of the various
offprints of his articles, this was the most popular—evidently because the
topic (Samaritan messianism) was of interest to Christian visitors to Nablus.

The tabernacle drawing by Jacob ben Uzzi was first published by the
writer.[8] The artist was probably the same Jacob ben Uzzi who published *The
Celebration of the Passover by the Samaritans* and several other (undated)
tracts on Samaritan religious practice.[9] It would be difficult to give a precise
date for this drawing: perhaps sometime in the 1930s.

In addition to these charts, I know of two other Samaritan tabernacle
drawings published by Western scholars. One appears in *The Samaritans:
Their History, Doctrines and Literature*, by Moses Gaster.[10] This chart was
clearly the work of Jacob ben Aaron (not mentioned by Gaster) and a sister-
drawing to the picture included here. Edward Robertson described two tabernacle drawings in *Catalogue of the Samaritan Manuscripts in the John Rylands
Library*,[11] although he provided a photograph of only one (330A), drawn
(and signed) by the priest Abisha (= Abisha ben Pinhas). Judging from Robertson's description of the undepicted MS (330), it is clear that it was the
drawing by Jacob ben Aaron that Gaster had published (something not mentioned by Robertson). Noteworthy is the fact that although the drawing reproduced by Gaster and described by Robertson was clearly the work of
Jacob ben Aaron, it is not precisely identical to the drawing presented here.
Some of the items are different in appearance, lacking, or located in a different place in the design (bearing in mind that the drawing by Jacob ben Uzzi
is also different from ben Aaron's). For convenience, I refer to this second
ben Aaron as "the sister-drawing," but the "sisters" are not "identical twins."

8. See n. 4.

9. Jacob ben Uzzi, *The Celebration of the Passover by the Samaritans* (trans. from Arabic by Abraham ben Zebulun; Jerusalem, 1934 [privately published]); see A. D. Crown,
A Bibliography of the Samaritans (American Theological Library Association Bibliography
Series 10; Metuchen, N.J.: American Theological Library Association/Scarecrow Press,
1984) nos. 1349–51.

10. Moses Gaster, *The Samaritans: Their History, Doctrines and Literature* (Schweich
Lectures, 1923; London: Oxford University Press, 1925) pl. 4.

11. Edward Robertson, *The Gaster Manuscripts* (Catalogue of the Samaritan Manuscripts in the John Rylands Library 2; Manchester: John Rylands Library, 1962) cols.
251–52, MS 330 [= Rylands Library no. 2107] and 330A [= Rylands Library no. 2081]
plate 11. A photograph of MS 330A appears also in Pummer, *The Samaritans* (pl. VIIa).

According to Barton, the prototype of the drawing by Jacob ben Aaron given here was the depiction of the tabernacle on the metal case of the Abisha scroll in Nablus. A pen-drawing of the design on this case was done by the Rev. Samuel Manning in 1873 and appears in his book *Those Holy Hills: Palestine Illustrated by Pen and Pencil.*[12] A comparison of Manning's drawing with the two pictures by Jacob ben Aaron indicates that the second drawing, the "sister-drawing" (published by Gaster [photograph] and Robertson [description]) was much closer to the original than the first drawing reproduced here—the most conspicuous feature being the placement of the menorah: on the left in the first picture but in the center in the "sister-drawing" and in Manning's pen-sketch of the prototype. The menorah also appears on the right in the illustration by Jacob ben Uzzi.

The Tabernacle, Its Furnishings and Utensils

The Court

The outer court is represented by a rectangular frame supported by sixty columns or posts with bases of alternating colors, numbered serially. In Jacob ben Aaron's drawing, there are twenty columns on each side along the length (corresponding to the north and south sides of the tabernacle) and ten columns on each side of the width (corresponding to the west and east sides). The total number of columns for each side agrees precisely with the specifications for the outer court in Exod 27:9–19. Jacob ben Uzzi's drawing differs in having twenty-two columns on each side along the length and nine each along the width. The frame of the court supported by the columns is represented in Jacob ben Aaron's drawing by blocks of alternating colors, with letters in the boxes spelling out the names of the twelve tribes of Israel, beginning in the upper right with Ephraim and (reading clockwise) ending with Gad. The dimensions of the court in the two drawings are not precisely to scale, which would be a length twice the width, according to Exod 27:18.

The court is the subject of the lower part of the frame. The objects of greater size appearing there are (1) the brazen altar (depicted with flame), (2) the multicolored vestment of the high priest (stylized by Jacob ben Aaron but represented realistically by Jacob ben Uzzi), (3) the laver, and (4) a screen

---

12. Samuel Manning, *Those Holy Hills: Palestine Illustrated by Pen and Pencil* (London: The Religious Tract Society, n.d.) 154.

identified as the door of the tent of meeting. Smaller objects include two trumpets (one of which is bent or curved) and various articles necessary for the sacrificial service. Note the following utensils in Jacob ben Aaron's drawing: (1) below the laver on the left, a jug with one handle and a ewer without handle, each identified as a *knw* (Exod 30:18); (2) below the laver to the right, the fire-pan of the altar of sacrifices (Num 4:14, 17:11); (3) on each side of the altar, two double-handled pots or basins (ash-pots?), the topmost pair identified as *mzrq*, and the lower pair as *mzlg* (Exod 27:3, 38:3; Num 4:14); (4) to the right of the altar, two pairs of knives; and (5) on the extreme right, a pair of hooks, with two pipe-like utensils between.

Jacob ben Uzzi's representation of the articles in the court differs slightly. The drawing of the screen before the tent of meeting differs in having five posts with two doors rather than six posts with three doors and is taller than it is wide (it is also incorrectly identified in English as the "holy of holies door"). Jacob ben Uzzi's depiction follows more precisely the description in Exod 26:36–37, in which the frame is said to have had five posts. Above the trumpets is a hanging incense censer, similar in design to a type used in oriental Christian churches. It is made of two bowls, one above the other, with a lid suspended above the lower bowl. To the right are two horn-shaped containers, most likely for storage and pouring of oil. A container for lamp oil is shown in the tabernacle next to the lamp (following Exod 27:20–21). These horns, then, probably represent containers for anointing oil for the high priest (following Exod 29:7, a text which also contains reference to the priestly garments, vv. 5–9) and should be viewed as belonging with the priest's vestment, shown on their immediate right.

The Tent

A greater amount of space is given to the depiction of the Holy of Holies and its furnishings than to the main part of the tent. The two sections are separated by a screen with a legend in Samaritan Hebrew/Aramaic giving the names of the high priests who were "the keepers of the holy tabernacle": Aaron and Eleazar, Ithmar and Phinehas, Abisha and Shashai, Bahki and Uzzi. There are three major items in the Holy Place: the menorah, the incense altar, and the table of showbread. The table and the menorah are in reversed positions in the two drawings. Small containers are shown on the top of the table. In Jacob ben Aaron's drawing, there are two smaller items in the Holy Place: a small, flat jar above the golden altar, identified as the jar for the manna, and a set of receptacles for the oil (matching jugs and plates) below the lamp. Jacob ben Uzzi's drawing has two unidentified objects below and to the left of the menorah, perhaps the containers for the lamp oil and manna and a set of knives and tongs below and to the right. There appears to be a piece of fruit hanging from the lower right branch of the menorah (the "sister-drawing" of Jacob ben Aaron published by Gaster and Robertson also seems to depict fruit hanging from the menorah).

The ark occupies the center of the Holy of Holies. Above are the two cherubim, represented as doves (with folded wings in Jacob ben Aaron's drawing, extended wings in the depiction by Jacob ben Uzzi). To the right of the ark is the rod of Aaron and to the left the rod of Moses. The two rods are depicted with sprouted branches, following the description of the sprouting of Aaron's rod in Num 17:23 (v. 8 in English translations). Both are drawn exactly the same (in Jacob ben Aaron's "sister-drawing," the rod of Moses is more fully developed).

Comparisons with Jewish and Christian Traditions

To my knowledge, the first person to compare the Samaritan depictions of the tabernacle with Jewish traditions was Samuel Manning.[13] He noted that the location of the door to the tent of meeting on the right-hand side, rather than in the center, was "as the Talmud describes it" and that the peculiar shape of the trumpets (especially the curved or bent one) "may throw some light upon a question much debated amongst students of the Talmud."[14] In the observations that follow, I discuss several more aspects of the Samaritan depictions which may be compared with Jewish and Christian traditions.

The Base of the Altar

At the base of the altar is a rounded mound (identified as "dust" in Jacob ben Aaron's drawing). This may imply that the altar rested on a mound of dirt, or it may allude to the ashes which had accumulated there. One may compare here a statement appearing in Josephus's description of the altar (*Ant.* 3.149.8): "The ground was in fact the receptacle for all burning fuel that fell from the brazier, the base not extending beneath the whole of its surface."

13. Ibid., 155–59. Manning's consultant was Mr. Van Straalen of the British Museum.

14. In regard to the trumpets, the Rev. Manning appears to have been a more astute observer than Edward Robertson, who in his catalog description of Jacob ben Aaron's "sister-drawing" described the trumpets as "two instruments, one curved like a hockey stick."

James D. Purvis

The Priest's Vestment

The vestment is shown with sleeves in Jacob ben Uzzi's drawing. It is my opinion that the two parts of the garment in Jacob ben Aaron's stylized depiction represent sleeves. Sleeves are not mentioned in the description of the priestly garments in Exod 28:1–43, but they are in Josephus (*Ant.* 3.162.5— on which see the comment by H. St. J. Thackeray, that outside Josephus, sleeves of the priest's coat are not mentioned in Jewish tradition).[15]

The Base of the Laver

Jewish and Christian translations of Exod 30:17 identify the *knw* as the base, foot, or stand of the laver. Jacob ben Aaron interprets the term as meaning a jug or ewer.

The Forks

Jacob ben Aaron labels two pairs of double-handled vases (ash-pots?) as *mzrq* and *mzlg*. These utensils are identified as forks or fleshhooks in Jewish and Christian translations of Exod 27:3, 38:3; and 1 Sam 2:13–14.

The Containers on the Table of Showbread

The variety of types of containers on the table suggests that not all were used for the same purpose, that is, for bread. One may compare here the tradition preserved in Josephus (*Ant.* 3:143:6, 3:256:7) that two golden cups filled with frankincense were placed on the table above (*hyper*) the bread. Two small cups appear also on the table of showbread depicted on the Arch of Titus.[16]

The Rods of Aaron and Moses

The location of Aaron's rod within the Holy of Holies agrees with the divine command to Moses, "Put back the rod of Aaron before the testimony, to be kept as a sign for the rebels" (Num 17:25 [v. 10 in English translations]). The Jewish Scriptures do not indicate that the rod of Aaron was placed in either the Shiloh or the Jerusalem Temple. But it is interesting to note a Christian tradition in Heb 9:4, where Aaron's rod (along with the jar

15. *Josephus IV, Jewish Antiquities, Books I–IV* (LCL 242; Cambridge: Harvard University Press, 1930) 393.

16. As noted by H. St. J. Thackeray, trans. (ibid., 383, 441).

of manna and the tablets of the law) was not only said to have been within the Holy of Holies, but within the ark itself. In the biblical story, the placing of Aaron's rod before the ark signified his special authority as priest against any usurpers of his prerogatives. The inclusion also of the rod of Moses in Samaritan depictions testifies to the special authority of Moses, the only prophet of the Samaritans. As will be seen, the depiction of the rods of Aaron and Moses and the pot of manna within the tabernacle has special significance for Samaritan eschatology.

The Significance of the Tabernacle Drawings for Samaritan Religious Thought

For the Samaritans, the tabernacle represents the true sanctuary of Israel. It is the only sanctuary the Samaritans claim to have had—and, they maintain, the only legitimate sanctuary in the history of the Israelite nation. The validity of any other sanctuary, tent or temple, in the history of Israel—Shilonite, Jerusalemite, or any other—is denied. The tradition preserved by Josephus of a Samaritan Temple having been constructed on Mt. Gerizim during the Hellenistic Period is also denied. The only legitimate sanctuary of Israel was the tabernacle constructed according to the pattern revealed to Moses on Mt. Sinai and established on Mt. Gerizim by Joshua. It was this sanctuary that was hidden away by divine action in the time of the schismatic priest Eli, and it is this sanctuary that will be restored at the end of this present age.

I turn now to describing aspects of the Samaritan drawings of the tabernacle that reflect their sectarian views and that also indicate matters stressed in their theology and religious traditions.

The Priest List on the Curtain Separating the Holy Place from the Holy of Holies

As has been noted, the Holy of Holies is separated from the Holy Place by a curtain on which appear the names of eight priests (listed as four pairs) called "the keepers of the holy tabernacle." According to Samaritan tradition, these were the high priests of the tabernacle from its inception to the time when the shrine was hidden away due to the anger of God over the schismatic action of Eli in establishing a rival cult center at Shiloh.[17] The period of time

17. For the story of the Eli schism and the hiding away of the tabernacle and the vessels, see the Samaritan chronicles: (1) For the older chronicles in Arabic, see Juynboll, *Chronicon*

of these pontificates is said to have been the Age of Divine Favor or Grace (the *rahûtâ*). This Age of Grace will be restored with the coming of the Samaritan eschatological prophet, the *Taheb*, who will recover the hidden tabernacle and restore its cultic operation. The hiding away of the tabernacle in a cave on Mt. Gerizim initiated the Age of Divine Disfavor (or the *fanûtâ*). Thus, the "sister-chart" of Jacob ben Aaron adds, following the list of priests, "And in the days of Uzzi the Lord hid the tabernacle; may the Lord restore it to us." A similar statement appears in the text of the drawing by Abisha (Robertson's MS 330A).[18]

The Fire on the Altar

Inasmuch as the tabernacle depicted in the Samaritan drawings is not only the sanctuary that was and is to be, but also the one that is now hidden away,

---

Samaritanum, aribice conscriptum, cui titulus est Liber Josuae (Leiden: Luchtmans, 1848) 43–44 [Arabic text] and 180–81 [Latin translations]; Edward Vilmar, *Abulfathi annales samaritani* (Gotha: Friderici Andrae Perthes, 1865) 38–39, and corresponding Arabic text. (2) For the older priest-lists in Hebrew (with annotations on the hiding away of the vessels in the time of Uzzi), see John Bowman, *Transcript of the Original Text of the Samaritan Chronicle Tolidah* (Leeds: University of Leeds, n.d.) col. 11A; Moses Gaster, "The Chain of Samaritan High Priests," *Texts and Studies* (London: Maggs Brothers, 1925–28) 1.483–502, esp. 494 [English translation]; M. Séligsohn, "Une nouvelle chronique samaritaine," *Revue des études juives* 44 (1902) 205–6; John Macdonald, *The Samaritan Chronicle No. II (or Sefer Ha-Yamim), from Joshua to Nebuchadnezzar* (BZAW 107; Berlin: de Gruyter, 1969) 42–43 [Hebrew text] and 114–15 [English translation]. The latter appears to be a modern Samaritan work, a pastiche derived from Jewish Scriptures and Samaritan sources, to which Macdonald assigned an unwarranted antiquity (an opinion shared by a number of scholars within the Samaritan community).

18. For a comparison of Jewish and Samaritan legends on the hidden tabernacle/temple vessels, see now Isaac Kalimi and James D. Purvis, "The Hiding of the Temple Vessels in Jewish and Samaritian Literature," *CBQ* 56 (1994), forthcoming. For Samaritan traditions on the *Taheb* and the restoration of the ancient tabernacle, see the texts from the fourth to the eighteenth centuries gathered together by Ferdinand Dexinger, "Der Taheb: Ein 'messianischer' Heilsbringer der Samaritaner," *Kairos: Zeitschrift für Religionswissenschaft und Theologie* n.s. 27 (1985) 1–172; note esp. the chart on p. 27; also published in book form under the same title, as *Kairos* (Religionswissenschaftliche Studien 3; Salzburg: Otto Müller, 1986). Josephus records that the Roman procurator Pontius Pilate was removed from office after an unwarranted attack on a large Samaritan crowd that had gathered to ascend Mt. Gerizim to find the lost tabernacle vessels (having been deluded by a pretender to the role of the eschatological prophet) (see *Ant.* 18.85–88).

it seems significant that the fire is shown on the altar. The Samaritan traditions concerning the hidden sanctuary and its vessels may be compared, in some respects, to Jewish traditions on the hiding away of the holy fire and the temple vessels at the time of the destruction of the Jerusalem Temple by the Babylonians. In Jewish writings, Jeremiah is most often represented as the one responsible for this (2 Macc 2:1–8; 2 Bar 6:7–9). These and other Jewish (and Jewish-Christian) traditions are treated (with comparisons to the Samaritan) by C. R. Koester in *The Dwelling of God: The Tabernacle in the Old Testament, Intertestamental Jewish Literature, and the New Testament.*[19]

The Rod of Moses and the Pot of Manna

As noted above, the inclusion of the rod of Moses in Samaritan depictions of the tabernacle testifies to the special authority of Moses for the sect. Moses is the only prophet recognized by the Samaritans. He is clearly the model of their eschatological figure, the *Taheb*. The title may (and has been) interpreted as meaning both 'the returning one' and 'the restoring one' (from the Aramaic root, *twb* 'to return'). The placing of the rod of Moses and the pot of manna within the tabernacle in Samaritan drawings has eschatological significance. According to the Samaritans, the legitimacy of the *Taheb* will be attested by his having Moses' rod and the manna, which will come into his possession when he uncovers the hidden sanctuary.[20]

The Trumpets

The inclusion of the two trumpets among the instruments in the outer court reflects the importance attributed to them by the Samaritans: "The Lord said to Moses, 'Make two silver trumpets; of hammered work you shall make them; and you shall use them for summoning the congregation. . . . The trumpets shall be to you for a perpetual statute throughout your generations'" (Num 10:1–2, 8). According to a Samaritan tradition, as reported in the Arabic Book of Joshua, the continual burnt-offering of the morning was offered before sunrise. As soon as the high priest had completed the sacrifice, he blew the trumpet from the summit of Mt. Gerizim. The trumpet blast was

---

19. C. R. Koester, *The Dwelling of God: The Tabernacle in the Old Testament, Intertestamental Jewish Literature, and the New Testament* (Catholic Biblical Quarterly Monograph Series 22; Washington, D.C.: Catholic Biblical Association, 1989) 48–49.

20. See Dexinger, "Der Taheb," 27.

continued by the other priests so that all the Israelites would know that it had been offered and that the time had come to arise and pray.[21]

Concluding Observation

The tabernacle, as the once and future sanctuary of Israel, occupies a central place in Samaritan theology. For a religion which was strictly aniconic (following the restrictive use of *icon*), representations of the tabernacle were not only proper vehicles of iconographic expression (in the broader sense of the term) but also provided an avenue through which the Samaritans could represent graphically the major (as well as the distinctive) claims of their religion. These included the significance of the law (the tablets of which were contained in the ark of testimony), Moses as the one true prophet of Israel, and the tabernacle (following Samaritan understanding) as the one true sanctuary.

I have two observations, offered as a final note. First, it is clear that tabernacle drawings have been a vehicle for artistic expression among the Samaritans because of the significance of the tabernacle in Samaritan theology. The Samaritan culture has always been, and remains today, a religion-dominated culture.[22] While there were certainly other aspects of Samaritan life that provided opportunity for artistic expression (marriage contracts, for example), tabernacle charts were deemed the proper vehicle. The marriage contract has been fully exploited as an artistic device in Jewish art. In contrast, Samaritan *ketubot*, if they are decorated, are decorated only with geometrical or floral designs.[23] Second, this study is concerned with Samaritan iconography, or *visual* art. It ought not to be inferred from what has been stated that the Samaritans have been lacking in esthetic appreciation. Their artistic expression has been primarily in music, the intonation of texts, and hymnody.[24]

21. See Juynboll, *Chronicon Samaritanum,* 38–39 [Arabic text] and 174 [Latin translation]. An English translation is found in John Bowman, *Samaritan Documents Relating to Their History, Religion and Life* (Pittsburgh: Pickwick, 1977) 73. Bowman stated that he knew of no parallel practice in the Jewish Temple in Jerusalem, but compare Sir 50:16–17, concerning Jewish practice at the time of the high priest Simon the Just (ca. 200 B.C.E.).

22. As pointed out and documented most recently by Nathan Schur in his informative *History of the Samaritans* (Beiträge zur Erforschung des Alten Testaments und des Antiken Judentums 18; Frankfurt am Main: Peter Lang, 1989).

23. See most recently Reinhard Pummer, *Samaritan Marriage Contracts and Deeds of Divorce,* vol. 1 (Wiesbaden: Harrassowitz, 1993) 21.

24. See especially and most recently Ruth Katz, "Samaritan Music," *The Samaritans* (ed. A. D. Crown; Tübingen: Mohr, 1989) 743–70. See also Benyamin Tsedaka with James Purvis, *Some Aspects of Samaritan Music and the Reading of the Law* (audio tape with text; Holon, Israel: A.B. Institute of Samaritan Studies, 1991) 28 minutes + 6 pp.

The Bible in Recent English Translation: The Word and the Words

Ernest S. Frerichs

❧•❧

F ACED WITH A VERITABLE DELUGE of English translations of the Bible in the past quarter century, the Bible reader, whether Jewish or Christian, is understandably confused about the multiplicity. In principle, it would appear that a commonly accepted single translation should be possible. The goal of a common Bible translation, serving the needs of both the Christian and Jewish communities, would seem to be attainable, at least with respect to a translation of the Hebrew Scriptures. Hypothetically, a committee of scholars, expert in the languages in question and in agreement with respect to the original text to be used, should be able to produce a translation that could be defended against all critics.

The reality is clearly very different from the presumption of an attainable common Bible translation. Bruce Metzger, in the preface to the most recent of these translations, the New Revised Standard Version (NRSV), counts 26 translations of the Bible since 1952, plus 25 additional translations or revisions of the New Testament alone.[1] A review of these translations reveals the reasons for the number of Bible translations in existence and why a commonly executed or commonly accepted Bible translation is improbable, now and perhaps forever.

Author's note: The topics covered in this paper were often discussed in my conversations with my late friend, H. Neil Richardson, a scholar and teacher who will be honored in memory by his students and colleagues for his commitments to accuracy and integrity in scholarship and in life.

1. B. M. Metzger, "Preface," *The Holy Bible: The New Revised Standard Version* (Oxford and New York: Oxford University Press, 1989), xii.

There are many reasons why a common Bible translation has never been achieved. The obvious difference between Jews' and Christians' definitions of *Bible* is only one consideration in a complex situation. The areas of disagreement extend to significant differences between Christian groups as well. There are, for example, the predictable areas of disagreement: which "books" are to be included in the Bible, how to translate particular words or passages, and which methods of biblical interpretation are to be honored. But many other reasons for the existence of multiple translations could also be given. Bible readers enjoy the security of knowing that a particular translation has been authorized for the use of their particular group. A specific religious community may require a particular translation of a passage and thus require a Bible version employing that translation. Given the popularity of Bible translations and the probability that one individual will own several translations, publishers of Bible translations have an economic interest in promoting a plurality of translations and a multiplicity of editions. Since many translations are the work of individuals rather than committees, they reflect the idiosyncrasies of the individuals who create them.[2] Various theological oddities and doctrinal emphases of particular religious communities, especially Christian communities, have been preserved in this fashion. There have been frequent attempts to provide a translation that meets the needs of all Christian communities. Success has eluded the translators and the sponsors, though the Revised Standard Version (RSV) of 1952, following its 1977 edition, was able to gain official authorization for use by Protestant, Anglican, Roman Catholic, and Eastern Orthodox churches. This official authorization, however, has not precluded the issuing of distinctive translations, also authorized for use, as in the case of the New American Bible translated under Roman Catholic auspices. It is rather the case, as Jonathan Sarna states, that "no single Bible translation has ever succeeded in meeting the needs of all biblically based faiths, and many churches have enthusiastically sponsored translations of their own, as if to emphasize their separate heritage, independent status, and unique claim to possess the truth."[3]

The multiplicity of English Bible translations is often attributed to the literary difficulties of translating and the variety of responses flowing from different philosophies of translation. The argument of this paper is that such literary issues are indeed important in explaining the variety of translations

---

2. See H. P. Scanlin, "Bible Translation by American Individuals," *The Bible and Bibles in America* (ed. E. S. Frerichs; Atlanta: Scholars Press, 1988) 43–82.

3. J. D. Sarna, "The Politics of Scripture: Jewish Bible Translations and Jewish-Christian Relations in the United States" [Unpublished manuscript] 1.

and editions, but no more so than other factors that may be termed political. My main concern here is with these "political" factors, their role in the translation and publishing process, and their contribution to the multiplicity of translations or editions.

A traditional problem, illustrative of our concern and revealing both political and theological considerations, is the question of their inclusion of apocryphal or deuterocanonical works. Longstanding disagreement on both the contents and the order of the apocryphal books has encouraged a multiplicity of editions, if not translations. The Eastern churches included such works in the Greek translation of the Bible, though Jerome omitted them from his version of the canon. This was the beginning of historical fluctuation on the problem. Jerome's view of omitting them was espoused by various medieval Christian spokesmen, and the ecumenical councils included them in the canon. The Protestant reformers objected to them, but the Council of Trent became their defender.[4]

One of the most widely discussed cases of disagreement concerned the use of the Apocrypha by the British and Foreign Bible Society in the early nineteenth century. The British and Foreign Bible Society (BFBS), founded in 1804, encountered pressure from those who opposed the circulation of Bibles containing the Apocrypha (primarily Scots). During the 1820s the Society was finally forced to cease publishing and distributing Bibles containing the Apocrypha. The effects of this activity in England were felt in the United States when the American Bible Society, founded in 1816, ceased to distribute Bibles with the Apocrypha in 1828. Cox points out that the inclusion of the Apocrypha in Bible Society editions in the United States and England was not renewed until after the middle of the twentieth century.[5]

The inclusion of the Apocrypha in recent translations has been accompanied by a significant rise in scholarly interest in them and in the creation of new translations. Concomitant with this increased scholarly interest in the apocryphal works has been a widespread interest in the definitions and history of the canon, both for the Hebrew Scriptures and for the Christian Bible.[6]

---

4. A. de Kuiper, "The Apocrypha," *Technical Papers for the Bible Translator* 25 (1974) 301–13.

5. See R. B. Cox, *The Nineteenth Century British Apocrypha Controversy* (Ph.D. diss., Baylor University, 1981).

6. See, e.g., S. Meurer, ed., *Die Apokryphenfrage in okumenischen horizont* (Die Bibel in der Welt 22; Stuttgart: Deutsche Bibelgesellschaft, 1989); S. Amsler, "La Politique d'Edition des Societes Bibliques au XIX Siecle et le Canon de l'Ancien Testament," *Le Canon de l'Ancien Testament* (Le Monde de La Bible; Geneva: Labor et Fides, 1984) 313–38.

Disagreements between Roman Catholic and Protestant scholars over the inclusion of the apocryphal or deuterocanonical works in Bible translation projects were published in a 1968 document, reissued in 1987 under the revised title *Guidelines for Interconfessional Cooperation in Translating the Bible.*[7] The *Guidelines* conclude that an edition of the Bible with Roman Catholic imprimatur must include the deuterocanonical materials, although a "great majority" of Protestants will not accept an edition of the Bible unless the apocryphal texts are clearly separated from the Hebrew Bible/Old Testament and the New Testament. The *Guidelines* make clear that it is "the aim of the Bible Societies to provide the Scriptures in the canon desired by the churches."[8]

Disagreement over the definition of the Apocrypha played a role less than twenty years ago in the creation of the 1977 edition of the RSV. Bruce Metzger provides the explanation in a footnote to a recent article.[9] The incident involved the gift of the RSV "Common Bible" to Pope Paul VI in 1973 by a group that included Metzger. Following the ceremony, Archbishop Athenagoras, who had taken part in the ceremony, remarked to Metzger that the gift had not really been a "Common Bible," since it lacked 3 and 4 Maccabees and Psalm 151, works accepted as deuterocanonical by Eastern Orthodox churches. This led to further translation between 1973 and 1975, followed by the 1977 edition, which included the three texts.

Given the differing approaches to the apocryphal and deuterocanonical materials, it was inevitable that there would be discussion about the appropriate way for these materials to appear in the recently issued NRSV. The conclusion was to print half-title pages for each of the Testaments and another half-title page for the apocryphal/deuterocanonical works. To preserve the differing views between Protestants and Roman Catholics, the compromise was to print a half-title page, worded: "Apocryphal/Deuterocanonical Books of the Old Testament." In addition to the wording of the title for this separate collection within the NRSV, the NRSV committee agreed to arrange the works in four groups, reflecting the traditions of several confessional bodies. A related debate concerned the title that would be given to the traditional Old Testament. Metzger reports that various suggestions included *The Hebrew Scriptures, com-*

---

7. The title in 1968 used the language of "guiding principles." This was replaced in 1987 with the term "guidelines." The work is published jointly by the United Bible Societies and the Secretariat for Promoting Christian Unity (*Guidelines for Interconfessional Cooperation in Translating the Bible* [Rome: Vatican Polyglot Press, 1987]).

8. *Guidelines*, 6.

9. B. M. Metzger, "The Processes and Struggles Involved in Making a New Translation of the Bible," *Religious Education* 85 (1990) 176 n. 2.

monly called, The Old Testament; The Jewish Scriptures; The Hebrew and Aramaic Scriptures.[10]

In addition to disagreement over the inclusion of the Apocrypha and the definition of that collection, an equally thorny issue has been whether any form of annotation may be included with the text. This issue has been largely responsible for the multiplicity of editions. The Bible Societies have had a guiding principle since the foundation of the British and Foreign Bible Society in 1804. Article I of the Statutes of the BFBS states that "the designation of this Society shall be the British and Foreign Bible Society, of which the sole object shall be to encourage a wider circulation of the Holy Scriptures, without note or comment; the only copies in the language of the United Kingdom to be circulated by the Society shall be the authorized version." The guideline "without note or comment" has been a source of debate over the years, especially during the last decade.

The stringent rule of 1804 has been modified after long and continuing discussion over the issue of "readers' helps."[11] Initially, the opposition to the phrase "without note or comment" may have been motivated by a desire to avoid the problems created by annotations in the margins of Bibles, since at least the Reformation. Theologically, this opposition to annotation is understandable, given the ability of divinely inspired Holy Scripture to speak directly to the reader.

Between blanket opposition and overt annotation lay the dilemma of whether annotation was ever justified. Considerable opposition was expressed to outright theological and christological titles or statements introduced into the text.[12] The nineteenth-century American Jewish community, which needed for the most part an English Bible translation rather than a Hebrew Bible, found the theological annotations of the Authorized Version available to them unacceptable and offensive. The result was the production of a text for Jewish readers by Isaac Leeser in 1853, a text which was still heavily influenced by the Authorized Version, but without theological annotation.

The question of overt theological annotation aside, many readers of the Bible have sought help; the challenge for the revisioners has been to include

10. Ibid., 181.

11. See within an extensive literature, P. Ellingworth, "Helps for Readers Which Really Help," *Bulletin, United Bible Societies* 124/125 (1981) 52–66.

12. See, e.g., J. H. Tigay, "Traditional and Modern Responses to the Christological Interpretation of the Bible," *Proceedings of The Rabbinical Assembly* 46 (1984) 119–29; F. Talmage, *Disputation and Dialogue: Readings in the Jewish-Christian Encounter* (New York: KTAV, 1975).

"notes or comments" that are helpful, without turning the annotations into direct theological statements. It must be recognized, however, that from certain perspectives there are subtle theological overtones in most forms of annotation, and those concerned with such subtleties will be more sympathetic to the tradition of translating "without note or comment." The challenge is to identify the reader's need and to agree on the form of help.

Symptomatic of a shift in attitude, if not yet policy, towards the United Bible Societies' old rule of thumb "without note or comment" are the conclusions of a 1980 meeting of the United Bible Society in Chiang Mai, Thailand. The focus of the shift is meeting the "real" needs of the reader. Ellingsworth, who wrote the readers' helps mentioned above, views the new trend as a positive change, even if it is no more than a recommendation to the national Bible Societies. Euan Fry, Translation Secretary of the Australian Bible Society, has also entered the discussion, trying to summarize the kinds of helps needed under the category of "notes." He defines notes as comments intended to help the reader understand literary features of the text, to help identify or explicate items in the text, or to give background information.[13] The application of these note principles is further extended to consider introductions to the individual books of the Bible, general introductions, headings, maps, charts, word lists, cross-reference systems, indexes, and pictures.

It should be clear that the shift toward greater freedom to include "notes or comments" in Bible versions will only increase the multiplicity of Bible editions needed to meet the expectations of various Bible readers. Publishing more editions containing notes without trespassing on theological issues will be difficult to achieve. Even if successful, the attempt will inevitably proliferate the varieties of Bible editions available from the publishers.

The issue of multiplying editions by including annotations in relation takes on special meaning when cooperation is needed in the production of interconfessional Bibles, particularly one to be used by both Protestants and Roman Catholics. The use of such documents as the previously cited *Guidelines for Interconfessional Cooperation in Translating the Bible* will help editors insure that notes are free of any denominational, sectarian, or doctrinal bias. One foreseeable problem of an ecumenical edition would be the choice of a Greek text for the translation of the New Testament. The *Guidelines* recognize that there are "certain constituencies" who will require that a New Testament translation be based on the Byzantine text-type, such as the *Textus Receptus*, despite the fact that this tradition is no longer accepted by a consensus of modern

13. E. Fry, "To Make A Good One Better—With Helps," *Bulletin, United Bible Societies* 124/125 (1981) 56–66.

critical scholars. Another predictable area of controversy in any interconfessional translation would be attempting to find a common exegetical basis for the translation. The resolution of this issue would be placed by the *Guidelines* in the hands of a joint commission that would draw up a list of "mutually acceptable commentaries and critical studies." An attempt was made in the *Guidelines* document to discuss the various forms of annotation acceptable for an interconfessional translation. On the whole, the *Guidelines* have succeeded in restraining this form of translation expansion and doctrinal assertion, though its concluding note is that "restrictions on the types of annotations in no way preclude different constituencies from employing the text in publishing commentaries as separate volumes to help the reader to understand and appreciate more fully the nature and significance of the Holy Scriptures in the light of their own traditions." [14]

What is clearly discouraged in the *Guidelines*' discussion of annotations is the use of section headings that assert or explain the theological import of a biblical passage from the perspective of the translators. Also rejected by the *Guidelines* would be the explanation of different Roman Catholic and Protestant beliefs in the notes relating to a particular passage.

If we take into consideration a variety of additional concerns, the deluge of Bible editions is even more explainable. Such concerns reflect the need, for example, for a Bible for children with the inevitable problem of defining what constitutes a translation for children, youth, or adults. Many types of study helps have been suggested for inclusion in a children's Bible: selected stories, illustrations, cartoon Bibles, and activity books. Other problems arise in the use of non-print media—audio scriptures, video, and similar questions. Some people question the production of condensed Bibles or paraphrase Bibles—the list of questionable products seems almost endless.

To summarize, I believe that the multiplicity of Bible translations and editions is inevitable and is an accurate reflection of the variety of reader groups who turn to the Bible. The variety is further informed by the needs of the readers: No single edition or translation will ever satisfy the many appetites of Bible readers.

14. *Guidelines*, 10.

Biblical Hermeneutics and Contemporary African Theology

Robert G. Rogers

❧·❧

Introduction

SOME CONTEMPORARY ANALYSTS OF AFRICAN CHRISTIANITY claim that African theologians of the 1980s have a different hermeneutical perspective from their predecessors of the 1960s and 1970s. Josiah Young, an African-American scholar, believes that the "liberation motif," so much a theme of Black South African theologians, has inevitably channeled the theological and biblical emphases of younger sub-Saharan theologians, thereby distinguishing them from their older counterparts who have been influenced more by the white missionary theology that shaped their initial understanding of Christianity. In this brief essay I will examine this claim, using a recent article by Young as a point of departure.[1]

Young divides black African theologians into two groups: the "Old Guard" and the "New Guard." (He states that the first category is not a negative term, but merely a reflection of a particular world view.) Such well-respected theologians as E. W. Fashole-Luke, Bolaji Idowu, John Mbiti, and Harry Sawyerr constructed their theologies during a time of intense nationalism, the period

---

1. Josiah Ulysses Young III, "African Theology: From Independence Toward Liberation," *Voices From the Third World* 10 (1987) 41–48.

when various African nations freed themselves from colonial rule. Committed to an "ideology of independence," as Young labels it, these theologians took Western Christian theology and defined it in African terms. The process was called "indigenization."[2] In this form of theologizing, African traditional values and experience became a passive partner, subordinated to the presumably superior European form of Christianity. The brevity of Young's article precludes the citation of extensive examples from these theologians. However, he strongly implies that their biblical hermeneutic was a Western-derived form that subordinated the African experience to a secondary position. "What they did was Christianize dimensions of African traditional religion."[3] His most strident critique of the "Old Guard" is that their theologies seem to ignore both the white supremacy of South Africa and the neo-colonialism of the "Black Elite" in many newly independent African nations.[4]

By contrast, Young writes, "New Guard" theologians of the 1980s reject the emphasis on indigenization. Although not South Africans themselves, these theologians have been dramatically affected by the experience and theological perspective of such well-known liberation theologians as Desmond Tutu and A. Boesak. The theme of liberation becomes a call to free African Christianity from the bourgeois values inherited from the West and in the process thereby affirm African traditional values.[5] Young places four theologians in this "camp": Eboussi Boulaga, Jean-Marc Ela, Ambrose Moyo, and Mercy Amba Oduyoye. Once again, the brevity of his article precludes extensive quotations from the works of any of the "New Guard." All four theologians refer to the Bible extensively in presenting their theologies, although Young fails to cite these usages.

If Josiah Young's analysis is correct, then the hermeneutical assumptions, indeed the whole focus of biblical interpretation, should differ significantly between the representatives of the two groups that he outlines. I now turn to an examination of the claims of these representative theologians, focusing particularly on their hermeneutical assumptions regarding the Hebrew Bible/Old Testament and its value to contemporary African theology.[6]

---

2. Ibid., 42. Roman Catholic scholars frequently use the terms "enculturation" or "adaptation" rather than "indigenization."

3. Ibid.

4. Ibid., 44.

5. Ibid., 45.

6. See the instructive article by Danuel N. Wambutda, "Hermeneutics and the Search for Theologia Africana," *Africa Theological Journal* 9 (1980) 29–39.

The "Old Guard" and Hermeneutics

Theologians in this group agree on the centrality of the entire Bible to African theological interpretation. Analyzing the sources for an authentic theology, Fashole-Luke states: "Now it is universally accepted by all engaged in this quest that the Bible is the primary and basic source for the development of African Christian theologies."[7] Mbiti concurs on the centrality of the Bible to the theological task, but he notes that it must reflect an African perspective.[8] More recently, Danuel Wambutda has analyzed the work of a number of African theologians, including those assigned to the "Old Guard," in what he terms their search for *Theologia Africana.* While speaking appreciatively of these theologians, Wambutda affirms that the process of deriving an authentic African theology is still evolving. "However, in the fervent search for an African Christian theology, one aspect which happens to be the most crucial in the whole enterprise and which seems to have hitherto remained elusive to it, is a properly biblically grounded reformulation of African thought from which a theology should naturally evolve, a point already hinted at."[9]

Turning more particularly to the Hebrew Bible/Old Testament, the theologians under discussion are in general agreement that this portion of the Bible is necessary for deriving an authentic African Christian theology. One cannot simply graft the Christian gospel onto African traditional religion, although there is general appreciation expressed for the value of traditional religions as part of the African heritage. Fashole-Luke very clearly rejects the notion that African traditional religion can provide a *praeparatio evangelica* that would substitute for the Old Testament. He contends that one cannot understand the meaning of Jesus without understanding the Jewish context in which he was nourished.[10] Fashole-Luke is very careful to avoid the claim that Africans had the full revelation of God before they encountered Christianity.[11] However, Professor Fashole-Luke is not opposed to the value of African traditional religion as a source of spiritual nourishment for African peoples. He even

---

7. E. W. Fashole-Luke, "The Quest for an African Christian Theology," *Ecumenical Review* 27 (1975) 265.

8. John S. Mbiti, *New Testament Eschatology in an African Background* (Oxford: Oxford University Press, 1977) 189.

9. Wambutda, "Hermeneutics and the Search for Theologia Africana," 31–32.

10. E. W. Fashole-Luke, "An African Indigenous Theology: Fact or Fiction?" *Sierra Leone Bulletin of Religion* 11 (1969) 6.

11. Fashole-Luke, "The Quest for an African Christian Theology," 264.

views it as an appropriate source for a meaningful African Christian theology. In the final analysis, he maintains the ultimate uniqueness of the *entire* biblical revelation.

> There is a sense in which African Traditional Religion can be regarded as the "Old Testament" for African Christian Theologies, but since the revelation of God was in the person of Jesus, a first-century Jew, all other revelations must be subjected to that full and final revelation. Perhaps when we have African Traditional Theologies written by practitioners of the religion in the vernacular languages, then this source for the creation of African Christian Theologies will be properly evaluated.[12]

John Mbiti is equally cautious in regarding African religiosity as *praeparatio evangelica*. In his substantial work entitled *New Testament Eschatology in an African Background*, Mbiti examines a dominant New Testament theme in light of the religious experience of his own people, the Akamba, in Kenya. For Mbiti, African concepts of time and history are inadequate to express a biblical understanding of eschatology. "Both linguistically and mythologically there is no notion in traditional African thought that the world will ever come to an end. The rhythm of nature ensures an endless continuity of human life and the world."[13] He notes that "the materialistic imagery in New Testament Eschatology is derived chiefly from a Hebrew background."[14] In effect, the Christian understanding of eschatology, while moving beyond traditional Jewish understandings of time and history, nevertheless is rooted in the Hebraic world. What then of a relationship between that world and the African religious world? Mbiti concludes that there are many interesting parallels between the African and early Old Testament cultural and religious backgrounds. In suggesting comparative studies of the two, he places them on an equal footing. Where the Israelite background is necessary for an understanding of a New Testament concept, however, the Hebrew Bible takes on unique significance. As he states in his conclusion, "the New Testament is an entirely different world with major themes for which there are no parallels in the African religious background."[15]

Harry Sawyerr makes the point even more strongly than Mbiti that African traditional religion is an inadequate substitute for the Hebrew Bible as background to the Christian Gospel. In his book entitled *Creative Evangelism:*

---

12. E. W. Fashole-Luke, "Footpaths and Signposts to African Christian Theologies," *Bulletin of African Theology* 3/5 (1981) 37.
13. Mbiti, *New Testament Eschatology*, 182–83.
14. Ibid., 62.
15. Ibid., 183.

Towards a New Christian Encounter with Africa, Sawyerr implies that the African view of reality provides a natural background or preparation for *both* the Hebrew Bible and the Christian gospel found in the New Testament.

> Whilst, therefore, we would advocate the assimilation of African religious thought forms, in an attempt to make Christian converts accept the Gospel message and turn away from their pagan concepts in forms of worship, we recognize that they do not provide adequate material with which to express the basic Christian concepts. Indeed, it seems to us imperative to recognize the role of the major Hebrew and Jewish religious concepts as expressed chiefly in the Old Testament. Gentile Christianity without a Hebrew basis seems to us empty.[16]

Sawyerr does offer some comparisons between the African and Hebrew thought worlds. In particular, he focuses on the concept of covenant, a pattern of relationship common to Africa and ancient Israel. Even here, though, Sawyerr finds the African concept to be an inadequate vehicle for understanding the biblical patterns of relationship. "For Israel, the covenant was a *diathaka* based on God's initiative; in Africa, a covenant is a *synthaka*—an agreement in which the human parties played an equal part."[17]

The remaining member of the so-called "Old Guard," Bolaji Idowu, takes a somewhat different approach to the value of African traditional religion, one rather sharply delineated from that of Sawyerr. Idowu is especially concerned to demonstrate that the model of God mediated by European missionaries is not the only legitimate one. Indeed, he claims that "God" was always present in African traditional religion.[18] In his definitive work, *Towards an Indigenous Church*, Idowu implies—without actually so stating—that African traditional religion serves as a *praeparatio evangelica* at least in terms of a knowledge of God. "There is only one God, the Creator of heaven and earth and all that is in them; the God who has never left Himself without witness in any nation, age, or generation. . . . It is necessary to find out what God has done, in what way He has been known and approached, in the past and present history of Nigerians, and upon what, traditionally, Nigerians base their faith now and their hope for the afterlife."[19]

---

16. Harry Sawyerr, *Creative Evangelism: Towards a New Christian Encounter with Africa* (London: Lutterworth, 1968) 33.

17. Ibid., 52.

18. E. Bolaji Idowu, "God," in *Biblical Revelation and African Beliefs* (ed. Kwesi Dickson and Paul Ellingworth; Maryknoll, N.Y.: Orbis, 1969) 21.

19. E. Bolaji Idowu, *Towards an Indigenous Church* (London: Oxford University Press, 1965) 25. See also his article "God," 28–29, for a discussion of the universalism of God.

Idowu notes a number of parallels between African traditional religion and that of the Hebrew Bible. Unlike Sawyerr, Idowu contends that modern Africans and ancient Israelites both view a covenant-relationship in much the same way. Of African traditional religion, he says: "One understands it properly when it is seen as a matter of strict covenant relationship: covenant with the divine and consequent covenant between man and man."[20]

Indeed, Idowu criticizes the missionary church for insisting that Africans learn about a new covenant-relationship when they already knew a living God through their own understanding of the covenant. "The African's covenant-relationship with his fellow man is a consequence often of his covenant-relationship first with an object of worship common to him and the fellow man."[21]

Members of the school of theologians under consideration do not present a specific hermeneutical principle by which to approach the Bible, particularly when considering the place of the Hebrew Bible. However, Fashole-Luke does recognize that African theologians (himself included) tend to fall into one of two categories, each of which has implications for biblical interpretation. Writing in 1978, he said: "It may well be that in the coming years the significant divide within the ranks of theologians will be between those who find the *raison d'être* of their endeavor primarily in the dialogue with African tradition and those who find it within a radical struggle for a new society freed from poverty and oppression."[22] Fashole-Luke would place himself in the former category of theologians, as would be the case with the other "Old Guard" theologians under consideration. Indeed, in 1975 Professor Fashole-Luke had called for those espousing Black theology in South Africa in the face of white oppression to move toward a universal perspective. "It is surely at this critical point that African theologians are challenged by the Gospel to raise African Christian theologies above the level of ethnic or racial categories and emphases, so that Christians everywhere will see that Christianity is greater and richer than any of its cultural manifestations, and that the Gospel of liberation is for the oppressed and the oppressor alike."[23] He does concede that Black theology is an authentic African Christian theology, but he suggests that it should be used primarily to deal with problems in which Blacks

20. E. Bolaji Idowu, "Religions on Peace," *Orita* 5/2 (1971) 89.

21. E. Bolaji Idowu, "The Predicament of The Church in Africa," in *Christianity in Tropical Africa* (ed. C. G. Baeta; London: Oxford University Press, 1968) 434.

22. E. W. Fashole-Luke, "Introduction," in *Christianity in Independent Africa* (ed. Fashole-Luke et al.; Bloomington, Indiana: Indiana University Press, 1978) 361.

23. Fashole-Luke, "The Quest for an African Christian Theology," 268.

oppress Blacks in newly independent African states.[24] Mbiti, too, acknowledges that *liberation* is a legitimate topic for African theologians to use in describing the call of the gospel. However, he believes that thus far the appropriate biblical basis for this theme has not been explicated by those theologians for whom it is most significant, especially those in South Africa. "This neglect of the biblical backing to the theology of liberation in Africa is a very alarming omission which calls for urgent correction, otherwise that branch of African theology will lose its credibility and respectability."[25] Wambutda, summarizing the work of earlier "Old Guard" theologians, wants to distinguish between African Christian theology and Black theology as propounded in South Africa. The former is trying to "evolve itself from the original cultural roots of the African into a biblical culture alien to itself," whereas the latter is attempting to "grapple with the rectification of oppression and discrimination for missionary purposes."[26]

We have seen that theologians labeled by Professor Young as "Old Guard" are in general agreement that African Christian theologians must be in dialogue with African tradition, including traditional religion, as they seek to present the biblical message to contemporary African people. Idowu, of course, is more optimistic than the others regarding the value of the traditional religious beliefs for an adequate understanding of Christian theology. In effect, each theologian advocates the principle of indigenization whereby the gospel in its fullest biblical expression is mediated through the experience of the African theologian. As early as the 1960s and early 1970s, Idowu, Mbiti, and Sawyerr were proclaiming that biblical theology must take seriously African perceptions of reality if it is to be authentic.[27] More recently (1981) Fashole-Luke has taken the principle of indigenization to its logical conclusion when he states: "I contend that only Africans, even detribalised Africans, descendants of slaves, can say what the shape, content and future of African Christian Theologies should be."[28]

All four theologians examined here agree on the necessity of sound biblical theology, particularly when interpreting the Hebrew Bible, as a basis for African

24. Fashole-Luke, "Footpaths and Signposts to African Christian Theologies," 39.

25. John S. Mbiti, "The Biblical Basis in Present Trends of African Theology," *Bulletin of African Theology* 1/1 (1979) 19.

26. Wambutda, "Hermeneutics and the Search for Theologia Africana," 38 n. 11.

27. See Idowu, *Biblical Revelation*, 14ff.; Mbiti, *New Testament Eschatology*, 189ff.; Harry Sawyerr, "The Basis of a Theology for Africa," *International Review of Missions* 52 (1963) 269.

28. Fashole-Luke, "Footpaths and Signposts to African Christian Theologies," 40.

Christian theology. Mbiti summarizes the view of the others when he says the following:

> Any viable theology must and should have a biblical basis, and African theology has begun to develop on this foundation . . . nothing can substitute the Bible. However much African cultural-religious background may be close to the Biblical world, we have to guard against references like the "the hitherto unwritten African Old Testament" or sentiments that see a final revelation of God in the African religious heritage.[29]

There may not be a central hermeneutical principle evident in these theologians, but there is agreement that there should be dialogue between African traditions and the Christian Gospel and that the biblical perspective, especially in its Hebraic mode, provides a corrective to any legitimate African Christian theology.

The "New Guard" and Hermeneutics

I turn now to those whom Young labels the "New Guard," African Christian scholars whose primary work has been produced in the 1980s, allegedly in response to the call for liberation in South African religious circles. A brief summary of the "liberation motif" in biblical theology is useful at this point, since the theologians to be considered in this section appear to start from a more common perspective than was the case with the "Old Guard."

As early as 1976, Ogbu Kalu and Manas Buthelezi were calling for scholars to use the hermeneutical perspective of liberation when interpreting the Bible. Kalu, not himself a South African, contended that theological reflection should apply to all of Africa, not just be limited to the South African experience. Specifically, he called for an "ideology of self-reliance," based on a reading of the biblical message of liberation and salvation. Kalu also affirmed that authentic African Christianity should seek liberation from philosophical/theological and economic dependence on the Western world.[30] Buthelezi, from a South African perspective, called for a biblical hermeneutic which took seriously the concrete contemporary situation of the people. In this way, "the content of the biblical message is transposed from the first-century situation to that of the hearer in such a way that the biblical-situational-indigenous elements are

29. Mbiti, "The Biblical Basis in Present Trends," 21.
30. Ogbu Kalu, "Theological Ethics and Development in an African Context," *Missiology: An International Review* 4 (1976) 459.

replaced with those of the twentieth-century hearer in South Africa."[31] Writing more recently (1983), Buti Tlhagale speaks of the exploitation of Black workers in South African and the need for "Black Theology" to address the situation. "A Black Theological reflection considers the tradition of entrenched privileges as being incompatible with the true Christian spirit as embodied in the Gospel tradition . . . both the Old and New Testaments underline the value of person in community . . . Black Theological reflection underscores the corporate nature of humankind."[32] In 1984, the Congress of African and European Theologians convened in Cameroon to consider the appropriate forms of theology for African peoples. This group reiterated the need for a new biblical hermeneutic of liberation "which reflected accurately the political realities. Any theological consideration regarding Africa must start with the study of our context which is a context of domination, oppression, and *anthropological poverty*."[33] Desmond Tutu, probably the foremost spokesperson for liberation theology in a South African context, argues strenuously that African Christian theology must address the harsh oppression of apartheid as well as any other forms of exploitation. "The God of Abraham, Isaac, and Jacob, the God of our Fathers, Father of Our Lord Jesus Christ, was known then first as the God of the Exodus, the Liberator God, and the theme of setting free, of rescuing captives for those who have been kidnapped, is one that runs through the Bible as a golden thread. It is an important part of the warp and woof of the Biblical Tradition."[34] A. Boesak echoes the theological perspective of Tutu and calls for a theology responsive to the political needs of the people. "Black Theology is the attempt of Black Christians to understand and interpret their situation in the light of the Gospel of Jesus Christ. . . . The Gospel, however, is a Gospel of liberation. Therefore, Black Theology is a theology of liberation."[35] Women theologians also cite the liberation motif as the basis for an appropriate biblical hermeneutic. Rosemary Nithamburi, a Kenyan theologian, believes that the

31. Manas Buthelezi, "Towards a Biblical Faith in South African Society," *Journal of Theology for Southern Africa* 19 (1977) 56.
32. Buti Tlhagale, "Towards a Black Theology of Labor," *Voices From the Third World* 6/2 (1983) 11.
33. "Report on 1st Congress of African and European Theologians in Yaounde, Cameroun, April 4–11, 1984," *Voices From the Third World* 7/2 (1984) 36.
34. Desmond Tutu, "The Role of the Church in South Africa," *Voices From the Third World* 8/2 (1985) 44.
35. A. Boesak, "Banning Black Theology in South Africa," *Theology Today* 28/2 (1981) 184. For a more recent treatment of liberation themes in Black Africa theology, see Itumeleng T. Mosala, *Biblical Hermeneutics and Black Theology in South Africa* (Grand Rapids: Eerdmans, 1989).

liberation of women in African cultural life is enhanced by a careful reading of biblical narratives. As she states: "In fighting for their liberation African women would be responding to God's activity of liberation for the oppressed as is revealed in the Old Testament and the New Testament."[36]

We can now examine those theologians specifically cited by Young as advocating a new hermeneutical approach to the Bible. Eboussi Boulaga and Jean-Marc Ela are both French-speaking Roman Catholics from West Africa. Each is critical of Roman Catholic missionary endeavors to "enculturate" or "indigenize" Christianity into African life, viewing such efforts as thinly-disguised forms of domination. Boulaga became so dispirited that he left the priesthood and returned to his native village to work there as a lay African Christian. Mercy Amba Oduyoye and Ambrose Mavingire Moyo, while being Protestants, nevertheless share with their Roman Catholic colleagues a sense of disillusionment with the role missionary Christianity has played in Africa. Indeed, all four theologians fit Fashole-Luke's category described earlier as Christians calling for "a radical struggle for a new society freed from poverty and oppression."[37] Writing in the 1980s, all four have been profoundly affected by the oppression of apartheid in South Africa. However, as Josiah Young failed to point out and we shall see, they approach scripture in rather different ways.

Boulaga is the more radical of the four "New Guard" theologians. He distrusts even the name "African Christianity" because it symbolizes African acceptance of domination imposed from without. "African Christianity will always be suspect as a mere religion of the herd, a theatricalization of the continuing subordination of Africa to the West in the neo-colonial context of a shameful, cowardly dependency in all areas—social, political, economic, and scientific."[38] Whereas he is a theologian who seeks liberation from Western domination, he moves beyond the more traditional pattern of citing biblical passages or stories to support this new understanding of religious freedom, even going so far as to say that the Bible "is altogether foreign to the questions that exercise us."[39] To a degree, he is reacting against what he perceives to be misguided uses of the Bible by Western missionaries. He is particularly suspicious of attempts to use "proof texts" to buttress one's argument.

---

36. Rosemary Nithamburi, "On the Possibility of a New Image for an African Woman," *Voices From the Third World* 10/1 (1987) 105.

37. Fashole-Luke, "Introduction," 361.

38. F. Eboussi Boulaga, *Christianity Without Fetishes: An African Critique and Recapture of Christianity* (trans. Robert R. Barr; Maryknoll, N.Y.: Orbis, 1984) 56.

39. Ibid., 203.

Yet Boulaga does not advocate abandoning the Bible as inappropriate to the experience of Christianity from within the African perspective. He views the Bible as a collection of types, myths, and stories, even images and words that can be useful to the community of faith. "The Bible is a treasury of metaphors, thanks to which we can represent our existence to ourselves, transpose it to others and for ourselves."[40] He calls for an "esthetic Christianity" that responds to biblical themes of a universal nature: e.g., the pain of defeat in exile or the joy and triumph of return. Appropriating such for the contemporary community of faith brings with it a shared experience with biblical peoples, and it becomes "the lived experience of a god and of reality."[41] Boulaga affirms that the stories of the Bible, more than dogmatic assertions based on a particular method of proof-texting, will provide the necessary stimulus for a Christianity appropriate to the African community. Such faith is dependent on a form of obedience to scripture "which alone gives the knowledge necessary for salvation: our powerlessness, our nothingness, as opposed to the omnipotence and all-reality of God."[42] Thus Boulaga views the Bible as a source of knowledge about a living God who is active in each generation with those who seek God's liberating power. Such a stance will make Christianity within Africa truly an African experience. "The contribution of African Christians to African civilization is yet to come. Their current power is but borrowed, subordinated, auxiliary."[43]

Ela has a much more traditional approach to the use of scripture than that of Boulaga. In a book entitled *African Cry*, he emphasizes the "liberation motif" of the Bible and chastises Western missionaries for failing to demonstrate that to those Africans whom they converted. "To be saved means to be delivered now, to be liberated already, from the forces of alienation that enslave persons."[44] He devotes an entire chapter in the book to "an African reading of Exodus." Differing somewhat from Boulaga, Ela affirms that the biblical story of Israelite liberation from slavery is a paradigm to be applied to African Christian experience. "The Exodus event is the grid permitting the deciphering of human history and the discovery of its deeper sense—that of an intervention of God revealing the divine power and love."[45]

40. Ibid., 204.
41. Ibid.
42. Ibid., 220.
43. Ibid., 223.
44. Jean-Marc Ela, *African Cry* (trans. Robert R. Barr; Maryknoll, N.Y.: Orbis, 1986) 30.
45. Ibid., 38.

Father Ela believes that the biblical experience of faith shows God's concern for political, economic, and social liberation as part of his schema of salvation. The God of scripture seeks to deliver humans from that which enslaves them. "This is a central message of the Exodus and the key to any rereading of Bible in history. . . . God reveals to humanity that to be saved means to be freed already, to be freed from the forces of alienation in the here and now."[46] As might be expected, Ela also quotes extensively from various Hebrew prophetic books. Like Boulaga, Ela is suspicious of "enculturation/indigenization." "The faith that will be able to say anything to these generations (of Africans) will not content itself with an Africanization of Roman Ecclesiastical models."[47]

Mercy Oduyoye brings an additional dimension to the discussion of biblical hermeneutics: an African woman testifying on behalf of liberation motif as a guiding principle for biblical interpretation. A West-African by birth, she views the emergence of newly independent African nations as the impetus for contemporary African theology. "In Africa, as we have seen, it is the experience of liberation from colonialism and the cry for this liberation that has stimulated theologies that struggle to be relevant to the realities of Africa."[48] She affirms that Christian theology in Africa is constructed from the vantage point of the "underside of history" and needs to be taken seriously in the larger Christian world.[49] More definitively than either Boulaga or Ela, Oduyoye analyzes the broad spectrum of theologians in Africa and then places herself within that context as feminist theologian and as self-conscious biblical interpreter. She particularly emphasizes the Hebrew Bible as providing the necessary key to an authentic African theology. The experience of covenant in African traditional life provides suitable background for those covenants explicated in both testaments of the Bible. However, Oduyoye does not go so far as to claim African traditional religion as *praeparatio evangelica*.[50]

The exodus from slavery in Egypt is the biblical story that offers the most to contemporary African Christians, according to Oduyoye. As biblical interpreter, she easily mediates between the experience of ancient Israelites and that of contemporary Africans. Both groups experience slavery and exploitation followed by God's liberation. The experience of Blacks in South Africa

46. Ibid., 90.
47. Ibid., 102.
48. Mercy Amba Oduyoye, *Hearing and Knowing: Theological Reflections on Christianity in Africa* (Maryknoll, N.Y.: Orbis, 1986) 80–81.
49. Ibid., 76.
50. Ibid., 109–19.

is likened to that of the Hebrews under the domination of the Pharaoh, but the story of God's activity reassures the exploited. "When oppressed peoples meet obstacles, the event of the exodus reassures them. Every triumph on the way evoked the Song of Miriam."[51]

As feminist theologian, Oduyoye applies the liberation motif to a reexamination of man and woman in the Scriptures. She especially stresses the *Imago Dei* concept in Genesis 1:26, deriving thereby the fundamental principle of equality. "Women and men are depicted by Scripture as being equally the objects of God's love."[52] Thus, God's plan for liberation as attested in the Bible brings hope to all oppressed Africans.

The work of Ambrose Moyo has already been alluded to in the previous section of this paper, where his general appreciation for "Old Guard" theologians was noted. However, he does fit appropriately within the broad theological spectrum of the "New Guard." He affirms that an authentic African theology per se has not yet emerged. The problem is that Christianity is still seeking to encounter the cultural and religious traditions of Africa. Although Moyo does not examine scriptural passages in any detail, he does suggest an approach that implies his indebtedness to the liberation motif. "Only from within the African cultures can we discover the Saviour of our oppressed, exploited, and poverty-stricken African world. We can only discover that Saviour when we have learned to feel, understand, see, and hear things the way Africa feels and understands its environment."[53] Whereas Moyo calls for dialogue between Christianity and African traditional religion, he does not affirm that the latter should take precedence over biblical revelation. Instead, he specifically calls for Christianity to "challenge the traditional self-understanding of the people of Africa, and in that serious challenge and confrontation, true African Theologies are bound to emerge."[54]

The liberation that Moyo seeks is that of the Church in Africa from the white missionary establishment. The failure of an authentic African theology to emerge is due in large part to the imposition of Western, white-imposed theology. He cites the example of African Independent Churches as being the only ecclesiastical structures free from missionary domination. He cites

---

51. Ibid., 89.

52. Ibid., 136. See also her article "In the Image of God: A Theological Reflection from an African Perspective," *Bulletin of African Theology* 6/7 (1982) 41–53.

53. Ambrose Mavingire Moyo, "The Quest for African Christian Theology and the Problem of the Relationship Between Fate and Culture—The Hermeneutical Perspective," *African Theological Journal* 12/2 (1983) 102.

54. Ibid., 98.

with approval their development of indigenous theologies but unfortunately does not cite any particular hermeneutical principles that they invoke in their approach to scripture. He claims that their theologies are not always systematic, "but they are relevant."[55]

Moyo concludes by noting that faith and culture are always inextricably interwoven. He cites interplay between various cultural patterns in the ancient Near East and biblical revelation in both testaments, an encounter that he considers both inevitable and appropriate. "Christian proclamation in an African cultural context must follow the same pattern."[56]

Comparisons and Conclusions

I began this paper by citing a claim made by Josiah Young regarding different groups of African theologians. Dividing theologians chronologically by decade, he affirms that those writing in the 1980s form a "New Guard," a contingent of African theologians whose concerns and biblical hermeneutics differ from those of their immediate predecessors writing in the 1960s and 1970s. It is now appropriate to pose the question: Is his typology a correct appraisal of the African theological scene?

There are some clear and significant differences between the two groups that he delineates. In general, "Old Guard" theologians are somewhat reluctant to enter into the political realm when they theologize, except as a response in some instances to perceived exploitation by Western missionaries. By contrast, "New Guard" scholars are strongly committed to a hermeneutic that is a response to the current "oppressive regime," whatever form that might take in their own particular situation.

A further difference, which Young rightly describes, could be characterized as "indigenization" versus "confrontation." The hermeneutical task of the "Old Guard" was to provide an African perspective on the Bible, affirming African religiosity without thereby giving credence to the idea of African traditional religion as *praeparatio evangelica* (Idowu perhaps being an exception to this statement). In evolving this approach, they sought to balance the universal claims of a Christian gospel that transcends cultural limits with the recognition that perceptions of biblical truth are finally rooted within a particular culture.[57] The

55. Ibid.
56. Ibid., 106.
57. For further discussion of the relation of gospel and culture in Africa, see the excellent article by Andrew F. Walls, "The Gospel as the Prisoner and Liberator of Culture," *Missionalia* 10/3 (1982) 93–105.

four younger theologians of the 1980s, by contrast, are less directly concerned with the philosophical conflict between Western cultural ideas and African thought and more prone to confront those structures that oppress or exploit, be they political or ecclesiastical, as the *sine qua non* of their theological approach. All "New Guard" theologians affirm the necessity of an African perspective on the Bible, and, in seeking this, they are willing to consider more favorably the contributions of African traditional religion than did the earlier theologians.

It is even debatable whether there is an exclusively chronological line of demarcation between theologians of the 1960s and 1970s and those in the 1980s. A number of African theologians (mostly Protestant) were active in the past decade and yet not cited by Young. These scholars are usually more traditional, even evangelical, in their approach to the Scriptures and Christian religion. One of these, Tite Tienou, implicitly criticizes the "New Guard" position as being too narrow in focus. He suggests that indigenous African theology should be tested for both its "Africanness" and its "correctness." The former is evaluated in terms of its meeting the needs of Africans within their total context; the latter is evaluated by faithful adherence to the entire Christian Scripture. "If we maintain the double concern of relating the totality of biblical revelation to the totality of the situation of African Christians, African theology will truly become a discipline at the service of the church."[58] In light of Tienou's comments, it is more accurate to suggest that the theologians selected by Professor Young are influenced by certain perceptions of political and social conditions in Africa. Other theologians of the 1980s, equally concerned and active, are influenced by other considerations—for example, the need for evangelism.

I have noted that there are some differences between "Old Guard" and "New Guard" theologians but have suggested that the latter category is not a complete and accurate portrait of theologians active in the 1980s. There clearly are significant similarities between all eight theologians cited by Young and examined in this essay. All agree that an African perspective on the Bible is essential to buttress a "living theology" appropriate to African Christian experience. African traditional religion is considered a worthy source for understanding African religiosity. "Old Guard" theologians are somewhat at variance on the degree to which dialogue between Christianity and traditional religion is useful. "New Guard" theologians do not have such dialogue as a major item on their theological agenda. Perhaps this lack gives credence to Young's thesis that theologians of the 1960s and 1970s were somewhat more

58. Tite Tienou, "Indigenous African Christian Theologies: The Uphill Road," *International Bulletin of Missionary Research* 14/2 (1990) 76.

concerned with indigenizing the gospel. Yet, there is general agreement among all eight (with the possible exception of Idowu) that the Hebrew Bible/Old Testament must not be replaced by African traditional religion as *praeparatio evangelica.* Hebraic themes of covenant and exodus are the theological linchpins for the biblical perspectives of the eight theologians considered. The liberation aspect of the exodus story is critical for those in the "New Guard" camp, but even they differ on the identification of the particular form of oppression from which the African Christian community should seek liberation.

Where does such analysis leave us in terms of the usefulness of the typology suggested by Young? A line of demarcation between two groups cannot be drawn simply on the basis of chronology. Some contemporary African theologians use a hermeneutic based on a "liberation motif." Others do not. A strict application of Young's typology might imply that "Old Guard" theologians, while appropriate for the concerns of earlier decades, are now "out-of-step" due to changed political conditions; only the "New Guard" approach is now relevant. Such theologians as Tienou, however, who speak to and for the concerns of many African Christians, belie this interpretation. Further, the similarities between so-called "Old" and "New" mitigate against strict separation of the two groups.

Even if Young's typology is somewhat rigid at points, perhaps even inaccurate, it correctly points out some differences which may be chronologically rooted. The decade of the 1980s has clearly seen the rise of political forces in opposition to such phenomena as apartheid. Even in Tienou's own terms, such political realities cannot be ignored; they will affect theology even though they may not become the *leitmotif* of a useful biblical hermeneutic.

What will the decade of the 1990s bring to African Christian Theology? Based on this brief analysis, it is possible safely to predict that there will be a variety of biblical hermeneutical perspectives present. One can only agree with the assessments of two theologians: one, Tite Tienou, an African evangelical, the other a European and former missionary, Andrew Walls. "African theology is impossible to define in such a way that all interested in the subject will be satisfied. One wonders if such an attempt is even wise."[59] "Perhaps the real test of theological authenticity is the capacity to incorporate the history of Israel and God's people and to treat it as one's own."[60]

59. Ibid., 74.
60. Walls, "The Gospel as the Prisoner and Liberator of Culture," 105.

Index of Authorities

Index of Scripture References

❧·❧

Index of Scripture References